A Synopsis Of The Works Of Josephus From The Beginning Of The Hasmonean Period To The Destruction Of Jerusalem By The Romans

Charles M. Woolf

Copyright © 2012, Charles Woolf

Book design by: a.zuccarello@gmail.com

All rights reserved. No part of this book may be reproduced in any manner without written permission from the publisher, except in the case of quotes used in critical articles and reviews.

ISBN: (13 digit) 978-1-938043-08-6

This book was published in the USA by:

ONE WORLD PRESS
890 Staley Lane
Chino Valley, AZ 86323
800-250-8171
balazuccarello@gmail.com
www.oneworldpress.com

Contents

Preface ix

The Life and Works of Josephus xiii

Historical Perspectives xvi

Hasmonean Pedigree... xxii

The Genealogies of Agrippa I, Agrippa II and
Herod (King of Chalcis) xxiii

Biological Relationships of Early Roman Emperors xxiv

Kingdom of Herod the Great at the Time of his
Death in 4 BC xxv

Territories Controlled by Three of the Sons of Herod
the Great and the Sister (Salome) Of Herod the Great
Following his Death xxvi

The Walls of Jerusalem During the Seige by the
Romans in 70 AD xxvii

Chapter 1 HASMONEAN PERIOD 1
Change from a Hasmonean Theocracy to a Jewish Monarchy 8
The War between Aristobulus and Hyrcanus for the
Kingdom [67-63 BC] 11
The Intervention of Antipater, the Idumean 12

The Role of Pompey 14
The Attempts of Alexander, Son of Aristobulus, to Overrun Judea ... 17
The Escape of Aristobulus from Rome and his Return to Judea 18
The Deaths of Aristobulus and his Son Alexander 18
Relationship Between Antipater and the Romans............................ 19
Herod: The Governor of Galilee 20
Death of Antipater 23
The Naming of Herod as Tetrarch and His Betrothal to
Mariamne the Hasmonean 24
Role of Antigonus, the Son of Aristobulus 25
The Naming of Herod as King by the Romans 27
Final War for the Kingdom Between Herod and Antigonus 29
The Marriage of Herod to Mariamne the Hasmonean 32
The Assault on Jerusalem by Herod and Sosius 32

**CHAPTER 2 EARLY YEARS OF THE REIGN OF
HEROD THE GREAT** 35
The Return of Hyrcanus to Jerusalem 35
The Death of Aristobulus the High Priest 39
The Death of Hyrcanus 48
Agreement Reached by Caesar Augustus [Octavian] and Herod 49
The Deaths of Mariamne and Alexandra 50
Honoring Caesar, Rome and Himself [Herod] by the
Building of Cities, Theaters, Amphitheaters, and Other Edifices 53
Building of Caesarea 56
How Caesar Enlarged Herod's Kingdom and the Relationship 57
Rebuilding of the Temple in Jerusalem 59

**CHAPTER 3 CALUMNIES IN HEROD'S FAMILY LEADING
TO THE DEATHS OF ALEXANDER AND ARISTOBULUS** 63
The Meeting Between Herod and Marcus Agrippa 65

How Disturbances in His Family Caused Herod to Name
His Eldest Son Antipater as His Successor 67
Psychological Profile of Herod, According to Josephus 73
The Affair Between Salome and Sylleus 76
Further Problems Facing Alexander and Aristobulus 78
How Sylleus Caused Caesar to Become Angry at
Herod and How this Precarious Situation was Resolved 79
Events Leading to the Deaths of Alexander and Aristobulus,
the Sons of Mariamne 85

Chapter 4 THE DOWNFALL OF ANTIPATER, HEROD'S ELDEST SON 91

Antipater Becomes Intolerable and Friction Arises
Between Herod and Pheroras 93
The Death of Pheroras 96
The Imprisonment of Antipater 100

Chapter 5 THE LAST DAYS OF HEROD THE GREAT 107

Chapter 6 THE DEBATE OVER WHO SHOULD REPLACE HEROD AS KING AND THE BEGINNING OF THE RULE OF ROMAN PROCURATORS IN JUDEA, SAMARIA, AND IDUMEA 115

The Beginning of Seditions Against Archelaus 116
The Case of the Spurious Alexander 125
The Banishment of Archelaus to Vienna, Gaul 127
The Beginning of the Rule of Roman Procurators 128
Events Occurring in Judea and in the Territories
 Ruled by Antipas and Philip 129
Death of Caesar Augustus 130
Sedition of the Jews Against Pontius Pilate 132
Mention of Jesus the Christ 133

The Three Major Sects of Jewish Philosophy 135

Chapter 7 AN ACCOUNT OF JOHN THE BAPTIST, THE EXILE OF HEROD ANTIPAS, AND THE RISE TO POWER OF AGRIPPA 141

John the Baptist 143
The Early Life of Agrippa 144
The Banishment of Herod Antipas 153
The Reign of Caius (Caligula) 154
The Uprising Against Caius by the Jewish People Over His Decision to Place His Statue in the Temple at Jerusalem 155

Chapter 8 EVENTS OCCURRING IN JUDEA WHEN CLADIUS AND NERO WERE EMPERORS OF THE ROMAN EMPIRE *161*

What King Agrippa did for Claudius 162
What Claudius Did for King Agrippa and the Jewish People 164
What Things Were Done After the Death of King Agrippa 170
Actions of Fadus and How Claudius Once Again Came to the Assistance of the Jews in Judea 171
The Famine in Judea and the Assistance of Queen Helena of Adiabene 172
Death of King Herod of Chalcis and the Bestowing of His Dominions on Agrippa II 177
Tumultuous Events Occurring During the Reign of Cumanus 178
Additional Honors Bestowed on King Agrippa II by Claudius Caesar 181
Death of Claudius Caesar 182
The Decision Nero Made Against the Jews in Caesarea and the Consequences of that Decision 185
The Death of James, Brother of Jesus 188
The High Priest Position in Judea 193

**Chapter 9 THE BEGINNING OF THE JEWISH
REVOLT AGAINST ROME** 197

The Beginning of Civil War in Jerusalem 205

The Calamities and Slaughters that Befell the Jews in
Caesarea and Elsewhere 208

The March on Judea by Cestius, the President of Syria 210

Preparation for War in Jerusalem 213

The Appointment of Vespasian to Command the
Army to Attack Judea 214

The Capture of Josephus 219

The War Continues in Galilee 223

Chapter 10 THE SEDITIONS WITHIN JERUSALEM 227

The Decision by Vespasian to Conquer Regions
Surrounding Jerusalem 235

The Reprieve Given Jerusalem Because of the Death of Nero 237

Concerning Simon of Gerasa 238

News from Rome 241

Conditions in Jerusalem Because of the Mischievous
and Seditious Behavior of John of Gischala 241

How Vespasian was Proclaimed Emperor by the Soldiers
in Judea and Egypt 243

Release of Josephus from Bondage 245

The Death of Vitellius 246

The Trip Made by Vespasian to Alexandria, and then to
Rome to Receive the Government. The March on
Jerusalem by Titus 248

**Chapter 11 THE DESTRUCTION OF JERUSALEM
BY THE ROMANS** 249

The Tragic Event That Shaped the Outcome of the
Coming Siege by the Romans 250

The March on Jerusalem by Titus 250

Titus Sends Josephus to Urge His Own Countrymen
to Seek Peace 253

The Crucifixion of Jews before the Walls of Jerusalem........................255

The Destruction of the Embankments Against the First
Wall by the Zealots 256

The Wall Built by Titus that Encompassed Jerusalem 258

Further Crimes of Simon of Gerasa 259

Josephus Presumably Killed by a Stone and Comments
by his Mother 260

Continuing Effects of the Famine in Jerusalem 262

The Breach of the First Wall by the Romans 262

The Capture of John of Gischala 270

The Destruction of Jerusalem Except for Three Towers
and the Capture of Simon of Gerasa 270

Chapter 12 THE TRIUMPH IN ROME AND THE DESTRUCTION OF REMAINING JEWISH STONGHOLDS 273

Concerning Herodium, Macherus, and Masada, Three
Jewish Strongholds that Remained Following the
Destruction of Jerusalem..276

The Siege Against Masada..280

Events Happening in Alexandria and Cyrene Following
the Assault on Masada by the Romans 286

Josephus in Rome 288

Epilogue 290

REFERENCES..293

Preface

My first exposure to the writings of Josephus was through my father (DeVoe Woolf), an educator and master teacher, who was a high school principal during most of his adult life. Because of his love of teaching, he agreed to teach a Sunday school class on the New Testament to adults just prior to and during the years of World War II. I attended this class during the war years on the few occasions I was on leave from the U. S. Navy. In attendance were about 120 persons. The class was taught at the same level as a course in religious studies at a university. He had no formal background in theology and spent many hours each week getting ready for the class, using references from many different sources. He referred repeatedly to Josephus in one of the classes that I attended, which especially interested me because at that time in my life, age 18, the name was unknown to me. I promised myself that at some future time I would read the writings of Josephus. Many years later I remembered that promise and obtained a copy of *The Life and Works of Flavius Josephus,* translated by William Whiston, A. M, Professor of Mathematics in the University of Cambridge, with an Introductory Essay by the Rev. H. Stebbing, D.D.

The writings of Josephus, commonly known as the Works of Josephus, consist of *Wars of the Jews, Antiquities of the Jews, The Life of Flavius Josephus*, and *Flavius Josephus Against Apion.* Because of the writing style of Josephus, the massiveness of his writings, and the intricateness of the subject matter presented in *Wars* and *Antiquities*, I soon realized that dedication is required to read completely the Works of Josephus. But I persevered, and became especially intrigued when I read about the beginning of the Hasmonean period, the career of Herod the Great, the conspiracies occurring among the members of Herod's family, what transpired in Judea following the death of Herod, the events leading to the Jewish revolt against the Romans, and the destruction of Jerusalem and surrounding areas by the Romans. In order to keep certain facts straight, I began keeping notes beginning with the rise of the Hasmonean period. The notes grew in quantity, and I eventually reached the decision that it might be worthwhile to expand them into a synopsis. At that time of my life I was Emeritus Professor of Zoology, Arizona State University, and the writing of the synopsis was a broadening diversion from research and academic pursuits in my professional field.

In the beginning the sole purpose was to produce a synopsis that might be of interest to relatives and some friends. The goal changed, however, upon the strong encouragement of some of the individuals who read the initial manuscript. They suggested that the synopsis would be of interest to other persons, and especially those of Christian and Jewish faiths, who wish to be informed about the events, according to Josephus, occurring in Judea and nearby regions from about 170 BC to 73 AD.

To keep the flavor of Josephus's writing style, many of the sentences were taken directly from his writings (or more precisely, from the writings of the translator), but because of the uniqueness of his writing style, it was necessary to paraphrase most of the sentences. His writing style was followed for the non-capitalization of certain words within sentences, such as the title preceding the name of a person (i.e., king Herod), names of various judicial and religious bodies (i.e., sanhedrin), and names of certain prominent and public places (i.e., the temple in Jerusalem). Most of the subject matter in the *Works of Josephus* for the specified time period has been omitted in this Synopsis. What is included is an attempt to present the main events from the beginning of the Hasmonean period to the destruction of Jerusalem and surrounding areas by the Romans. Notes and commentaries appear in footnotes.

Readers are encouraged to use the wealth of the internet for obtaining information about historical cities, fortresses, and geographical regions mentioned by Josephus. Photos of historical sites, or the ruins of them, that are available on the internet, such as Masada, Herodium, and Macherus, give added insight about what transpired at those sites during the designated periods of time. Readers should also view the photos available on the internet of the Model of Jerusalem in the Israel Museum in Jerusalem showing the Second Temple, other structures built by Herod the Great, and the walls around Jerusalem at the time of the destruction of Jerusalem by the Romans.

The photo of the Second Temple Model on the cover of this book is reproduced here with the kind permission of The Israel Museum, Jerusalem (Credit line: Photo © Holyland Tourism 1992, Ltd. By Garo Nalbaldian, Courtesy The Israel Museum, Jerusalem).

The Life and Works of Josephus

Josephus was born in Jerusalem in 37 AD. He was of priestly and royal lineage, being a descendant of the Maccabees (Hasmonean blood-line), and was named Joseph, son of Matthias. Because of his heritage, Josephus was favored with an aristocratic education. He was educated in major Jewish schools in Jerusalem, those of the Pharisees, the Sadducees, and the Essenes, where he concentrated on Jewish religious philosophy. He became fluent in the Aramaic and Hebrew languages and also acquired a limited knowledge of the Greek language. In addition to formal studies, he entered a mentor-student relationship under a monk who lived in the Judean desert under sparse conditions. After 3 years of this educational experience, Josephus returned to Jerusalem and began his career as a priest and public official. One of his first noteworthy achievements was a trip to Rome where he negotiated for the release of fellow priests who had been retained by Nero.

At the beginning of the Jewish revolt against the Romans, when Nero was the Roman emperor, Josephus was given the responsibility of being governor and commander of an army in Galilee. He fulfilled his duties as a Jewish governor and general but maintained the view that a war against the Romans was futile. The Romans controlled the world known to them and the Jews had no chance of a military success against this power. It was his conviction that it was best to live at peace with them, and to seek for the religious freedom they had experienced under certain previous emperors. When the Roman general Vespasian and his son Titus arrived in Galilee and Judea, the Jewish forces were eventually subdued. Josephus was taken captive in 67 AD but was spared being sent to Nero for execution when he presented himself to Vespasian and "prophesied " that he (Vespasian) and eventually his son (Titus) would be named emperor. Intrigued and flattered by what Josephus said (which soon came to pass), Vespasian retained Josephus as his prisoner and granted him certain favors. His chains were removed in 69 AD when Vespasian accepted the acclamation of his troops and others, to become emperor.

Josephus accompanied Vespasian and Titus to Alexandria from where Vespasian sailed to Rome. Josephus then returned to Judea with Titus for the final siege of Jerusalem, which fell in September, 70 AD. The destruction of Jerusalem by the Romans was a tumultuous event for Josephus, and especially because his wife, parents and other relatives were in the city. During the assault on Jerusalem, Josephus was used by Titus to encourage the Jewish people to surrender. In speeches made while standing in front of the walls surrounding Jerusalem, Josephus addressed the Jews lining the tops of the walls and exhorted them to allow the Romans to enter the gates of the city peacefully, as the only means of saving themselves and Jerusalem and the Temple from destruction. His pleas were treated with scorn by his fellow Jews who accused him of being a traitor and a coward because of his association with the Romans. Many Jews had come to Jerusalem for the Passover and found themselves trapped. Others had come there believing that Jerusalem would be a sanctuary from the Romans because of the assumed impenetrable walls. Some had come there believing that God would protect them in this holy city. The blockade of the city by the Romans and unfortunate events occurring within the city caused many of the inhabitants to die from starvation. The Jews fought valiantly, but to no avail. According to Josephus, over one million Jews perished from the long siege by the Romans, either from starvation or by the sword. The plundering and destruction of Jerusalem by the Romans was massive. When the walls around Jerusalem finally fell, the Temple was destroyed.

With the fall of Jerusalem and the destruction of the Temple, Josephus traveled with the triumphant Titus to Rome. In Rome, his imperial patrons permitted him to live in an apartment in Vespasian's residence (vacated when Vespasian became emperor), granted him Roman citizenship, protected him from his enemies, granted him large tracts of land in Judea (from which he realized an income), gave him an annual stipend, and commissioned him to write historical treatises. At the time he obtained Roman citizenship he took the name of his patron Emperor Vespasian, whose full name was Titus Flavius Vespasianus. Thus, Joseph, the son of Matthias, became Flavius Josephus, a Roman citizen. Vespasian was succeeded as emperor by his son Titus, who was succeeded by his brother Domitian. Vespasian served as emperor from 69AD to 79AD, Titus from 79AD to 81 AD, and Domitian from 81AD to 96 AD. The period from 69 AD to 96 AD was known as the Flavian dynasty.

As a Roman citizen with the emperors (Vespasian, Titus, and Domitian) as his literary patrons, libraries and military archives were made available to Josephus, and he spent the rest of his life as a historian and author. His four surviving works are the *Wars of the Jews, Antiquities of the Jews, The Life of Flavius Josephus*, and *Flavius Josephus Against Apion. Wars* and *Antiquities* were major works. Each was written in Aramaic, his native tongue, and then translated into Greek. Only the Greek versions have survived.

His first work *Wars* was commissioned by Vespasian, and was published in about 75 AD when Josephus was 38 years of age. It begins with the uprising of the Jews, led by the Maccabees (Hasmoneans), against the forces of Antiochus IV, and concludes with the last resistive efforts of the Jews in Judea and nearby regions, and notably at Masada, following the destruction of Jerusalem and the Temple by the Romans.

The second book, *Antiquities,* was completed in about 93 AD, about 18 years after the publication of *Wars*. Domitian was emperor when it was completed. The objective of *Antiquities* was to give a complete history of the Jewish people from their origins to the time just prior to the Jewish revolt against the Romans. This long and ambitious undertaking reviews the early Hebrew Scriptures, beginning with Genesis, bridges the gap between the periods of the Old Testament and New Testament, and recants much of the earlier information, with additional details, found in *Wars*. In *Antiquities* Josephus gives detailed accounts of the Hasmoneans, events leading to the capture of Judea and Galilee by the Romans, the rise and long rule of Herod the Great, the intrigues and seditious calumnies among the members of Herod's immediate family, the impact of the Roman emperors on events occurring in Jerusalem and surrounding areas, and the circumstances in Judea leading to the Jewish revolt against the Romans.

His minor works *Life* and *Against Apion* appeared after the publication of *Antiquities*. *Life* was mainly a defense of his personal activities during a 5 month period as a Galilean commander and his account of the revolt against the Romans appearing in *Wars*. *Against Apion* was a defense of the Jewish religion, history, philosophy, customs, and culture. In this work he championed the laws of Moses, stating that the attributes of these laws are comparable to the highest aspirations of Greek philosophers.

The writings of Josephus cannot be overestimated. They give a history of the Jewish people from antiquities to about 73 AD, and they also give a valuable background for events described in the New Testament. They are also the only surviving account of the destruction of Jerusalem and the Temple by the Romans in 70 AD and the battle at Masada three years later.

Historical Perspectives

The early history of the Jewish people is given in the Hebrew Bible and recounted in *Antiquities* written by Josephus, going back to Genesis. According to these accounts, God ordered Abraham to leave his home in Mesopotamia (ancient country between the Tigris and Euphrates rivers, now part of Iraq) and to travel to a new land which God promised would belong to his descendants. This promised land (a land of "milk and honey"), known as Canaan, was a narrow strip between the Mediterranean Sea and a desert, which since pre-historic times had been a route of migration and commerce between Egypt and Asia Minor. Tradition states that a large group of Abraham's descendants eventually settled in Egypt where they were reduced to slavery. They finally fled to freedom under the leadership of Moses, assumed to be in about 1200 BC. After wandering in the desert, the tribes finally settled in Canaan where they fought among themselves and were continually challenged by their neighbors. When threatened by the Philistines, inhabitants of the southern coast of Canaan, the tribes united under the rule of Saul of the tribe of Benjamin. Saul died fighting the Philistines, and was succeeded by David of the tribe of Judah. David was successful in conquering the city of Jerusalem, which had been controlled by a Canaanite tribe. He made Jerusalem into the capital of his empire, and his son Solomon erected the Temple in Jerusalem which became the major spiritual center of the Jewish people.

The unity within the Jewish kingdom became unstable after the death of Solomon. The tribes in the north considered themselves more culturally and economically advanced than those in the south. The inhabitants of the north also chafed under Solomon's autocratic behavior during the later years of his life, and resented serving under kings from the south. The rebellion led to the splitting of the kingdom into a northern kingdom known as the Kingdom of Israel, and a southern kingdom known as the Kingdom of Judah.

The two kingdoms soon found themselves threatened by the empire of Assyria that was invading nearby territories. The Kingdom of Israel could not defend itself from the powerful aggressors from the north and in 722 BC the Kingdom of Israel ceased to exist. Because the Kingdom of Judah, including the city of Jerusalem, was of little economic value, it was not invaded by the Assyrians, and the inhabitants of this kingdom accepted the dominating presence of Assyria in the region.

With the slow disintegration of the Assyrian Empire, the Egyptians saw an opportunity to obtain Judah and the lands north. The Egyptians moved northward as far as the Euphrates, conquering all before them, but they soon faced a rising new empire led by king Nebuchadnezzar II of Babylonia. The capital of this empire was Babylon, the ancient city on the Euphrates River. The Egyptians were driven back to the Nile by this new conqueror, who in the process destroyed Jerusalem and the Temple (586 BC) built by Solomon, and deported a large number of the inhabitants, including the influential and skilled craftsmen, to Babylon. Those that remained in Judah following the takeover by king Nebuchadnezzar retained a strong faith that their promised land and Temple would eventually be restored to their full glory. The refugees in Babylonia and elsewhere also retained this same faith.

Cyrus the Great, the founder of the Persian Empire, conquered Babylonia in 536 BC. The Persian Empire eventually extended from the Indus River in northwestern India to the Mediterranean Sea including the areas south of Syria. In a momentous decision, Cyrus permitted the Jewish exiles in Babylonia to return to Jerusalem and rebuild the Temple. In an epistle to the governors in Syria, he wrote: "I have given leave to as many of the Jews that dwell in my country as please to return to their own country, and to rebuild their city, and to build the Temple of God at Jerusalem on the same place where it was before." Many chose, however, to remain in Mesopotamia. Josephus states that the number of Jews who came out of captivity and departed for Jerusalem was 42,462. These exiles took the leadership in rebuilding the Temple, the walls of Jerusalem, and urging allegiance to the laws of Moses. Great authority was given to the high priest who could claim descent from Aaron (brother of Moses). The area in which they settled, with Jerusalem being their major city, became known as Judea, or the land of the Jews.[1]

---

1   With the passage of time these people occupied the region extending from Syria to Egypt. The name Judea was retained for a broad area containing Jerusalem and the Temple. Areas north of Judea were named Samaria and Galilee. The area south of

The name Judea was taken from the word Judah, as in Kingdom of Judah.

Alexander the Great, the most celebrated conqueror of the ancient world, was born in 356 BC in Pella, the capital city of Macedonia. Macedonia was an ancient kingdom north of Greece, now part of Greece, Bulgaria, and Yugoslavia. His father, king Philip II of Macedon, was an outstanding leader who organized the Macedonian army, converting it into an efficient fighting force. He proceeded to invade Persia, but was assassinated in 336 BC when he only 46 years old. His son Alexander, who had been tutored by Aristotle, succeeded him to the throne even though he was only 20 years old. Alexander quickly subdued all uprisings following his father's death and turned his attention to the Persian Empire, the wealthiest empire extending from the Mediterranean to India.

Alexander launched his invasion of the Persian Empire in 334 BC. He led his troops through Asia Minor and then turned south to Egypt. Gaza fell after a siege of 2 months and Egypt surrendered without a fight. In Egypt he founded the city of Alexandria at the mouth of the Nile River. He then returned north, conquered Babylonia, and the Persian capitals of Susa and Persepolis. After 3 years of fighting he had conquered all the Persian Empire. From there he led his troops into Afghanistan and western India. Although intending to invade eastern India, his troops rebelled from exhaustion and refused to go any further. Alexander reluctantly returned to Persia where he reorganized his empire and army.

Alexander had been brought up to believe that Greek culture represented the only true culture and all persons of other cultures were "barbarians," but he soon reached the conclusion that

---

Judea acquired the name Idumea, and an area east of the Jordan River was named Perea. The entire region was eventually named Palestine by the Romans, with Palestine being a Hellenized version of the word Philistine. This region retained the name Palestine until after World War II when by action of the United Nations in 1947, the state of Israel was carved out of the region as the homeland of the Jewish people.

individual Persians were as intelligent and worthy of respect as individual Greeks. Thus, he developed the concept of creating a joint Greek-Persian culture and kingdom with himself as the ruler. Although he intended to make additional conquests, he fell ill with a fever and died at age 32 in Babylon in 323 BC.

An impact of Alexander's conquests was the spreading of the Greek culture throughout all countries that he had conquered. After his death there was a two decade struggle for power among his generals. His empire was eventually divided among three of the victors, and two of the resulting empires (the Ptolemaic and Seleucid) would eventually rule Judea.

With the death of Alexander the Great, Judea was attached to the domain of Egypt. One of Alexander's leading Macedonia generals (Ptolemy Soter) became governor of Egypt, and in 304 BC declared himself king (Ptolemy I, king of Egypt). Ptolemy I placed Greeks and Macedonians in key government and army positions, and acquired great wealth through trading networks linking India, east Africa, and the Mediterranean. He made Alexandria his capital and established libraries and museums there. The Ptolemies demanded tribute from the Jews living in Judea, but granted them religious freedom. During this period of time a large number of Jews settled in Alexandria. Even though these Jews were under strong Hellenic influences, they were able to retain their traditional religious values. It was in Egypt during the reign of the Ptolemies (in about 250 BC) that the sacred Jewish books were translated from Hebrew into Greek.

In 198 BC Judea was wrested away from the Ptolemies by the Seleucids, whose capital was Antioch (now located in southern Turkey). The initial ruler (Antiochus I) of this dynasty was Seleucus Niccator, one of Alexander's Macedonian generals. The Syrian Greek king, Antiochus III the Great, ruled a vast empire from the Mediterranean across Syria and Persia, but with the passage of time and the slow disintegration of the empire from within, Antiochus IV began a program of suppressing with force all cultures that were different from his own Graeco-Syrian culture. Although many Jews favored the Hellenized way of life, most Jews opposed the oppressive program of the Syrian king, who demanded that the practice of circumcision and the observance of Sabbath rituals must cease, and all sacrifices must be offered to his gods rather than to the Hebrew God. He then plundered the Temple in Jerusalem, ordered that the Jews build temples and idol alters in every city, and sacrifice swine on those alters. Because of the fear of the severe consequences if they opposed Seleucid rule, many Jews abided by the demands of the Hellenistic Syrians. .

But an older and influential man living in the village of Modein (northwest of Jerusalem), took a stand against this religious persecution. Mattathias, who had been a revered priest and resident of Jerusalem, refused to sacrifice swine. The year was 163 BC, and his defiance led to the Maccabean revolt and eventual Jewish independence from the Seleucids.

That is the beginning of the story.

HASMONEAN PEDIGREE

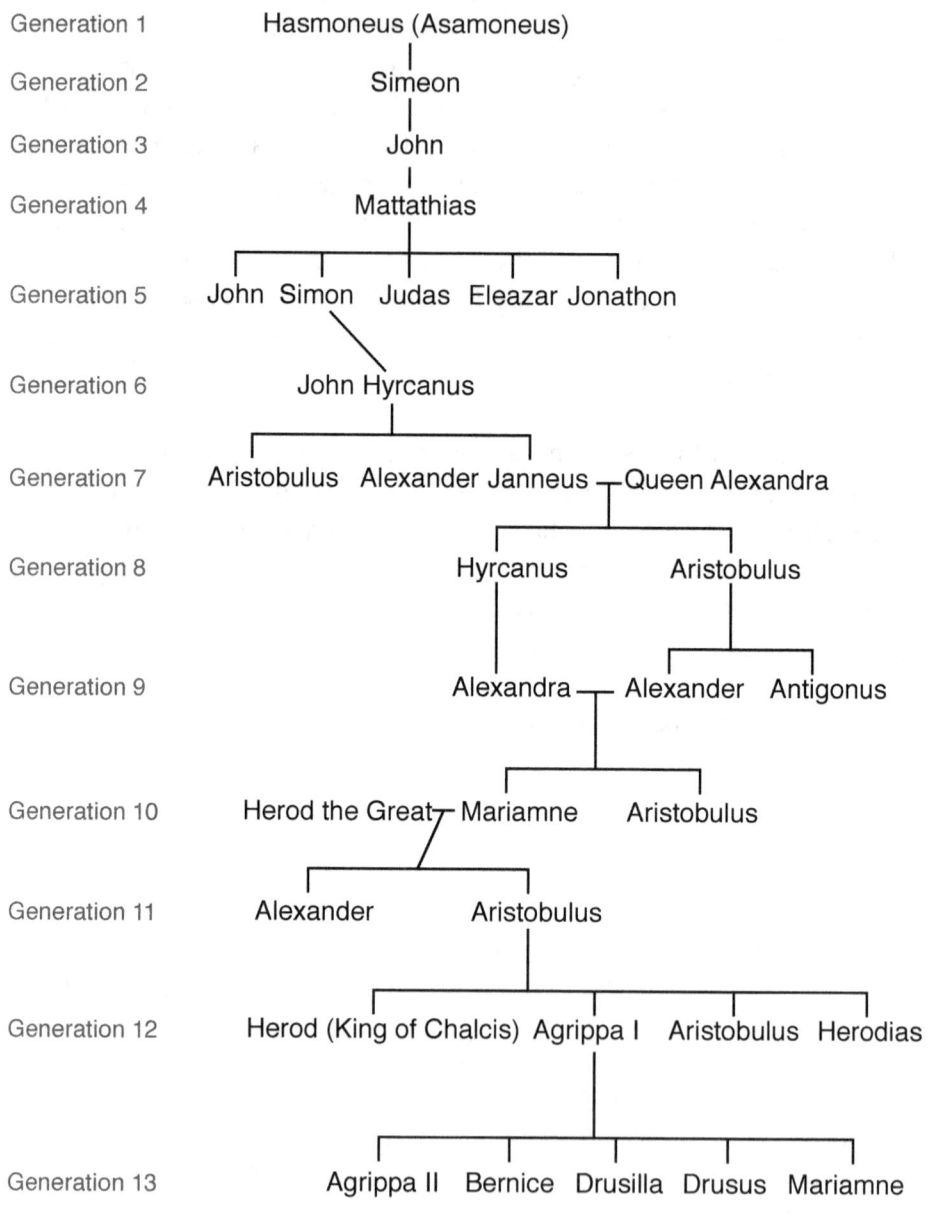

THE GENEALOGIES OF AGRIPPA I & AGRIPPA II

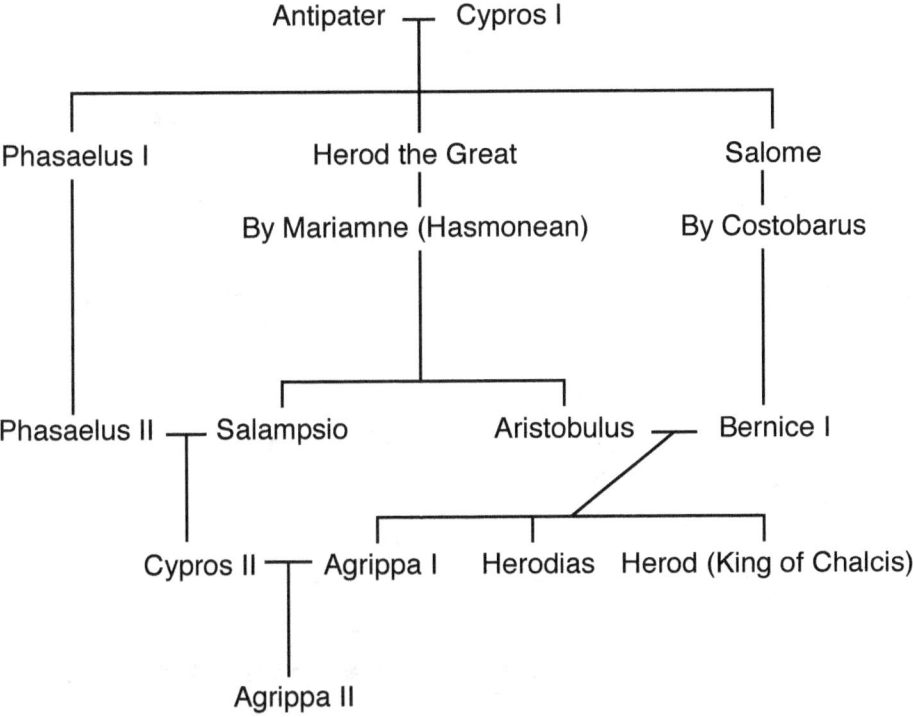

[Both parents of Agrippa II were of Hasmonean lineage through Mariamne who was one of the wives of Herod the Great. Herodias, sister of Agrippa I, was initially married to Philip (Herod) who was the half brother of Herod Antipas. The father of Philip (Herod) and Herod Antipas was Herod the Great. The daughter of Philip (Herod) and Herodias, named Salome, was the damsel of biblical fame (Mark 6:14-28) who danced before Herod Antipas. Prior to that event, Herod Antipas had divorced his wife and married Herodias, even though it was against Jewish Law for a man to marry his brothers wife.]

BIOLOGICAL RELATIONSHIPS OF EARLY ROMAN RULERS

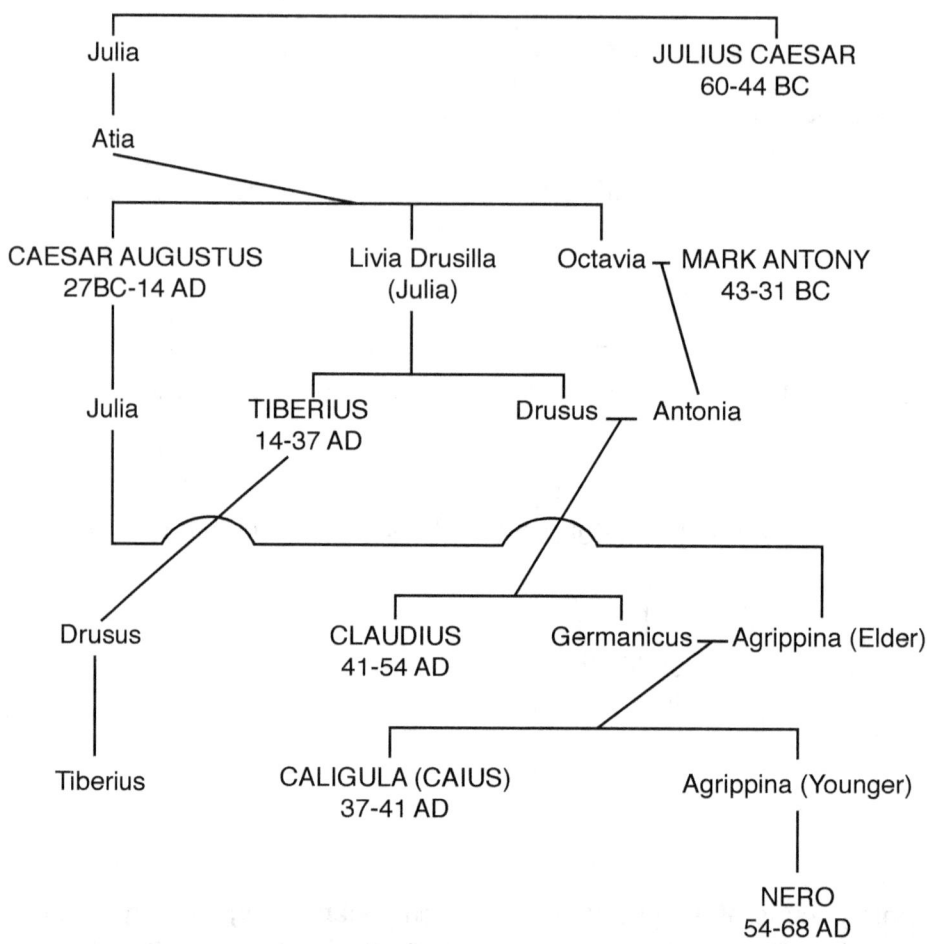

[With the support of the Roman Senate, Julius Caesar served as the supreme Ruler with various titles, including Consul and Dictator. Octavian (Augustus), Mark Antony, and Lepidus were rulers (Trimvirs) of different divisions of the Roman world from 43 - 31 BC. Caesar Augustus is acknowleged to be the first true Emperor.]

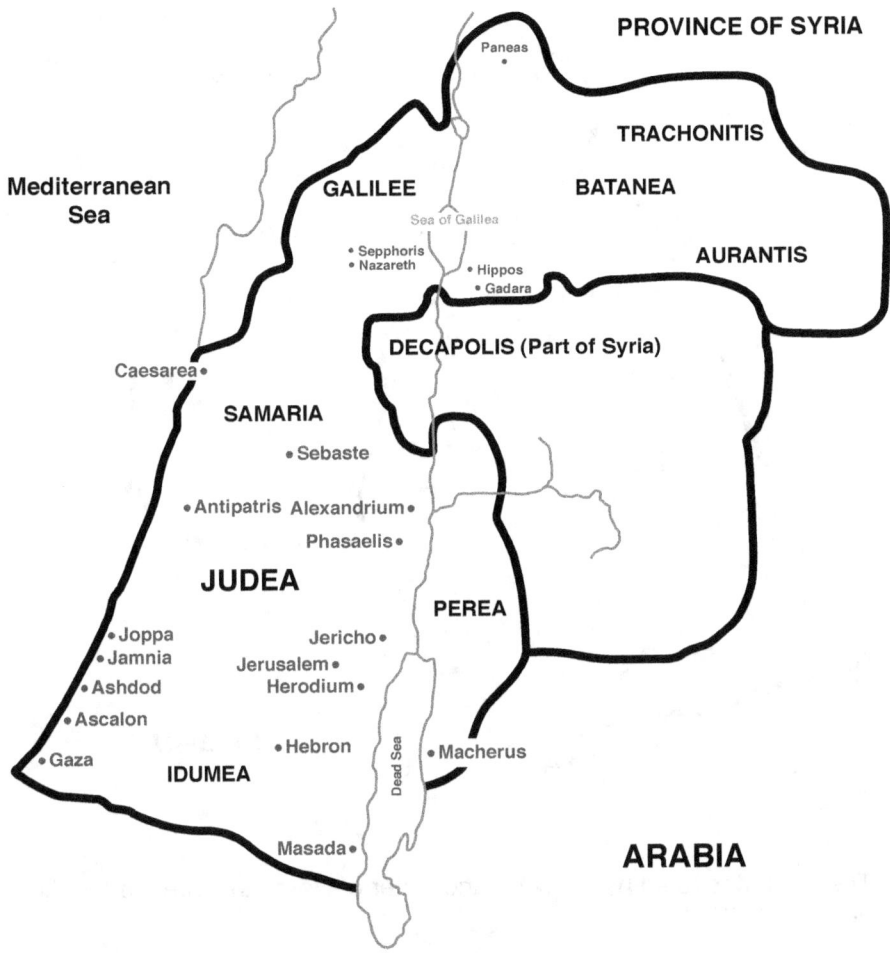

The Kingdom of Herod the Great prior to his death in 4 BC. The seaport of Ascalon was controlled by Rome.

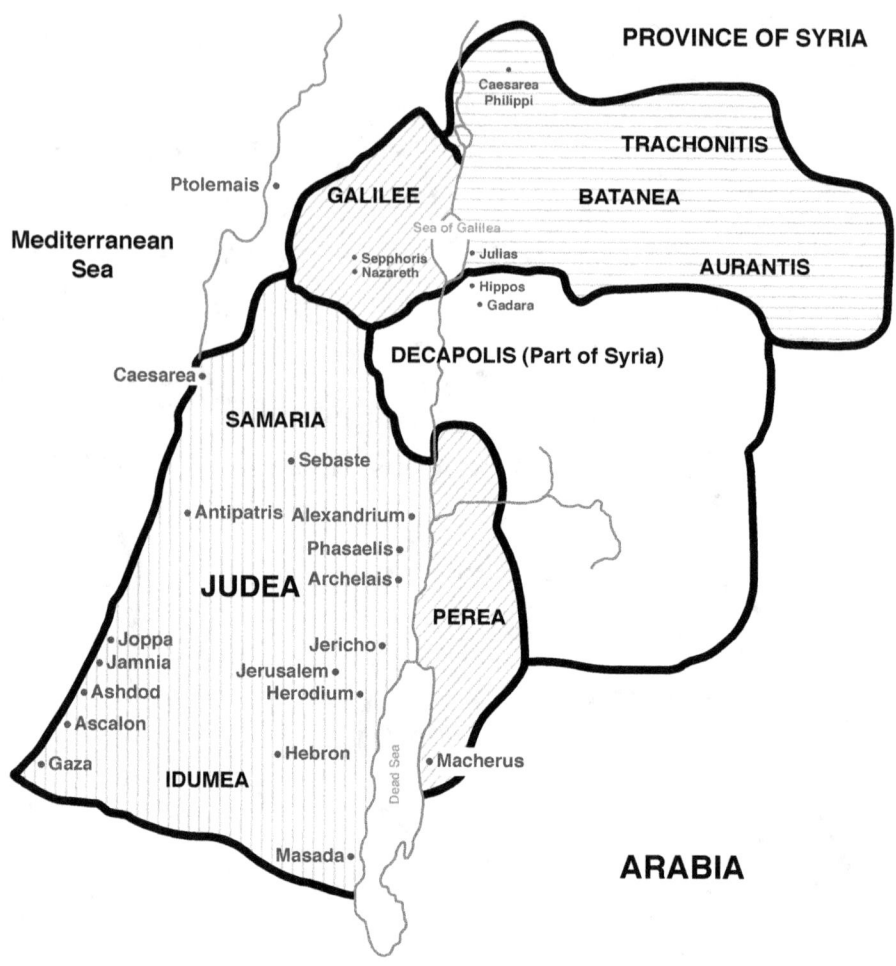

The territories ruled by the sons and sister of Herod the Great after his death in 4 BC:

    Ethnarchy of Archelaus: Vertical Lines
    Tetrarchy of Antipas: Slanted Lines.
    Tetrarchy of Philip: Horizontal Lines
    Territories of Salome: Cities of Ashdod, Jamnia, and Phasaelis

    Ascalon and Gaza were assigned to Syria

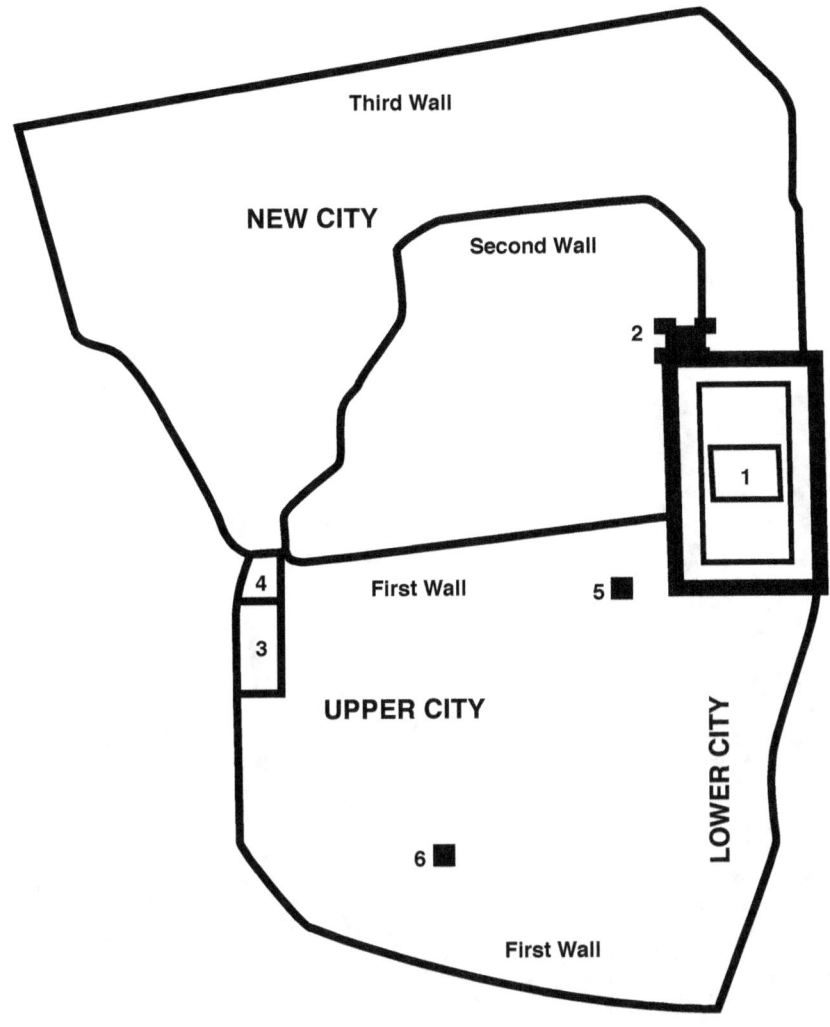

Chapter 1

HASMONEAN PERIOD

King Antiochus [Antiochus IV]) made an expedition against Jerusalem, and pretending peace, he obtained the city by treachery. Led by his covetous inclinations he pillaged the temple and removed the gold and ornaments, the golden candlesticks, the golden altar, the veils which were made of fine linen and scarlet, and anything he deemed of value, leaving the temple bare of all its treasures. He then pillaged the entire city, slaying many of the inhabitants and making ten thousand others captives, including wives and children. He also burned down many of the finest buildings, and when he had overthrown the city walls, he built a citadel in the lower part of the city, fortified it with high walls and towers, and stationed within it a garrison of Macedonians. He also built an altar upon God's altar in the temple, and slew swine upon it.

And throughout Judea he forbade the Jews from worshiping their God, and instead, forced them to worship his gods and to live the Grecian way of life. He made them build temples and idol altars in every city and village, and to offer swine upon those altars every day. He also commanded them not to circumcise their sons and threatened to punish anyone who transgressed this injunction. He appointed overseers to compel the Jews to do what he commanded. Many Jews complied with the king's commands, either voluntarily or out of fear. The best men, and those with the noblest souls, continued to worship God according to their own dictates, but if they were discovered by the overseers they were whipped with rods, their bodies were torn to pieces, and they were crucified while they were still alive and breathing. New born sons who had been circumcised were strangled, and their mothers were hung on crosses with their dead sons draped about their necks. If any sacred book of law was found, it was destroyed, and the possessor was first tormented and then slain.

Now at this time [167 BC] there was a man named Mattathias from Modin (also spelled Modein) whose great grandfather Hasmoneus (also spelled Asamoneus) had been a revered priest (order of Joarib) and a resident of Jerusalem. Mattathias lamented to his children about the sad state of their affairs under the Hellenistic Syrians, including the religious persecution, the plundering of the temple, and the ravaging of their city. He informed them that it was better to die for the religious laws of their country than to live under such deplorable conditions. Mattathias had five sons, related to Hasmoneus as follows:

Generation 1 → Generation 2 → Generation 3 → Generation 4
  Hasmoneus   Simon   John   Mattathias

→ Generation 5 (Sons of Mattathias)
John, Simon, Judas, Eleazar, Jonathan

One of the king's generals (Apeles) came to Modin to compel the Jews living there to adhere to the commands of the king. The general attempted to entice Mattathias, a person with the greatest character among them, to sacrifice a swine on a pagan altar in the manner ordered by the king, believing that if a person with his reputation would conform to the edicts of the king, his fellow-citizens would follow his example. Mattathias said that he would not do so, stating that he and his sons would not forsake the religious laws of their country. As soon as he had ended his speech, one of the Jews in the audience approached the altar and made the sacrifice as commanded. Mattathias, with great indignation, drew his sword, ran towards the Jew who had made the sacrifice, and slew him. He and his sons also slew the king's general and a few of the men who were with him. Mattathias then knocked over the pagan altar and cried out, "If any one be zealous for the laws of his country and for the worship of God, let him follow me." He and his sons then fled to the desert, leaving all their belongings behind. Large numbers of Jewish families followed Mattathias and his sons to the desert, where many of them were forced to live in caves.

The king's generals and men living in Jerusalem pursued the Jews into the desert and initiated an attack against them on the Sabbath, a day of the week when Jews refused to fight or even defend themselves. About a thousand persons, including women and children, were smothered in caves from fires started by the Syrians. Those who escaped this massacre went to Mattathias and asked him to be their leader. One of his first actions was to convince them that if they were to survive they must not obey the Sabbath law so rigorously, because surely the Syrians would plan to fight all major battles on the Sabbath. He argued that they would all perish if they refused to fight on the Sabbath. This speech persuaded them, and from that day on it was agreed, "We will fight on the Sabbath if it is necessary to do so." Mattathias assembled a great army and went to battle against the Syrians and those Jews who by choice had gone over to the Syrian side. He also commanded that those males who had not been circumcised should be circumcised immediately.

After a year Mattathias became ill and called for his sons. He appointed his third son Judas to be the general of the army because of his courage and strength, announcing that "He (Judas) will avenge your nation and bring vengeance on your enemies." Mattathias then died and was buried at Modin.

Whereupon, Judas took control of the army and the administration of public affairs. His army overthrew the forces of the local Syrian generals in Judea and Samaria. When king Antiochus heard of these events, he was very angry and sent other armies against Judas, but Judas was victorious, believing that God was on his side.[1]

Judas assembled the people and told them that because of these many victories which God had given them, they should go to Jerusalem, purify the temple, and offer the appointed sacrifices. Upon their arrival they found the temple deserted, its gates burned down, and weeds growing in the temple. He then began to purify it by cleaning it, hanging up new veils, adding doors, and bringing in new altars made of gold. When all was ready, they lighted the lamps that were on the candlestick, offered incense upon the altar, laid the loaves (shew-bread) upon the table, and offered burnt offerings upon the new altar.

Judas celebrated the festival of the restoration of the sacrifices of the temple for eight days, and honored God by hymns and psalms. He made a law for posterity that they should hold an eight day festival honoring the restoration of their temple, and it was to be called lights.[2]

All five brothers, John, Simon, Judas, Eleazar, and Jonathan, were active leaders in the revolt against the Syrian Greeks. Judas, who had been appointed military leader by his father, was eventually

---

[1] The name Maccabeus was later bestowed upon Judas, the third son, because of his zealous attacks against the Syrians. The name (from the Greek) means "hammerer." Thus, it was said that Judas "hammered" the Syrians. Judas Maccabeus proved to be an influential leader and a military genius who defeated four Seleucid armies in quick succession. The Maccabeus appellation has historical significance because the members of this distinguished family became known as the *Macabees*. They belonged to the Hasmonean blood-line in honor of their important ancestor Hasmoneus.

[2] This Jewish festival, called Hanukkah, occurs in December, and marks the reconsecration of the temple of Jerusalem after its recapture from the Syrians. Associated with this festival is the miracle of the burning of a day's supply of pure olive oil for eight days until fresh jars of clean oil could be brought into the temple. This accounts for the eight days during which candles are kindled during Hanukkah. The eight-branched candelabrum has become a symbol of the holiday. Songs and stories associated with the festival refer to the Macabees (particularly to Judas Maccabee) and to their victory.

named high priest in addition to being the general. With the high priest title, he became the spiritual leader of the people.

The battles continued even after the initial successes against the Syrian Greeks. Eleazar was killed in one of the battles, leaving four brothers. In addition to military battles, the brothers also had to deal with discontent within Judea, and with minority groups attempting to gain control. In one major battle, desertions occurred in the army headed by Judas because the invading Syrian army was vastly greater in number. After putting up a courageous battle, Judas was wounded and eventually died [161 or 160 BC]. Simon and Jonathan were able to retrieve his body, by an agreement with the enemy, and carry it to the village of Modin where he was buried. Judas had been high priest for three years when he died. He has been forever revered for gaining freedom for his nation and delivering the Jewish people from slavery under the Syrians.

Jonathan was the successor to Judas. In the beginning he was appointed general of the army, but eight years after the death of his brother Judas, he was also named high priest [152 BC]. While preparing for a battle against the Syrians, Jonathan sent his brother John to an Arab city to negotiate support. An ambush was laid for John and he was killed. His death left only two of the original five brothers: Jonathan and Simon. Jonathan was also killed by treachery. A Syrian general (Trypho) who had offered cooperation and support, encouraged him to travel to Ptolemais without his main army. Believing that Trypho was sincere, he went to Ptolemais relatively unguarded, where he was taken captive by Trypho. With Jonathan in bonds, Trypho then put together a large army and made plans to make war against Judea. Because of the situation they faced, the people of Jerusalem were terrified. Simon encouraged them in a speech to defend their city from Trypho. His words to the multitude were so inspirational that they cried out that if he would be their leader they would obey whatsoever he would command them to do. Simon accepted this role, assembled all the soldiers that were fit for war, and made haste in rebuilding the walls of the city, making them higher and stronger.

Trypho and his army then marched to Judea, bringing Jonathan with them in bonds. He offered to release Jonathan for a price, but Simon knew that Trypho was a deceitful person and even if the money were given, Jonathon would not be set free. This situation was troublesome because the people would be distraught if Jonathan, their high priest, were killed merely because the money was not sent. The only solution was to give Trypho the money and hope that Jonathan would be released. The money was sent to Trypho, and as expected, Jonathan was not set free. Trypho then planned an attack against Jerusalem by way of Idumea, but a severe snowstorm prevented him from doing so. Instead of continuing with the battle, he killed Jonathan, gave order for his burial, and returned to Antioch. At the appropriate time, Simon sent soldiers to Basca to retrieve his brother's bones, which were then taken to Modin and buried. All the people made a great lamentation over the death of Jonathan, who had served as high priest for 7 years and leader of the people for a longer period of time.[3]

With the death of Jonathan the multitude acclaimed that Simon should be their high priest and leader [143 BC]. Simon served for eight years and became known as Simon the Great because of his military successes against the Syrians. His death came by treachery. The husband of his daughter was Ptolemy, the Greek ruler from Alexandria. Ptolemy attacked Syria and then moved southward with the goal of invading Judea and taking Jerusalem. He believed

---

[3] During his tenure as high priest Jonathon realized that an isolated high rock plateau (later named Masada), with precipitous sides, near the west side of the Dead Sea, had the potential of being a formidable fortress, where persons on top with adequate supplies, including weapons, food, and water, could defend themselves for a long period of time from a large army of enemies. In case he might have need for such a fortress, Jonathon built barracks and storehouses on top, and winding and narrow trails leading to the top that could be readily defended. He also built cisterns on top for the capture of rainwater. At a later in time in history Masada was greatly improved as a fortress by Herod the Great.

that his military efforts would be successful in Judea if he could first eliminate his father-in-law Simon and his three sons, thereby leaving the Jewish people without a leader. In an effort to bring this about he invited Simon, Simon's wife and two of Simon's sons to a feast in a city outside of Jerusalem. There, by treachery he killed Simon and placed Simon's wife and Simon's two sons in bonds. Ptolemy also sent soldiers to kill Simon's third son, named John Hyrcanus, but this son learned of the plot and was able to escape to Jerusalem.

John Hyrcanus, who inherited the high priest position [135 BC] upon the death of his father, then made an expedition against Ptolemy who had retired to a fortress near Jericho. During the siege of this fortress Ptolemy brought John Hyrcanus's mother and his two brothers to the wall and threatened to throw them down unless John Hyrcanus called off the siege, but his mother spread out her arms and encouraged him not to do so. Ptolemy then had her beaten and torn to pieces. He then killed her two sons, and fled to Philadelphia.

After many years at war with the Syrians and Egyptians, John Hyrcanus eventually put an end to most of the seditions against the Jewish people. He also successfully administered the government for 39 years before he died. John Hyrcanus was highly revered as a spiritual leader, with three of the highest privileges that could be given by God—the government of his nation, the dignity of the high priesthood, and the gift of prophesy. It is of historical importance that his death brought to an end the Hasmonean theocracy of the Jewish nation, whereby the high priest, who was perceived to be divinely inspired, was the ruler of the people without any other title. This form of government, carried out by John Hyrcanus and the preceding Hasmoneans (i.e., members of the Maccabee family) was not followed by the succeeding rulers who, instead, established Jewish monarchies, to the anguish of the Jewish people, with the ruler being king, with or without the title of high priest.

Change from a Hasmonean Theocracy to a Jewish Monarchy

Upon the death of John Hyrcanus [104 BC], his eldest son Aristobulus became the high priest. One of his first acts was to create a Jewish Monarchy by placing a crown on his head and announcing that he was king in addition to being high priest. Although he was fond of his brother Antigonus, next to him in age, and treated him well, he placed his other three brothers in prison. He also placed his mother in prison because she disputed with him over the form of government that he had established. He eventually starved her to death in prison, and then had his brother Antigonus killed because of the fear that he might be assassinated by him. He then went into depression, became physically ill, and died after reigning only one year. Following his death his wife Salome let his three brothers out of prison and announced that one of them, Alexander Janneus, who was the oldest would be king. Thus with the death of his brother and the decree of his mother, Alexander Janneus obtained the government with the titles of king and high priest [103 BC].[4]

Alexander Janneus soon found himself embroiled in battles with both the Syrians and Egyptians. He also found himself in a turmoil with his own people who revered his father John Hyrcanus and considered him unworthy to be their high priest and king. In expeditions against the Syrians, there were many deserters, and in some battles Alexander Janneus found himself fighting Jews who had joined with the Syrians in an effort to overthrow his monarchy. He sought revenge against these deserters and any other Jew who opposed him. In one battle against Syrian-Jewish forces he captured a large number of Jewish deserters, placed them in bonds, and took them back to Jerusalem. He then carried out a barbarous act. He ordered that about 800 of the captured men should be crucified in the sight of the populous of the city, and in sight of him while he was feasting with his concubines. And while the captured men were hanging on the crosses and still alive, he ordered that the throats of

---

4   Alexander Janneus is known historically as a heinous Hasmonean monarch because of his atrocities against those who opposed him.

their wives and children should be cut before their eyes.

Alexander Janneus served as king for 27 years. When he became ill and was dying in a fortress beyond Jordan, his wife Alexandra came to him weeping and lamenting. She bemoaned that because of the hatred of the people towards him, she and their young children had no future after his death. The Pharisees, who had strong influence among the people, had been especially critical of Alexander Janneus because of his atrocious behavior as king. In order to retain the kingdom for her and his children, Alexander Janneus informed her that he would commit the kingdom to her, but to obtain the needed support of the Pharisees, he told her that upon his death she should proclaim herself immediately as the leader, return to Jerusalem as on a victory march, report immediately to the leaders of the Pharisees, and place some of her authority into their hands. She was to promise them that no major decisions would be made without first consulting with them. Alexander Janneus then died [76 BC].

Alexandra followed her husband's counsel. After proclaiming that her husband had named her to be queen and regent, she gave the Pharisees great authority and ordered the multitude to be obedient to them. This pleased the Pharisees. Their anger towards Alexander Janneus was pacified, and as a result he was given a glorious funeral. The Pharisees gave their support to Alexandra, and the multitude soon grew to love her, and especially because she pronounced great displeasure at the many barbarous offenses of her husband. Even though Alexandra gave much authority to the Pharisees, she as queen and regent took care of many of the affairs of the kingdom. She also increased the size and effectiveness of the army so that it was a defensive threat to hostile neighbors. Because of these actions, the country was at peace.

Alexander Janneus committed the government to his wife Alexandra even though he had two sons, Hyrcanus and Aristobulus.

The elder son Hyrcanus showed no interest in public affairs and preferred a quiet private life. The younger son, Aristobulus, however was an active and bold man. Alexandra made Hyrcanus high priest because he was the elder son, and also because he preferred to allow the Pharisees to have all the responsibilities in public affairs. For that reason the Pharisees were pleased with the appointment of Hyrcanus as high priest. However, the appointment of Hyrcanus as high priest disturbed Aristobulus because in that position Hyrcanus had the potential of being a man of great influence. Aristobulus was a scheming man of great ambition who believed that he would be a better ruler than Hyrcanus, and he resented the fact that Hyrcanus, who was a passive man, had been named high priest. Aristobulus feared that when their mother died, Hyrcanus and the Pharisees would rule jointly, but with all the power going to the Pharisees because his brother preferred a quiet life. He knew that he would have no future in the government under this arrangement, and being an ambitious man, he began waiting for an opportunity to seize the government as king.

Even though the country was at peace during her years as queen and regent, Alexandra soon found herself in a political turmoil. The Pharisees demanded that she execute the men who had participated in the actions of her husband when he ordered that the 800 army deserters should be crucified and their wives and children should have their throats cut. When she failed to do so the Pharisees took matters in their own hands and proceeded to cut the throats of several of the accused men. Others who had participated called upon Alexandra and told her that she should force the Pharisees to stop this persecution, arguing that they had served Alexander Janneus their king with honor, and had followed faithfully his wishes and commands. It was reproachful that their lives were now threatened and dishonored in such a manner. Aristobulus, who defended these men in front of Alexandra, suggested that one solution would be to place them in various fortresses throughout the kingdom where they could not be harmed by the Pharisees. Alexandra agreed to this plan, and it was carried out, to the dismay of the Pharisees.

Alexandra soon became very ill, and Aristobulus resolved that now was the time to seize the government. He left Jerusalem in secret and conferred with the men in the various fortresses whom he and his mother had protected from the Pharisees. He knew that he would have the support of these men because he had come to their assistance at a critical time in their lives. He convinced them that their lives would be in grave danger if upon his mother's death the Pharisees took over the control of the government. Aristobulus was able to obtain the allegiance of these men, and soon he had put together a formidable army. The Pharisees and their supporters in Jerusalem were alarmed at these events. Accompanied by the high priest Hyrcanus, they called upon Alexandra and inquired how she intended to respond to these ominous events. Her reply was that she had little interest in public affairs now that the strength of her body had failed her, and the Pharisees should do whatever they thought was proper. She soon died [67 BC] at the age of 73, after serving as queen for nine years. During those nine years she had kept the nation in peace.

The War between Aristobulus and Hyrcanus for the Kingdom [67-63 BC]

Upon the death of his mother, Hyrcanus, as high priest, assumed the leadership of the Jewish people, and immediately his brother Aristobulus made war against him. During a battle at Jericho, many of Hyrcanus's soldiers deserted, and joined his brother's army. Realizing that he had no chance of winning the battle, Hyrcanus fled to Jerusalem and sent a message of understanding to his brother, proposing that Aristobulus should be king, and that he, as high priest, would live quietly without meddling in public affairs. They agreed upon these terms publicly in the temple, where they took oaths, shook right hands, and embraced each other in sight of the multitude. At the conclusion of this ceremony, Aristobulus, as king, departed for the palace, and Hyrcanus, as high priest, went to the former house of Aristobulus. But knowing the influence of the high priest on the multitude, Aristobulus soon broke the agreement by decreeing that he as king should also hold the office of high priest, and thereby took it away from Hyrcanus.

The Intervention of Antipater, the Idumean

A rich and influential Idumean, named Antipater, had been appointed by Alexander Janneus as general of Idumea (kingdom located south of Judea). Antipater, born into a prominent family, rose to a high position in Alexandra's court when she was queen and regent, and was on the scene when her two sons Aristobulus and Hyrcanus competed for the throne. Antipater married Cypros, an Idumean and the daughter of a noble Arab. She bore him four sons (Phasael, Herod, Joseph, and Pheroras) and a daughter (Salome). His second son was eventually named king by the Romans and was later known historically as Herod the Great.[5]

Antipater was suspicious of Aristobulus, and was worried about what might happen to his own personal power base with Aristobulus as king. Antipater began cementing his friendship with neighboring Arabs to the east (Petra) and west (Gaza), and initiating private conversations with influential Jews, arguing that Aristobulus had obtained the government improperly by going to war against his brother Hyrcanus, who was older and who by birthright should be the leader. Antipater also spoke to Hyrcanus warning him that Aristobulus was being advised by friends that he could not rightfully claim the government while Hyrcanus was still alive, and therefore

---

5   Josephus states that *Jews are Jews by nature and from the beginning, but Idumeans were not Jews from the beginning*. The Idumeans were defeated by John Hyrcanus, and were told to become Jews or leave the country. Becoming Jews meant becoming circumcised, uniting under one country, and living according to Jewish law. The original Idumean population was a composite of the people living south of Judea, and had a large Arabian component.. Thus, the Idumeans were not Jews in the beginning, and the offspring of Antipater were, at the most, only half Jew because of their Arab mother. This heritage was of great historical concern for Herod the Great (a half-Jew who was later appointed King by the Romans.

Hyrcanus's life was in jeopardy. At first Hyrcanus paid no attention to these warnings because he trusted his brother and preferred not to become involved in public affairs. Antipater persisted and advised him to seek the protection of Aretas, the king of Arabia. Hyrcanus finally consented after being assured by Antipater that Aretas would receive him and not deliver him to his enemies. Antipater and Hyrcanus stole out of Jerusalem at night and went to Petra, southeast of the Dead Sea, where Aretas dwelled in his palace. Antipater and Aretas were good friends, and Antipater urged Aretas to accompany Hyrcanus to Jerusalem with his army and drive Aristobulus out of Jerusalem, allowing Hyrcanus to assume the government. Aretas agreed to do so if Hyrcanus would give him 12 cities that his father Alexander Janneus had taken from the Arabians. This arrangement became a pact between them.

Aretas attacked Aristobulus's army outside of Jerusalem and forced Aristobulus to retreat behind the walls of the city for safety. At this time many members of Aristobulus's army deserted and went to the cause of Hyrcanus. Thus, there were Jews on the inside (including many priests) aligned with Aristobulus, and Jews on the outside, aligned with Hyrcanus, who were fighting each other. The Jews on the outside brought Onias into their camp and ordered him to pray on their behalf against the forces of Aristobulus. Onias was a righteous man whose prayers had previously ended a serious drought. When he refused to do so, they threatened him, and thus he was compelled to give a prayer. So, he prayed as follows: "Oh God, the king of the whole world. Since those that stand now with me are thy people, and those that are besieged are also thy priests (people), I beseech thee, that thou wilt neither harken to the prayers of those against these, nor bring to effect what these pray against those." As soon as he had finished, he was stoned to death by those Jews who were unhappy with this prayer.

In the meantime the Roman statesman and general Pompey[6]

---

6   Pompey (106 BC - 48 BC) was one of the great statesmen and generals of

sent a general named Scaurus to Damascus and eventually into Judea. Aristobulus and Hyrcanus sent ambassadors to him asking for military assistance, and each offered money for his support. Scaurus sided with Aristobulus, believing that it would be easier to defeat those on the outside than those on the inside who were well fortified. So he went into battle against Aretas and Hyrcanus and their armies of Arabians and Jews. After inflicting damage, Scaurus returned to Damascus. Aristobulus then came out of the city with a great army and fought Aretas and Hyrcanus. Much damage was done to both armies, but neither achieved a victory.

The Role of Pompey

Pompey then arrived in Damascus and both Aristobulus and Hyrcanus appeared before him requesting his assistance. Antipater was also present, supporting the cause of Hyrcanus. In addition, groups of individuals appeared before Pompey stating that they represented the Jewish people. They told Pompey that the nation of Jews was against both Aristobulus and Hyrcanus because the people did not wish to be under a kingly government. They wanted their leader to be the priest of the God they worshipped, a form of government they had enjoyed in previous generations. They noted that although both Aristobulus and Hyrcanus were the descendants of righteous Hasmonean priests, the government had changed in recent generations in order to enslave the people.

Hyrcanus complained that he was older than Aristobulus and that he had been deprived of his birthright by Aristobulus. He also stated that the people had revolted against Aristobulus because he

---

the Roman Empire. His early military adventures were in Africa, Sicily, and Spain, but one of his greatest achievements was extending and reorganizing the eastern areas of the empire, including Syria and Judea. At one time he was a colleague of Julius Caesar and was part of the First Triumvirate including himself, Crassus and Julius Caesar that ruled the empire. Later he became involved in the civil war as an opponent of Julius Caesar. His forces were finally beaten by those of Julius Caesar at Pharsaelus in 48 BC. Following this defeat Pompey fled to Egypt where he was treacherously assassinated at the orders of king Ptolemy who chose not to offend Caesar by receiving Pompey.

was a man of violence and disorder. Antipater then argued strongly on behalf of Hyrcanus, stating why he was entitled to be king.

Aristobulus argued that Hyrcanus was not a forceful leader, his passive behavior was contemptible, and because of Hyrcanus's lack of leadership, he had been forced to take over the government or it would have been transferred to someone else, such as the Pharisees. He also claimed that the title of king was claimed by his father, and therefore he was entitled to it. He also said that because he was a Hasmonean, he was entitled to the position of high priest, a position he, as king, had taken away from Hyrcanus when Hyrcanus expressed a preference for a private life. Aristobulus then requested that certain witnesses be allowed to speak on his behalf. These witnesses offended Pompey and his court because of their youth, manner of dress (purple garments, fine heads of hair, and ornaments) and especially their insolence. They appeared as if they were marching in a pompous procession rather than pleading their case in a court of justice.

Pompey chastised Aristobulus for his arrogance and informed both Hyrcanus and Aristobulus that he would settle this situation at a later time. In the meantime, he ordered them to behave and to wait for his decision. Aristobulus left for Jerusalem in a contemptuous manner, assuming that Pompey would not be of assistance to him. He prepared for war against Hyrcanus and also against Pompey if necessary. Because of these actions Pompey became angry, gathered his army, and made an expedition against Aristobulus.

When Pompey's army approached Jerusalem, Aristobulus repented of what he had done, went to meet Pompey and promised to give him money and to receive him in Jerusalem. Pompey forgave him and sent a general and soldiers to the city to receive the money, but Aristobulus's soldiers in the city rebuffed them, and they returned to Pompey without the money. When this became known to Pompey, he became very angry, and placed Aristobulus in bonds.

Josephus

Pompey then made a siege on Jerusalem and used battering rams to knock down walls and gain entry into the city. Hyrcanus, who was still hoping to be named leader by Pompey, assisted Pompey by encouraging Jews, both inside and outside the city, not to support the forces loyal to Aristobulus. The siege was bloody. The Romans killed 12,000 Jews, but only a few Romans were casualties. In the siege of the city Pompey was careful not to cause any damage to the temple, but he did something that only the high priests had been able to do throughout the ages. He entered the inner sanctum of the temple (holy of holies) and viewed all that was there—the golden table, the holy candlestick, the pouring vessels, the great quantity of spices, and the treasure of sacred money. Pompey did not touch any of it because of his regard for religion and also for the religious beliefs of others.

Pompey ordered that the temple should be cleansed and offerings should be given according to Jewish custom. Because Hyrcanus had been useful to him in his war with Aristobulus, he also granted that the high priest position should be restored to Hyrcanus. Pompey then secured Judea and surrounding areas, placed them under the jurisdiction of generals, and returned to Rome. He took with him Aristobulus and Aristobulus's two daughters and a son named Antigonus. Another son, Alexander, had been able to avoid being captured by fleeing away from Jerusalem. Thus, Aristobulus was deprived of his kingdom after serving as king for 3 years and 6 months.

> *"Jerusalem and the surrounding areas were now under the control of the Romans [63 BC], an event that was hastened because of the actions of Aristobulus and Hyrcanus who sought the political assistance of Pompey, a powerful Roman statesman and general."*

To secure the positions around Jerusalem, the Roman general Scaurus made an expedition into Arabia and attempted to conquer

Petra, but the initial assault failed because the city was fortified by its geographical location. He then set fire to places around it, and would have caused more damage if his army had not suffered because of famine. Antipater came to his aid by providing him with provisions from Judea sent by Hyrcanus. General Scaurus also sent Antipater to king Aretas in Petra to persuade him to buy peace with money. Antipater and Aretas had been friendly in the past, and Antipater was able to convince Aretas that it would be prudent to pay what was requested because his situation was precarious. With the payment, Scaurus withdrew his army out of Arabia, and Petra was preserved from destruction by the Romans.

The Attempts of Alexander, Son of Aristobulus, to Overrun Judea

Alexander, the son of Aristobulus, who had managed to escape from Pompey, was able to assemble a large army consisting of 10,000 armed footmen and 15,000 horsemen. With this formidable militia he fortified Alexandrium, Hyrcanium, and even Macherus on the east side of the Dead Sea. Hyrcanus was unable to oppose him because he was busy repairing the walls of Jerusalem destroyed by Pompey, but Gabinius, who had been sent to Syria to replace Scaurus as commander of the Roman forces, made an expedition against Alexander. A battle broke out between Gabinius and Alexander near Jerusalem, during which the Romans slew 3,000 of Alexander's army and took a similar number alive. Gabinius then made a siege against Alexandrium. As this battle continued, Alexander despaired of ever obtaining the government, and with the strong encouragement of his mother he sent an embassage to Gabinius asking that he be pardoned for his offenses. As payment he promised to give up all his fortresses (Hyrcanium, Macherus, and Alexandrium). Knowing that Roman lives would be saved by this agreement; Gabinius pardoned Alexander, and then began to demolish the fortresses.

Alexander's mother, who was concerned about the welfare

of her husband Aristobulus, two daughters, and her son Antigonus, who were being retained in Rome, went to Gabinius and asked for his assistance in obtaining their release. Because she had been instrumental in helping him acquire the fortresses without any battle, and therefore had benefited the Romans, Gabinius agreed to grant what she had requested concerning these persons.

The Escape of Aristobulus from Rome and his Return to Judea

In the meantime, Aristobulus had been able to escape from Rome and return to Judea. Many Jews ran to him because of his former glory and the hope that he would deliver them from the Romans. As soon as he had a sizable force he took Alexandrium, which had been demolished by Gabinius, and began building a wall around it. He retreated, however, to Macherus when Gabinius sent a large army against him. After a brief battle at Macherus, the Romans captured Aristobulus and returned him to Rome where the senate put him in prison. However, his son Antigonus and his two daughters were allowed to return to Judea, at the request of Gabinius who had promised to reward the wife of Aristobulus for helping to deliver the fortresses to him.

Gabinius then went to war against the Parthians, and in his absence from Judea, Alexander, the son of Aristobulus, once again tried to get the Jews to revolt. He raised a formidable army and began killing the Romans that were still in the country. Fearful of what was going on in Judea, Gabinius returned and met Alexander's army at Mt. Tabor, defeated them, and took Alexander as a prisoner. Soon after doing so, Gabinius returned to Rome and was replaced by Crassus as commander of the Roman forces.

The Deaths of Aristobulus and his Son Alexander

When Julius Caesar[7] came to power in 60 BC, he freed

---

7 Julius Caesar (100 BC - 44 BC) was born in Rome. When he was 42 years old he was appointed governor of northern Italy, the coastal region of Yugoslavia and the southern coast of France. Using forces at his command he then conquered regions in

Aristobulus from prison and sent him to Syria with an army to help settle matters in that area, believing that Aristobulus had influence in that country. Aristobulus was not keen about serving the Romans, and did so only because it was a means of being released from prison. But soon after arriving in Syria he was poisoned by followers of Pompey. His body was eventually returned to Judea by Mark Antony, where he was buried in the royal sepulcher. Pompey also ordered that Aristobulus's son Alexander should be slain because he was guilty of so many offenses against Rome. As a consequence Alexander was beheaded at Antioch.

Relationship Between Antipater and the Romans

Antipater was an able diplomat who made friends with Arab kings of areas surrounding Judea, and was an influential and self-serving advocate of Hyrcanus in his controversy with his brother Aristobulus. For political reasons and to further his own cause, Antipater was also a strong friend of the Romans and catered to them at every opportunity.

Upon the death of Pompey, Antipater was named by Julius Caesar to manage Jewish affairs, and when Julius Caesar made war against Egypt, Antipater and Hyrcanus came to his assistance. When Mithridates, the Roman general, marched on Egypt, Antipater joined him with a Jewish army. Antipater encouraged Egyptian Jews not to oppose the Romans, showing them epistles from Hyrcanus (high priest) urging them to cultivate a friendship with Julius Caesar and to supply the Roman army with provisions. The Egyptian

---

France, Belgium, Holland, Germany, and parts of Switzerland. His success as a general made him a hero in Rome, but this success also produced political enemies who were fearful of his objectives. At the completion of his military term he was ordered back to Rome unaccompanied by his army. Fearing assassination, he defied this order. The result was a civil war between troops loyal to him and those loyal to the senate. The war lasted 4 years, with the last battle being fought in Munda, Spain in 45 BC. He returned to Rome and was acclaimed as dictator for life. He was assassinated at a senate meeting in 44 BC by a group of conspirators.

Jews complied as requested, and many joined the fight against the Egyptians.

In the war with Egypt, Mithridates's army found itself in a serious military situation and faced defeat. Antipater with his Jewish army came to the rescue, and by a flanking movement, saved the Roman army. Mithridates sent an account of this battle to Caesar, openly declaring that Antipater was the reason for the victory and for his own preservation. Caesar commended Antipater for his actions.

At the conclusion of the war with the Egyptians, Julius Caesar honored Antipater and Hyrcanus for their meritorious service to Rome. He bestowed on Antipater the privilege of Roman citizenship and granted him freedom from taxes wherever he lived. **He also awarded Antipater with a territory to oversee as procurator, and allowed him to choose the territory. Antipater chose to be procurator of Judea and the surrounding areas, including Galilee. Julius Caesar also confirmed Hyrcanus as high priest and ethnarch.**[8] With this new authority Antipater admonished the Jewish people to behave, and to live peacefully under his leadership. If they lived according to his dictates, they could enjoy their possessions, but any uprising would bring his wrath, that of the high priest, and that of the Romans. Because he had been given the authority to do so by the Romans, **Antipater then appointed his eldest son Phasaelus as governor of Jerusalem and the places about it, and made his next oldest son Herod governor of Galilee [47 BC].**

Herod: The Governor of Galilee

As governor of Galilee, at age 25, Herod found himself embroiled in a situation with far reaching consequences. A gang

---

[8] An ethnarch is the title of a ruler that is less than a king. In this case the title was mostly honorary because Hyrcanus was a passive individual who preferred not to become involved in public affairs, and Antipater, as procurator, was the actual ruler. However, in the revered position as high priest, Hyrcanus had great influence on the multitude.

of robbers, captained by Hezekiah, was terrorizing the region of Galilee and parts of nearby Syria.[9] Herod went after these robbers and killed their leader Hezekiah and many of those who served under him. He was praised by many inhabitants of the region for his actions, and also by Sextus Caesar, a relative of Julius Caesar, who was president of Syria. Phasaelus, Herod's brother, who was governor of Jerusalem, was jealous of the acclaim given Herod, and in order to be similarly praised he made an effort to be a just governor and to have the good will of the people. The overall result was that the people praised Antipater for his appointments. Although many honored Antipater as if he were the absolute ruler of the country, Antipater, being a wise political leader, was careful not to diminish the influence of Hyrcanus, who was high priest and ethnarch.

Many influential Jews, however, became jealous and highly suspicious of Antipater because of his power. They also became displeased with him because he would prevail upon Hyrcanus, as high priest and ethnarch, to obtain money for the rulers in Rome, and when it was provided by Hyrcanus, Antipater would send it Rome as if it were a gift from him. These influential Jews also complained to Hyrcanus that Antipater and his two sons had assumed the leadership of the government, even though he as high priest and ethnarch was the official ruler. They also condemned Herod as a violent and ambitious man, who often acted in a tyrannical manner. Even though Herod had been praised by the Syrians and many Jews for having rid the country of Hezekiah and his gang of robbers, the influential Jews acclaimed that Herod had committed a grave sin by killing these persons because Jewish law prevents any such killings unless the persons have been condemned to death first by the sanhedrin.[10] The mothers of the robbers complained

---

9   Although Josephus described Hezekiah as a robber, he may have been a rebel who was revolting against Roman rule.

10   In Jerusalem, the sanhedrin was the supreme council and tribunal consisting of 70-72 members, having jurisdiction over religious matters and important civil and criminal cases. In provinces, it consisted of only 23 members, having jurisdiction over minor civil

about the deaths of their sons and grumbled daily in the temple that Herod should be punished for his actions. Hyrcanus was moved by these complaints and as high priest was obligated to summon Herod to trial before the members of the sanhedrin, knowing that if Herod was found guilty of the charges against him by the sanhedrin, he would be put to death. Hyrcanus found himself in a difficult situation. As high priest he was expected to follow Jewish laws, but he was dealing with a charge against a son of Antipater, who was his friend and who had been his benefactor. Hyrcanus also received a message from Sextus Caesar, president of Syria, which stated that he should clear Herod of the charges against him. Sextus Caesar also threatened Hyrcanus if he did not do so.

Upon the recommendation of Antipater, Herod appeared before the sanhedrin in Jerusalem not as a private person but accompanied by many well armed guards. The presence of these guards was threatening to the members of the sanhedrin who sensed that their lives would be in danger if they found Herod guilty of the charges against him. Not knowing how to handle the situation they became silent. In the beginning none of his accusers had the courage to make any charge against him. But sensing that the sanhedrin would eventually pronounce the sentence of death on Herod, Hyrcanus postponed the meeting to another day, and then secretly urged Herod to flee the city. Herod escaped to Damascus. Later he conferred with Sextus Caesar, and resolved that he would not obey any future summons by the sanhedrin.[11] Herod was also furious with Hyrcanus for allowing the charges to have been made against him.

When Sextus Caesar made Herod general of the army of Celesyria (an appointment paid for by Herod), Herod began a march towards Jerusalem with the goal to assault the city. But his father

---

and criminal cases.

[11] Because of his fury against the members of this sanhedrin, Herod later had them all killed.

Chapter 1 Hasmonean Period

Antipater and his brother Phasaelus intercepted him and convinced him not to fight Hyrcanus who had befriended him in the past and who had also prevented the sanhedrin from sentencing him. Besides, since it is God who turns the scales of war, it would not be wise to fight against the high priest, who had bestowed many benefits upon him and who had done nothing severe against him. Herod was persuaded by these arguments, and believed that it was sufficient for his future to have made a show of his strength before the nation. The case against Herod was then eventually dropped by lack of any further action by the sanhedrin, mainly because of the power Herod now possessed and the support he received from the Romans.

Death of Antipater

After the assassination of Julius Caesar[44 BC] by Cassius and Brutus in the senate-house, Cassius went from Rome to Syria to be commander of the Roman forces stationed there. One of his first acts was to demand additional taxes from the Syrian and Jewish people. Antipater appointed various persons to gather the taxes, including Herod and Malichus, a Jewish commander. Herod did exactly what was expected of him in Galilee, and was praised by Cassius for his actions. Herod thought it was highly prudent to cultivate a friendship with the Romans, even though carrying out their mandates caused ill will among many Jews. Malichus was negligent in collecting the taxes in his designated areas, which made Cassius so furious that he planned to have Malichus killed. Sensing the seriousness of the situation, Hyrcanus pacified Cassius by sending him money of his own. Because of this timely intervention Malichus was now indebted to Hyrcanus.

After Cassius left Judea, Malichus began plotting against Antipater believing that his death would allow Hyrcanus, as high priest and ethnarch, to be the true leader of the people rather than merely a token leader. An opportunity presented itself when Antipater was invited to dine with Hyrcanus. Malichus bribed Hyrcanus's butler (and food-server) to poison the food served to

Antipater. The scheme was successful and Antipater died by this treachery. Even though Malichus denied any involvement, Herod suspected who had orchestrated the death of his father. He sent Cassius a message informing him of the assassination of his father, and Cassius replied that Herod should avenge his father's death. Cassius also sent orders to the commanders of his army at Tyre that they should assist Herod in the execution of Malichus. A trap was set, and Herod arranged to have the commanders ambush Malichus and stab him to death.

The Naming of Herod as Tetrarch and His Betrothal to Mariamne the Hasmonean

Following the death of Antipater, Mark Antony[12] traveled to Syria. A delegation of eloquently speaking Jews met with Mark Antony there to accuse Herod and those about him of tyrannical behavior, hoping that Antony would remove Herod as leader. When Antony asked Hyrcanus who governed the best, Hyrcanus replied, "Herod and his friends." Whereupon, Mark Antony, partly out of respect for the deceased Antipater, named Herod and Phasaelus as tetrarchs, committed the public affairs of the Jews to them, and wrote letters to that effect. Being a stronger and more forceful leader than Phasaelus, Herod began to assume the government. The affinity between Herod and Hyrcanus was made stronger because of the marriage betrothal between Herod and Mariamne, the granddaughter of Hyrcanus and the daughter of Alexandra (Hyrcanus's daughter

---

12   Mark Antony was a loyal supporter of Julius Caesar and served with him during his conquest of Gaul. After Caesar's assassination, he attempted to arouse the people against those assassins. With growing political influence he became a candidate to succeed Caesar, along with Octavian who was Caesar's great-nephew and adopted son. Julius Caesar, who had no sons of his own, had prepared Octavian for a political career. In 43 BC Octavian, Antony and Lepidus formed the Second Triumvirate, a board of three, to rule the empire. The triumvirs agreed to divide up the empire, and Antony took over the administration of the eastern provinces, including Syria and Judea. One of Antony's early actions was to summon Cleopatra, Queen of Egypt, to Tarsus to provide him assistance in the war with the Parthians. She arrived with gifts and captivated Antony. He returned to Alexandria with Cleopatra where they spent the winter of 41-40 BC in a romantic relationship.

).[13] At this time Herod was married to Doris (an Idumean) by whom he had his eldest son Antipater.[14]

Role of Antigonus, the Son of Aristobulus

With the beheading of his brother Alexander in Antioch, the sole surviving son of Aristobulus was Antigonus. Antigonus had been returned to Judea from Rome by Gabinius at the request of Alexandra, the mother of Antigonus. Antigonus was an ambitious man and because he was a Hasmonean and the only remaining son of Aristobulus, he believed that he was the proper heir to the throne. He had the support of many Jewish people, who attested that Herod had no right to this position because he was not a Hasmonean and was only a half-Jew because his mother was an Arab. Antigonus formed a large army of loyal Jewish supporters and in his first major skirmish with the forces of Herod, Antigonus was driven from Judea. Antigonus then made an agreement with the son of the king of Parthia, whereas, Antigonus would give the Parthians a large sum of money and 500 women of Jewish stock from principal families, if they would assist him in obtaining the government and killing Herod.

Parthian generals made a siege on Jerusalem, and by subterfuge convinced Hyrcanus (high priest and ethnarch) and Phasaelus (tetrarch) to leave the city as ambassadors to the commander of the Parthians in an effort to bring peace. A trap was set for them and they were made prisoners by the Parthians. Distressed by this news and fearing the consequences, Herod made the decision to flee Jerusalem with his close relatives, including his mother Cypros, his sister Salome, his future wife Mariamne and her mother Alexandra, and his youngest brother Pheroras, in addition to wives, children, and all their servants. Accompanied by armed men they left at night

---

13   Mariamne was the product of a first cousin marriage because her father was Alexander, the son of Aristobulus who was Hyrcanus's brother.

14   Doris was Herod's first wife and Mariamne became his second wife and the first of other polygamous wives.

under cover of darkness and made their way southward to Masada. There was great sadness among them because they had been forced to leave their own county. Herod experienced melancholy because of the situation, and the grave dangers that faced his family. During the journey he was especially alarmed when the wagon carrying his mother overturned. This accident almost resulted in her death. His overall apprehension was so great that he considered killing himself, but he was restrained by those close to him just as he was drawing his sword to do so. There were skirmishes along the way with the Parthians, and each time the forces of Herod were victorious. At one locality there were hand to hand battles with Jewish forces loyal to Antigonus who tried to ambush them. Herod and his army were able to put these opponents to flight. To honor this great victory Herod later built at this locality a beautiful palace, and a city about it, and named it Herodium in honor of himself.[15]

Following the defeat of the Jewish forces loyal to Antigonous, Herod and his army hastened to Masada, but before reaching that destination Herod rendezvoused with his brother Joseph at a place in Idumea. The decision was made to disband most of the troops that the two brothers had brought with them, and Joseph was to command the men guarding Masada. This towering fortress near the western shore of the Dead Sea was well supplied with grain, water, and other provisions, and was safe from attack because of its location and fortification. Believing that his family and future wife Mariamne were now safe, Herod traveled to Petra in Arabia.

The following day the Parthians plundered Jerusalem, the palace, and the countryside. With forethought Herod had sent a great deal of his money to Idumea, where it was safe from the Parthians. With this victory Antigonus was then brought back to Judea by the Parthians, where he received Hyrcanus and Phasaelus as his prisoners. Antigonus was greatly distressed because the

---

15   Herod later decreed that he should be buried at Herodium. A tomb was prepared at Herodium for this purpose.

women from prominent Jewish families he had promised the Parthians had escaped, with many being at Masada. He was also aware that Hyrcanus (his uncle) was a threat to him because they both shared Hasmonean blood and Hyrcanus was high priest and ethnarch. Fearing that Hyrcanus might receive the government from the Jewish multitude, he had Hyrcanus's ears cut off, thereby assuring that Hyrcanus could no longer serve as high priest because of his maimed condition.[16]

Fearing that he was going to be killed, Phasaelus (with arms bound and under chains) pounded his head against the wall, thus committing suicide. It was also reported, however, that physicians, under the orders of Antigonus, infused poison into the head wound, which caused the death of Phasaelus.

With the support of the Parthians, Antigonus now assumed the position as king [40 BC].

The Naming of Herod as King by the Romans

Herod traveled from Masada to Petra hoping to obtain financial assistance from Malchus the king of Arabia, whom he had been kind to in the past. Malchus had also previously received large financial loans from Herod's father Antipater, and had pledged fidelity to Antipater. Through messengers, Herod requested a loan or a gift from Malchus, and expected to be received favorably by him. Herod intended to use the money to bribe the Parthians to release his brother Phasaelus. He took with him the son of Phasaelus who was only 7 years old. He offered to leave his nephew as hostage for repayment of any loan of money that Malchus might give him. But Malchus did not want to receive Herod and sent a message to him that the Parthians, whom he did not want to antagonize, would take offense if he aided Herod. This was only a pretense because he chose not to make amends for the financial assistance given him previously by

---

16   The law of Moses states (Levit, 21:17-24) that high priests that officiate are to be complete and without blemish for all parts of their body.

Antipater, assuming that the outcome of Herod's conflict with the Parthians might excuse him from the need to make payment of the loan. Turned away by Malchus, whom he now viewed as his enemy, Herod departed for Egypt, where, with the assistance of Cleopatra, he obtained passage by sea to Rome. Soon after rebuffing Herod, Malchus repented of his actions, and sent messengers to intercept him. However the messengers were unable to overtake Herod's fast moving party. On the way to Egypt Herod also learned about the death of his brother Phasaelus, which grieved him greatly.

In Rome Herod met with Mark Antony and related the problems that had befallen him at the hands of the Parthians, including the death of his brother, how Hyrcanus had been detained by them, and how they had made Antigonus king. Antony commiserated with him, recalled the friendship he had had with his father Antipater, and affirmed that he would be of assistance to him. Antony also expressed his hatred for Antigonus, whom he declared was now an enemy of Rome.

A meeting of the senate was convened. Herod was introduced and the senators were reminded of the past good will that existed between his father Antipater and the Romans, and the benefits they had received from Antipater. At the same time Antigonus was accused, and declared to be an enemy because he had sided with the Parthians and had assumed the government and title of king without consulting with Rome. Antony informed the senators that it was to their advantage that Herod should be named king. The senators made a decree accordingly, and when the senate meeting was ended, Antony and Octavian [17] went out of the senate house with Herod between them. But though Herod received the kingdom from the Romans [40 BC], he could not serve as king until he had wrested the kingdom away from Antigonus.

---

17   Antony and Octavian were two members of the Second Triumvirate who ruled the Roman empire.

In the meantime Antigonus made an assault on Masada hoping to capture members of Herod's family. Even though the fortress was safe from attack, the inhabitants were in dire straits. They had ample grain and other provisions, but a severe drought had plagued the area and they were in dire need of water. Conditions were so severe that Joseph, Herod's brother, made plans to escape to the Arabians with 200 hundred persons, including family members. Joseph expected to be received favorably by Malchus, who had repented of his refusal to give financial assistance to Herod, but during the night when they planned to make their escape, it rained and the cisterns became filled with water. This act of God rejuvenated the people, and they were able to defend themselves against the attacks by Antigonus.

Final War for the Kingdom Between Herod and Antigonus
With the support of Rome, Herod sailed out of Italy for Ptolemais, gathered together an army and marched through Galilee where he met opposition from Antigonus's forces. To his advantage Herod had the support of Roman troops as he fought his way across Galilee in the direction of Judea. His immediate goal was to reach Masada and save his relatives who were under siege. Before proceeding on to Masada, it was necessary for him to take Joppa because it contained forces that were loyal to Antigonus, and it was important that no enemies would be at his rear when he made his assault on Jerusalem. After he had successfully taken Joppa, Herod made full flight for Masada. He had a strong army and even though Antigonus laid snares and made ambushes at various different locations, they had little effect. Herod soon reached Masada and retrieved the members of his family.

From Masada, Herod and his army traveled to Jerusalem and made their camp west of the city. Herod then proclaimed to the people in the city, who lined the walls, that he had come for the good of the people and for the preservation of the city, and he would not bear any old grudge at even his enemies. He urged them to open the gates and allow his army to enter the city in a peaceful manner. In the exchange of words Antigonus proclaimed that it was not proper for the Romans to have given the kingdom to Herod because he was only a private man, an Idumean, and only half-Jew. It was only just that the kingdom should be bestowed on a member of the royal family, which was the custom of the people. As a Hasmonean and proper heir to the throne, he was being deprived of the kingdom by the Romans.

Since his efforts to enter the city peacefully were rebuffed, Herod then ordered his army to assault the city, but the followers of Antigonus who manned the walls and who therefore had the advantage of height and the protection given by the walls and towers, successfully prevented Herod's soldiers from gaining entrance into the city. Herod then realized that a successful assault on the walls would require the construction of embankments and towers, and he faced other problems. Time would be required to build the embankments, and there were two serious complications--the army was running short of food, and the winter season was approaching. The Romans were becoming increasingly disgruntled because of the food shortage, and they complained that they did not want to spend the winter camped on the outskirts of Jerusalem. The Roman commander Silo, who had accepted bribes from Antigonus, had actually encouraged his men to grumble about the living conditions. Silo then announced that he planned to move his army away from the area because of the scarcity of food. Herod pleaded with him and his captains not to depart, and promised that he would solve the food shortage problem. He had his friends in Samaria send grain, wine, oil and cattle to Jericho, and although Antigonus attempted to intercept them, he was not successful and the Romans had ample food to meet their needs. Deciding that no military actions should be taken against the walls of Jerusalem that winter, Herod allowed the Romans to spend the winter in hospitable regions of Samaria, Judea, and Galilee, where they rested and laid their weapons of war aside.

Herod did not wish to be idle. He sent his brother Joseph with 2,000 armed footmen and 400 horsemen to put down an opposition in Idumea. He himself then departed for Samaria where he left his mother, his future wife Mariamne, and other family members in a safe location. From there he moved on to Galilee to take villages and cities held by forces loyal to Antigonus. After attending to these matters he went to Antioch and from there hurried north to assist Antony who was embroiled in a battle at Samosata, a place on the Euphrates. The road from Antioch to Samosata was controlled by Parthian barbarians who attacked travelers at key passages. By fighting courageously, Herod and his army defeated these Parthians, and when Herod approached Samosata, Antony, out of deeply felt gratitude, sent his army to meet Herod and to pay respect for his valor. Antony also embraced him and saluted him in an emotional manner. It was apparent to all who observed this tribute to Herod that a mutual bond of admiration existed between these two men. Antony soon departed for Egypt, but before doing so he gave orders that General Sosius and his large Roman army were to assist Herod in the assault on Jerusalem.

With great sadness, Herod then learned that his brother Joseph had been killed. He had left his brother Joseph in command of the armed forces in Judea with the instruction that he should not attack Antigonus until Herod had given the order, but Joseph took matters into his own hands. When Herod moved north and was not available for consultation, he made an assault on Jericho. Joseph was slain in the battle, and Herod learned to his great anger that when Antigonus obtained possession of Joseph's body, he cut off his head. At a later time Herod took revenge by cutting off the head of the commander who had slain Joseph.

The battles that winter in Judea and Samaria between Antigonus's army and the combined armies of Herod and Sosius were intense, with both sides having large numbers of casualties. But eventually the tide turned against Antigonus. Plans were then made by Herod for the assault on the walls of Jerusalem, and he camped his army close to the city. This was three years after he had been named king by the Romans.

The Marriage of Herod to Mariamne the Hasmonean

In order to assault the walls surrounding Jerusalem, bulwarks and towers were constructed. Trees were cut down on the outskirts of Jerusalem to build these structures. Leaving an army behind to build and protect these structures, Herod then went to Samaria to marry Mariamne, daughter of Alexander and the granddaughter of Hyrcanus. Herod believed that he could solidify his position with the Jewish people by banishing his first wife (Doris) and first son (Antipater), and marrying Mariamne, a Hasmonean princess. He was also deeply in love with Mariamne, who was renowned for her beauty.[18]

The Assault on Jerusalem by Herod and Sosius

Following the wedding Herod returned to Jerusalem with an additional army. There he rendezvoused with Sosius who also arrived with a large number of horsemen and footmen. The assault on the walls of Jerusalem then began. Herod and Sosius proceeded to build embankments and towers against the walls, to batter the walls with their engines of war, and to scale the wall. The Jews within the city fought with alacrity. With their bows they attempted to force their enemy away from the walls, and they made sallies outside the walls in an effort to burn the engines of war, embankments and towers. But they faced a huge and well equipped army. The first wall was taken in 40 days, and the second wall in 15 more days. In a short time the outer court of the temple and the lower city were also taken.

The slaughter and plunder then began. All parts of the city became filled with persons who had been slain by the rage of the

---

18 Because of Mariamne's royal heritage, the offspring of this marriage could claim Hasmonean blood, a fact of great importance in the future lives of Herod and his family members.

Romans because of the long duration of the siege, and also because of the zeal of the Jews who were on Herod's side. Both armies murdered continuously in the narrow streets and in the houses, even though Herod besought them to spare the people. There was no pity taken of either infants or the aged. Nor did they spare the weaker sex.

Antigonus then came down from his citadel and fell at the feet of Sosius, who took no pity on him. Sosius insulted him beyond measure by calling him Antigone (i.e., a woman, and not a man), and then had him put into bonds and guarded closely.

Herod, who had finally overcome his enemies, now had to restrain the Romans who rushed to see the temple and the sacred things in the temple. Herod used entreaties and threats, and even sometimes force, in order to restrain them. He also protested the ravage that had occurred in the city, and asked Sosius whether the Romans would empty the city both of money and men, and leave him king of the desert. And when Sosius insisted that this plunder was permitted because of the long siege the soldiers had undergone, Herod replied that he would give every one their reward out of his own money. By this means he saved the destruction of what remained of the city. He gave a noble reward to every soldier, a proportional present to their commanders, and a most royal present to Sosius. The Romans then marched away from Jerusalem. Sosius took Antigonus with him in bonds, and delivered him to Antony in Syria.

Herod feared that if Antigonus were taken to Rome as a captive he might be able to convince members of the Roman senate that he was the rightful heir to the throne because of his royal heritage. To prevent this from happening, Herod gave Antony large sums of money as a bribe to have Antigonus killed. Antony had also reached the conclusion that Herod's fears were well founded. He had heard that the nation had grown seditious out of their hatred for Herod (whom he had appointed as king) and continued to bear good-will towards Antigonus. In order to quiet the Jews concerning this troublesome matter, he had Antigonus beheaded at Antioch.

The death of Antigonus and the beginning of the reign of king Herod [37 BC] ended the rule of the Hasmoneans, 126 years after the Maccabees established the government.

CHAPTER 2

EARLY YEARS OF THE REIGN OF HEROD THE GREAT

Herod, with the support of the Romans, took full control of Jerusalem as soon as Antigonus was taken captive. With decisive actions, he took wealth from the rich, plundered many of the ornaments of the city, and sent gold and silver to Antony and other friends in Rome. He slew 45 of the principal men who had supported Antigonus, and out of vengeance, he also killed members of the sanhedrin who had brought him to trial many years previously. He made it clear to all that he was a king to be feared. However, there was a situation that he could not control: He was not a Hasmonean, and in the minds of the multitude he was not entitled to be king. Herod was a practicing Jew who was born in Idumea. Although his father Antipater was a "Jew by birth," his mother Cypros was of Arab origin. Furthermore, he lacked any Hasmonean heritage. In the minds of the Jewish people, he was a foreigner who was king only by the decree from Rome. A complicating situation for Herod was the heritage of his wife Mariamne. She was a Hasmonean who had male Hasmonean relatives, including a brother and a grandfather (Hyrcanus) who was the former high priest.

The Return of Hyrcanus to Jerusalem

The Parthian generals had taken Hyrcanus to Parthia, and eventually to the city of Babylon, where many Jews were residing. Hyrcanus was treated well by the king of the Parthians, who learned that he was from an illustrious family. The king released him from his bonds and gave him a place to live in Babylon. Because he had been high priest and ethnarch in Judea, the Jews there honored him as their high priest and their king even though he had a deformity. When Hyrcanus heard that Herod had assumed the Judean government as king, he yearned to return to Jerusalem, believing that Herod would treat him well because he was married to his granddaughter Mariamne, and also because he had saved Herod from a death sentence that would have been imposed by the sanhedrin. The Jewish people in Parthia urged him not to go. Not trusting Herod, they feared for his life if he returned to Jerusalem. They also argued that because he was maimed, he would not be received with the dignity that he deserved, while among them he was highly revered as high priest and king. Nevertheless, Hyrcanus wanted to return to Jerusalem, and he sent a message to Herod asking that he be allowed to do so. Herod replied immediately stating that he would be welcome in Judea. Herod had a motive in wanting Hyrcanus to return to Jerusalem. Learning that he was highly respected as the high priest and king among the Jews in Parthia, Herod desired to have Hyrcanus close by so he would have control of him. Even though Hyrcanus could not serve as the high priest in Jerusalem because of his deformity, he was a political threat to him because he was a Hasmonean and many Jews would seek to have him as their king. So Herod received him with honor and set him above all the rest at feasts, and thereby deceived him. He called him "father" and made every effort to cover up his true intentions concerning him.

The Saga Concerning Who Should Be High priest

A high priest was demanded by the Jews of Judea. Hyrcanus could not serve in this position, and Herod, being fearful of the consequences, did not want to name any descendant of Hasmoneus to that position who might be living in Judea or elsewhere. In order to resolve this dilemma, Herod sent for an obscure priest living in the Babylon area whose name was Ananelus, and bestowed the high priest position upon him. Ananelus was from a stock of high priests

Chapter 2 Early Years of the Reign of Herod the Great

and from a people who had been carried away as captives to the Babylon area.[19]

Alexandra, daughter of Hyrcanus and mother of Mariamne, viewed that naming Ananelus as high priest was an act of great indignity. Alexandra had produced two children: Mariamne (who was married to Herod) and Aristobulus (who was then about 16). Alexandra argued that Aristobulus (who was a Hasmonean) was entitled to be high priest even though he was only 16 years old. She wrote to Cleopatra, Queen of Egypt, and urged her to intercede with Antony on behalf of Aristobulus.[20] Antony hesitated getting involved in this matter.

Antony's friend Dellius soon came to Judea to handle some affairs. He was taken back in awe at the tallness and handsomeness of the young boy Aristobulus and the great beauty of his sister

---

19   Ananelus was from a family line (purported to be the descendants of Aaron, the brother of Moses) that had provided high priests prior to the time the position became vested in the Hasmonean line.

20   Cleopatra was the last Macedonian ruler of Egypt; a line that was initiated by Ptolemy at the death of Alexander the Great in 323 BC. She was of pure Macedonian descent without any Egyptian blood. When her father King Ptolemy died in 51 BC, the throne passed to her and her 15 year old brother (Ptolemy XIII). A civil war soon broke out between them and Cleopatra knew that to gain the kingdom she had to have the support of the Roman rulers. When Julius Caesar arrived in Egypt in 48 BC in pursuit of Pompey, who had been murdered four days previously, Cleopatra took steps to captivate him. He defeated the anti-Cleopatra forces led by her brother Ptolemy XIII, and succumbed to the amorous charms of Cleopatra, allegedly becoming the father of her son who was named Caesarion. She was in Rome when Caesar was assassinated, but she soon returned to Egypt. Her alliance with Mark Antony began when he summoned her to Tarsus to assist him in the war with the Parthians. She was then 28 years old, and they began a relationship that lasted for 11 years. They allegedly had an Egyptian marriage (not recognized in Rome), and Antony became the father of three of her children. Her dream was to be queen over the area once ruled by the former Ptolemy rulers, extending from Egypt to southern Syria and including Judea. She used her charms to entice Antony to grant her territories in Syria and Judea, including Jericho with its lucrative balsam groves and date palm trees. In order to obtain further territories in Judea, if not all of Judea, she was most willing to become involved in intrigues against Herod, and even with women in his palace, hoping to cause his downfall.

Mariamne. He acclaimed that these two "children seemed not derived from men, but from some god." He urged Alexandra, the mother of these children, to send drawings of both of them to Antony, who, he said, would be so struck with the beauty of both of them that he would grant Alexandra whatever she requested. It was Dellius's plan that based upon the drawings and descriptions of Aristobulus and Mariamne, Antony would be enticed to have lewd pleasures with both of them. Antony was ashamed, however, to ask for the damsel because she was married to Herod, and he also knew Cleopatra would reproach him if he did, but in the most decent manner that he could conceive, he did send for Aristobulus. Herod sensed that this handsome sixteen year old boy from a noble family would be treated dishonorably by Antony. Not wanting this to happen to the son of Alexandra and the brother of his wife Mariamne, he wrote back to Antony and said that there would be a state of war and an uproar among the Jews if this boy were to go out of the country. It was their hope that eventually he would be king, and they would fear that he might be killed or kept in exile if he left the country. Because of this letter to Antony the matter was closed.

Herod's wife Mariamne then joined with her mother and vehemently urged that the high priest position be bestowed on her brother. Herod finally consented to do so, with her firm understanding, and also that of her mother Alexandra, that Aristobulus would be high priest and deal only with religious matters, and he would be king and take care of all civil matters. With this understanding, Herod took the high priest position away from Ananelus and bestowed it upon Aristobulus, hoping that this act would restore peace in his family. But still being suspicious of his meddlesome mother-in-law Alexandra, Herod ordered that she dwell in the palace, stay out of public affairs, and be monitored constantly by guards. Alexandra soon learned to hate this existence and to despise Herod. She wrote to Cleopatra, gave a list of her complaints, and asked for assistance. Cleopatra urged her to sneak away from Herod, come to Egypt and bring her son with her. Alexandra then made plans for them to be taken out of the palace secretively in coffins, one for her and one for her son. Once at the seashore, they would board a ship for Egypt. Their attempt to escape failed because a servant informed Herod of their plans. Herod caught them in the act of trying to escape, but because he did not want to offend Cleopatra, he did not show much offense at the act. He swore to himself however, that he had to get rid of Aristobulus, who had become a political threat to him.

The Death of Aristobulus the High Priest

Aristobulus was greatly admired by the people. He was tall and handsome and at age seventeen brought great dignity to the high priest position. They rejoiced at his presence and his Hasmonean heritage. Herod, who was fully aware of the feelings of the people, vowed to bring to action what he had intended against this young man. Herod invited Aristobulus to a party near some fish-ponds in Jericho, where he was encouraged to go swimming with some of the servants. Once in the ponds, the servants began to submerge his head under water in a playful manner. The play became more vigorous, and as ordered by Herod, his head was finally kept under the water until he drowned. Thus, Aristobulus, the high priest, was slain at the orders of Herod, but his death was explained as an accident. Following his death the high priest position was given back to Ananelus. At a later time it was bestowed on Jesus, son of Phabet.

Herod claimed innocence, but it was widely known, however, that he was responsible for the murder of his brother-in-law. Alexandra and Mariamne were greatly grieved. Alexandra wrote to Cleopatra and urged her to insist that Antony bring charges against the persons, including Herod, who had murdered Aristobulus. She also argued that it was not proper for Herod to have been made king of a country that did not belong to him, and that he should be punished for the horrid crimes against those of royal blood. Cleopatra was adamant on behalf of Alexandra and demanded that Antony take action. Antony finally responded to her demand, and when he was in Laodicea he commanded that Herod appear before him and answer the charges against him.

Herod was in great fear because of Cleopatra's accusations, and he knew that Cleopatra was attempting to turn Antony against him. He had no choice but to appear before Antony. Knowing that he might not return to Judea, he named his uncle Joseph, who was married to his sister Salome, as procurator of the government and in charge of public affairs in his absence. He also gave him private instructions that if Antony put him to death, he was to kill Mariamne, stating that because of his great love for her he did not want to be separated from her by death. But the real reason was jealousy. Because of her beauty he knew that she would be sought by others. He also knew that Antony was infatuated with her and might attempt to possess her upon his death. He did not want this to happen. At that time his uncle Joseph was governor of Idumea, an appointment given him by Herod.

While Herod was away, Joseph spent many hours with Mariamne. He even confided with her that Herod had proclaimed to him that he could not endure a separation from her, even after he was dead, and therefore that she would be killed if he were killed. The women (Mariamne, Alexandra, and various others) were not convinced that this proclamation was an expression of great affection for Mariamne. Instead, it was evidence that they could not escape destruction from this tyrannical person even after his death. They became alarmed when the rumor swept the city that Herod had been tortured and killed by Antony. Alexandra panicked and proposed that she, Mariamne and Joseph should flee away to the Roman troops that were camped outside the city, and when in their sanctity ask that they be delivered to Antony. She believed that Antony would be so captivated by Mariamne once he observed her, that he would restore the kingdom to the Hasmoneans. Letters soon arrived, however, from Herod, proving that the rumor of his death was false.

Chapter 2 Early Years of the Reign of Herod the Great

Herod arrived in Laodicea with many extravagant presents for Antony and was able to convince him that he had done no wrong. Herod's presents were more convincing than Cleopatra's arguments, who was in Laodicea with Antony. Antony ruled "that a king has to do what a king has to do." This conclusion greatly disappointed Cleopatra who had hoped to add Herod's kingdom to her own. To at least partly satisfy her, Antony added Celysria to her kingdom.

Herod soon returned to Jerusalem. There he heard many malicious rumors about the continuing intrigues of Alexandra, including her plot to flee away to the Romans, and because of Mariamne's beauty, to have Antony return the kingdom to the Hasmoneans. Herod became even more furious with Alexandra, restricted her to her living quarters and had her watched carefully by guards. Salome (Herod's sister) also told Herod that a rumor was circulating that her husband Joseph and Mariamne had many "criminal conversations" (e.g. adulterous encounters) during his absence. Herod became insanely jealous, but Mariamne denied any wrongful conduct. He believed her, but then in an expression of mutual love, she said "Yet was not that command thou gavest, that if any harm came to thee from Antony, that I should perish with thee, a sign of thy love to me?" Herod then "believed" that Joseph and Mariamne had been involved in criminal conversations, because Joseph would not inform her of his private order unless they had been intimate. In a fit of jealousy he ordered that Joseph be killed. Salome did not come to her husband's assistance. Instead, she implied that the charge of criminal conversations might be true, thereby hoping that Mariamne would also suffer from the calumny. If the calumny would lead to Mariamne's death, then the loss of her husband Joseph would make it worthwhile. Salome, who was an Idumean, hated the beautiful Mariamne and her haughty mother Alexandra who were prone to flaunt their royal dignity because of their Hasmonean lineage.

At this time Cleopatra, who was with Antony in Syria, became even more mischievous and made many requests of Antony, taking advantage of their relationship. She coveted all the kingdoms from Syria to Egypt, including Judea and Arabia, and requested that these lands be given to her. Antony relented on most of these requests, but reluctantly gave her cities on the coastline from the river dividing Phoenicia and Syria to Egypt, except Tyre and Sidon which he kept as free cities, although she pressed him to give her these cities as well. With these additions to Cleopatra's kingdom, Herod lost valuable properties on the coastline, only because of the influence Cleopatra had on Antony. She was a person for Herod to fear.

Knowing that Cleopatra coveted Judea and was making continuing attempts to have Antony remove him as ruler and give Judea to her, Herod made an increased effort to refurbish the fortress Masada in Idumea, making it into a veritable fortress for himself in case of need. At Masada he could defend himself against the Egyptian armies of Cleopatra and the Roman armies if Antony, out of his passion for Cleopatra, succumbed to her request and removed him as king. The fortress was also being refurbished as a refuge from another possible danger. Herod knew that the Jewish people longed for a Hasmonean ruler, and events might occur that caused him to be overthrown by the Jews. If so, he would seek refuge against them and any other enemy at Masada. This fortress on the western shore of the Dead Sea was first built and named Masada by Jonathan the high priest and brother of Judas Maccabeus. And it was at Masada that Herod left his family when he went to Rome to receive the government. It served well as a fortress at that time because the armies of Antigonus were unable to penetrate it. To make it even more impregnable, Herod built a wall around the entire top of the rock at the edge of the steep precipices. This wall was about one mile in length and about 20 feet in height. On the wall at spaced intervals he erected 38 towers, each about 75 feet tall. A sumptuous palace was built within the wall with costly baths, with some of the floors made of stone of different colors. Many large pits were carved

Chapter 2 Early Years of the Reign of Herod the Great

out of the rock to serve as reservoirs for the storage of water, and one large area with fertile soil was reserved for agricultural purposes. Huge storerooms were built to store grain, oil, wine, dates, edible seeds of various plants, and other food substances. Weapons of war were stored there to equip 10,000 men. It was a fortress in a desolate part of Idumea that Herod could defend against any enemy with conventional weapons of war for a long period of time, and longer than any enemy would likely continue its siege.

Cleopatra was also mischievous by scheming with Costobarus over the future of Idumea. Costobarus was an Idumean by birth who was appointed to be governor of Idumea by Herod following the death of Joseph, who had been married to Salome. Soon after the death of Joseph, Herod gave Salome to Costobarus in marriage. Costobarus was a principal person among the Idumeans whose ancestors were priests to the god Koze, who had been worshipped by the Idumeans. Although the Idumeans had been forced to follow the Jewish laws and customs, many still longed to worship their own gods. With the passage of time Costobarus reveled in the position and the power that he had. He became so impressed with himself that he began to question why he was subject to Herod, and why the Idumeans should be subject to Jewish customs. He formulated a plan that would allow him to rule the country free of Herod, and would also allow the Idumeans to worship their own gods without any Jewish influence. He wrote to Cleopatra and urged her to influence Antony to take Idumea away from Herod and give it to her, and if this were done, he would be her loyal subject and rule faithfully as governor under her. It was not his wish to be part of her government, but it was his opinion that freeing himself of Herod's influence would allow the Idumeans the freedom to worship their own god, and might allow him to obtain the government for himself at some future time. Cleopatra, who was pleased with this overture, attempted to obtain Idumea from Antony, but he did not accommodate her. When Herod became aware of Costobarus's scheme he was ready to kill him, but did not do so because of pleas from his sister Salome and his mother

Cypros to save his life. So Herod forgave Costobarus and promised to pardon him entirely, even though he remained highly suspicious of him.

Previously Antony had given Jericho to Cleopatra. This area only 15 miles from Jerusalem was known for its balsam and date palm trees, and farming in the area was a big source of revenue. The balsam tree, which was a source of a precious drug, grows only in that area. Date palm trees were in abundance there, and the dates made a fine wine. Fearful of having Egyptians so close to Jerusalem, an arrangement was proposed by Herod that he would farm the land and send all the revenues to Cleopatra. For lands in Arabia that Antony had similarly given to Cleopatra, Herod volunteered to collect the revenue from the Arabians and forward them to Cleopatra. One of these areas in Arabia was adjacent to the Dead Sea, and bitumen from that sea, which was mined by the Arabians, was a good source of income for Cleopatra. She approved of this arrangement because it did not require any outlay of funds, or commitment of workers or troops. It also presented an opportunity for the Jews and the Arabs to become involved in controversies, for her benefit.

On her way back from Syria, Cleopatra passed through Judea. One reason was to view her farms in Jericho. Herod felt obligated to entertain her lavishly, and to give her many gifts. She spent many hours with Herod and endeavored to engage him in "criminal conversations," but Herod sensed that it was a trap and he avoided becoming involved with her. He told his close associates that it would be best for him, and also even best for Antony, if he had her killed. But he did not do so because Antony would not approve and the result might be fateful for him. Eventually, he escorted her out of the country, laden with gifts, on her way back to Egypt.

Soon after Cleopatra returned to Egypt, Herod found himself involved in a war with the Malchus, the king of Arabia. This occurred at about the time Antony and Caesar [Octavian] were

Chapter 2 Early Years of the Reign of Herod the Great

getting ready for their major naval battle at Actium in 31 BC for supreme power of the Roman Empire.[21] Herod raised a large army to be of assistance to Antony, but Antony said that he did not need his support. Instead, he ordered Herod to go to war against Malchus, the king of Arabia, because both he and Cleopatra now considered this king to be untrustworthy. Although in the beginning Malchus paid the revenues from his lands that he owed Cleopatra and were collected by Herod, he soon became very slow in making payments, and then became unwilling to pay them without deductions. Antony commanded Herod to punish Malchus for this transgression. This war, actually requested by Cleopatra, played to her advantage. There would be an opportunity to obtain his kingdom if either king were killed in battle, but since she coveted Judea more than Arabia, she hoped that the Arabians would be victorious. In an effort to tip the scale, she sent an Egyptian army to monitor the situation.

---

21   The pact between the triumvirs Antony and Octavian was made strong when Antony married Octavian's sister Octavia. This marriage occurred after Antony had spent the previous winter with Cleopatra in Alexandria. At this time Antony controlled the eastern provinces and Octavian controlled the entire west except Africa which was assigned to Lipidus, the third member of the Second Triumvirate. Octavian also controlled Italy even though it was supposedly neutral. Lipidus was eventually forced into retirement when he opposed Octavian's leadership in the west. With his removal from the triumvirate, the empire was now ruled by Antony and Octavian. For a few years there was an uneasy truce between them, but with time a competition for power took place. When Octavian criticized Antony publicly for his gifts of territories to Cleopatra, it was clear that a confrontation was eminent. The division between them was heightened when Antony divorced his wife Octavia and renewed his amorous relationship with Cleopatra. Octavian obtained Antony's will which gave convincing evidence that Cleopatra's power over Antony was a threat to the existence of the empire. The battle lines were then drawn, with each leader obtaining support from his constituents, and Octavian declared war on Antony and Cleopatra. The decisive battle occurred at Actium (cape on the western portion of Greece) in 31 BC between the combined naval forces of Antony and Cleopatra and those of Octavian. The forces of Octavian were victorious, and Antony and Cleopatra fled to Egypt. The following year (30 BC), the war came to an end with the suicides of Antony and Cleopatra. The death of Cleopatra brought an end to the reign of the Macedonian rulers in Egypt. The Roman senate then gave Octavian the title of Augustus, and he became known as Caesar Augustus. He became the first emperor and ruled the Roman empire for 40 years. Characterized as a true statesman, he demanded total allegiance and servitude to Rome from all subjects throughout the Roman empire. His long tenure as emperor attests to his effectiveness as a ruler.

The general had instructions that if the Arabians were brave and successful, he should do nothing, but if the Arabians were being beaten by the Jews, then he should attack the Jews.

Not knowing that he might have a disadvantage because of the presence of the Egyptian army, Herod and his army marched across the Jordan River to engage the Arabians. The Jews fought with alacrity in the first battles, and defeated the Arabians. They soon had the Arabians in full flight. The Arabians were almost completely destroyed, when the Egyptians came to their rescue. At this time the Jews were fatigued and ready to enjoy themselves in quietness after their victory. The attack by the Egyptians was unexpected, and the Jews were not prepared for it. The Egyptians had fresh horses and were ready for battle. The Egyptians also chose to attack in an area that was better known to them than the Jews. The result was disastrous for the Jews and many were slaughtered by the Egyptians. The Arabians became rejuvenated at this turn of events, and returned to join in the fight against the Jews. With reduced forces, Herod was forced to retreat, but he continued to fight by making sudden incursions against the Arabians in selected locations. He used all means to increase the size of the army and to make it ready for additional attacks against the Arabians. This happened at the time of the battle at Actium between the naval forces of Octavian and the combined naval forces of Antony and Cleopatra. It also happened in the seventh year of the reign of Herod (i.e., seven years after he defeated Antigonus and took command of the government, but ten years after he had been named king by the Romans).

Also at this time a devastating earthquake hit Judea, killing thousands of people and toppling homes and cities. The men in the armies out in the fields were not damaged by this sad event. When the Arabians heard about the damage caused by the earthquake, they took delight, believing that their enemy would not be able to continue fighting. They attacked the Jews with confidence, and the Jews were so devastated by all that had happened that they offered little resistance. Herod revitalized them by emphasizing that God was on their side in this war against the Arabians, and he led them across the Jordan to engage the enemy once again. With renewed spirit and confidence the Jews put the Arabians to flight. Knowing they were defeated, the Arabians sent ambassadors to Herod to propose terms of accommodation, but Herod would not accept them, being desirous of seeking revenge against his enemy. Seven thousand Arabians were then killed, and 4,000 were taken prisoner. The war came to an end with the Arabians being amazed at Herod's warlike spirit following the previous calamities. They were in such awe of him that they proclaimed him *ruler of their nation* (which was an honorary title). Herod then returned home to Jerusalem with glory because of his victory and the honor bestowed on him.

The celebration was short-lived. Octavian had won (31 BC) the decisive naval battle against the forces of Antony and Cleopatra at Actium. With depleted forces, Antony fled to Egypt where he was getting ready for the alleged "last" battle, which he would surely lose. Herod's kingdom was in jeopardy, because it seemed logical that Octavian would now dispose of Herod because of his long friendship with Antony. His friends were in despair, and his enemies were hopeful that Octavian would replace Herod with someone who would be more acceptable to the Jews. Herod was aware of the feelings of the Jews and who the candidate might be. The only person with royal Hasmonean dignity who could be a candidate at this time was Hyrcanus. It was Herod's conviction that he did not want to be replaced by a Hasmonean, and even if Octavian allowed him to remain as king, it would be best to get rid of any person who by blood had a claim to the throne in case of any future uprising. Although Hyrcanus stayed out of public affairs, and was of no personal threat to Herod, persons such as Alexandra (Hyrcanus's daughter and his wife's mother) were contentious, and Herod knew that she was capable of spiteful behavior on behalf of her father. How could he justify killing Hyrcanus who, with a mild temper, did not meddle in public affairs and preferred to live a quiet life free of conflict?

The Death of Hyrcanus

An opportunity soon presented itself. Alexandra urged her father to write to Malchus the governor of Arabia. The letter should state the many injustices that Herod had leveled on the family, and request that he give them protection away from Jerusalem. Alexandra argued that if Octavian rules against Herod, as he probably would, then the Hasmonean lineage might return to power once again in Jerusalem with Hyrcanus as king. Hyrcanus wanted no part of this plan, but Alexandra persisted, and finally he wrote the letter asking for horses and the protection of horsemen as they traveled away from Jerusalem to a sanctuary, awaiting the results of the showdown between Octavian and Herod.

The letter was to be sent by a trusted courier, but the courier showed the letter to Herod, hoping to receive a just reward. Herod instructed him to deliver the letter to Malchus, and also to show him Malchus's reply. Malchus responded to Hyrcanus's letter by saying that he would receive Hyrcanus and all those who accompanied him. He also said that he would send forces to protect them on the journey. At a social occasion, Herod asked Hyrcanus in a casual manner, without showing any sign of displeasure with him, if he had received any messages recently from Malchus. Hyrcanus replied, "Yes. Letters of Salutation." When asked if he had received any presents from Malchus, he replied, "Yes, four horses to ride." Herod then twisted these statements into evidence of treason and bribery. He showed Malchus's letter to the sanhedrim and made charges against Hyrcanus. Even though Hyrcanus denied any wrong doing, the sanhedrim found him guilty and he was put to death.

It was realized by many that this execution was contrived by Herod. Being a mild mannered person, there was no manifestation of treason or bribery in Hyrcanus's letter to Malchus. In fact, he merely asked for safe passage and protection in case Octavian acted against Herod. Those who knew the true situation understood that since Hyrcanus truly wished a private life and had no interest in being named ruler, or involving himself in public affairs, he could not have been guilty of treason and bribery. Hyrcanus was over 80 years of age when he was put to death. He had been named high priest of the Jewish nation at the beginning of his mother's (Alexandra's) reign. After her death, he took the government himself and held it for 3 months, and then lost it to his brother Aristobulus, who also took the high priest position away from him. He was renamed high priest by Pompey and later confirmed as high priest and ethnarch by Julius Caesar. He remained in that position for 40 years until he was made a captive of the Parthinians and maimed by Antigonus. Being a passive person, he remained in the background during the 40 year period and allowed others to run civil matters.

Agreement Reached by Caesar Augustus [Octavian] and Herod

After he had arranged to have Hyrcanus condemned to death by the sanhedrim, Herod went to meet Caesar Augustus at Rhodes. Fearing that an uprising might occur in his absence at the instigation of Alexandra, he instructed his brother Pheroras to take over the government in his absence, and he placed his mother Cypros and sister Salome and the rest of his family at Masada. Because his wife Mariamne did not get along with his mother and sister, he placed his wife and her mother in a fortress at Alexandrium [north of Jerusalem near the border of Judea and Samaria], where they were heavily guarded by Sohemus, who had been faithful to Herod. Herod instructed Sohemus that if he were killed by Caesar, both Mariamne and Alexandra were to be slain immediately. He also instructed Sohemus and other close advisers, that the kingdom should be preserved for his sons and his brother Pheroras in case he did not return.

At Rhodes, Herod took off his crown in the presence of Caesar and gave an eloquent presentation. He stated that he had been a faithful supporter of Antony because Antony represented Rome as the administrator of the eastern provinces, and it was proper that he demonstrated full allegiance to him. He also stated that he would now be an equally faithful supporter of Caesar. Herod told Caesar that he had advised Antony that Cleopatra was a detriment to him, a cause of many of his problems, and it would be wise if he put her aside. Caesar was impressed with his frankness, and pronounced that he wanted him to remain as king. So Herod returned to Judea with the full support of Caesar. Caesar passed through Judea soon after with his army on the way to do battle against Antony in Egypt. Herod entertained him at Ptolemais, and gave many provisions to his army. He honored Caesar, presented him with gifts, and they became close friends.

The Deaths of Mariamne and Alexandra

Even though Herod returned home to Jerusalem with great joy because of the relationship he had been able to establish with Caesar, he found his home life in disarray. Mariamne and Alexandra knew that they had been placed in the fortress at Alexandrium not for their protection but as a form of imprisonment. Mariamne had also learned from Sohemus, who had confided in her (after gifts had been given to him), that both she and Alexandra were to be killed if Herod were slain by Caesar. She was greatly depressed with the decree that she could not live "beyond" Herod.

Upon his return, Herod went immediately to Mariamne, assuming that she would share his happiness, but she did not greet him warmly and actually grieved at his success. When Herod's mother (Cypros) and sister (Salome) knew of this open difference between Herod and Mariamne, they exploited it by gossiping about Mariamne in an effort to excite his jealousy and hatred. There were strong negative feelings between the Hasmoneans (Mariamne and Alexandra) and the commoners from Idumea (Cypros and Salome),

Chapter 2 Early Years of the Reign of Herod the Great

and both sides were now in open warfare against each other.

The year was 30 BC and Herod learned that Caesar had conquered Egypt and both Antony and Cleopatra had committed suicide. With this news Herod hastened to meet Caesar in Egypt. **Caesar greeted him as an old friend and added to his kingdom, giving him jurisdiction over all the areas that he had lost to Cleopatra, including Jericho, and the maritime cities Gaza, Anthedon, Joppa, and Strato's Tower. He was also given jurisdiction over additional cities on the coast (including Azotus and Jamnia) and two cities east of the Sea of Galilee (Hippos and Gadara) on the Syrian border.**

Herod returned to Jerusalem hoping to find more peaceful conditions in his family, but such was not the case. One day at noon he called his beautiful wife to his bed, but she would not lie down by him, and instead accused him of killing her brother (Aristobulus) and grandfather (Hyrcanus). Salome then sent Herod's "cup-bearer" to Herod with the information that Mariamne had given him presents and told him to give a love potion to Herod, but since the love potion was a composition that she had given him, and he did not know what effect it might have, he thought it wise to inform Herod of the situation. The story was false; it had been contrived by Salome, but was told to give the implication that Mariamne was attempting to poison Herod. Herod went into a rage and tortured Mariamne's eunuch to find out what he knew about the potion. The eunuch knew nothing about it, but did say, under torture, that her hatred for Herod stemmed from what Sohemus had said to her-- that she and her mother should be killed if Caesar killed Herod. With this statement Herod had evidence that Sohemus had given confidential information to Mariamne and he concluded therefore that they must have had "criminal conversations" at Alexandrium. In a fit of jealousy he ordered that Sohemus be seized and slain. He also ordered that Mariamne be brought to trial. With the help of his sister, his mother, and others, he made elaborate accusations against her concerning the potion, and after listening to the evidence, the court passed a sentence of death on her. Thus, Mariamne, who was innocent of the charges against her, was executed by order of her husband.

Herod went into deep mental depression over the death of Mariamne. He would call for her, and would have his servants call for her, as if she were alive. He would spend long periods of time in desert places lamenting his loss. Physicians attempted to cure his disease with various remedies, without success. Alexandra, knowing about his mental instability condition, then attempted to stage an uprising, stating that in case Herod did not recover from his illness, steps should be taken to give the government to her and to Mariamne's sons. Herod eventually recovered from his illness and was made aware of Alexandra's activities. He gave orders that she should be slain immediately, and it was done.

At this same time Herod ordered that his brother-in-law Costobarus should also be slain. Previously Herod wanted to kill Costobarus because he had schemed with Cleopatra to have Idumea taken away from him and given to Cleopatra. He did not do so because his wife Salome and his mother Cypros had pleaded for Herod to forgive him. Salome now changed her attitude towards her husband. She had quarreled with him and sent him a bill of divorce, not according to Jewish law, but by her own authority. She informed her brother that Costobarus was guilty of seditious events. During the siege of Jerusalem leading to the downfall of Antigonus, the sons of Babas, who were Hasmoneans and distant relatives of Hyrcanus, were strong supporters of Antigonus. They urged the people to keep the government in the hands of the Hasmoneans. They had regal dignity and support among the people because of their Hasmonean lineage. When Herod took over Jerusalem, he ordered that they be slain, but Costobarus protected them and secretively hid them on one of his farms in Idumea, hoping that at some future time they might be of political advantage to him. Herod attempted to find them and Costobarus denied under oath knowing their whereabouts. When Herod learned from his sister about the location of the sons of Babas (where they had been for 12 years), he ordered that they be found and killed. Because of his crime Costobarus was shown no mercy by Herod and was killed immediately.

Honoring Caesar, Rome and Himself [Herod) by the Building of Cities, Theaters, Amphitheaters, and Other Edifices

Many years of peace now followed. Herod was in complete control of the kingdom as a powerful client-king under Rome, with no threat from any Hasmonean. The extent and power of the Roman empire also protected his kingdom from external intrusions. To honor Caesar, Herod began a program of having solemn games every fifth year including chariot races, wrestling matches, and other sporting events. He built a theater in Jerusalem and a very great amphitheater in the plain. He spared no expense in constructing and decorating these edifices. Inscriptions in the theater praised the great actions of Caesar, and trophies from nations he had conquered were on display. Precious garments and stones adorned the theater and the sites of the games. He invited contestants from other countries, and gave prizes to winners of events. He extended these games to other cities and areas under his authority, with the goal to demonstrate his own grandeur. The multitude believed, however, that these events were contrary to Jewish law, and especially when he had persons who were condemned to die fight with wild lions and other animals. To have men killed by wild beasts to the delight of spectators was totally against their customs. Trophies were given to the winners of contests, and the Jewish people considered these trophies, adorned with metal, to be images. Competing for them and cherishing them, was a form of idol worship, which was contrary to Jewish law.

Because Herod was disobeying Jewish laws, a plan was designed to assassinate him in the theater. Ten men vowed to slay him with daggers, but a spy informed Herod of the plot, and the conspirators were seized and killed. The spy was then in turn seized by some of the people, who killed him, pulled him apart limb by limb, and fed his limbs to dogs. Herod retaliated by torturing persons, including women, until he learned who had killed the spy. Entire families were then destroyed, and this is how Herod controlled the minds of the people whom he ruled.

When Herod defeated Antigonus and took over the government [37 BC], the Hasmonean palace stood on a high elevation in Jerusalem southwest of the temple. Not wishing to occupy that palace, because of its identification with the Hasmoneans, Herod remodeled the citadel northwest of the temple, known as Baris (or the tower), and made it into a citadel-palace. He named it Antonia in honor of his benefactor Mark Antony, who administered the eastern provinces at that time. He resided in this palace, also known as the Antonia Tower, with his Hasmonean wife Mariamne. Herod soon decided that Antonia was not satisfactory as his palace because of its close proximity to the temple. He chose another location in the upper city with a clear view of areas surrounding the city. There he built a magnificent palace that was a city by itself with many buildings and two large and beautiful apartments named *Caesareum* and *Agrippium* after Caesar Augustus and Marcus Agrippa. The forty foot wall enclosing the palace was marked by three massive towers named after three persons who had been the dearest to him. They were his Hasmonean wife Mariamne, his brother Phasaelus, and his friend Hippicus.[22]

Prior to building his new palace Herod began construction [27 BC] of a fortress in Samaria called Sebaste,[23] which was a day's

---

22   Construction began on this palace in about 23 BC, about six years after the death of his Hasmonean wife Mariamne, whom Herod had slain out of love and jealousy. Herod's brother Phasaelus and his friend Hippicus had lost their lives while serving courageously in war. When Jerusalem was destroyed by the Romans in 70 AD, the three towers (*Mariamne, Hippicus,* and *Phasaelus*) were left standing because of their eminence.

23   Sebaste was named after Caesar Augustus, where Sebastos is the Greek name for Augustus.

journey from Jerusalem. He built a temple in Sebaste in honor of Caesar as a reward for those who had assisted him in his wars, and to give further eminence to the fortress. Sebaste was noted for its fertile soil and fruit trees and Herod placed settlers there to serve as a military force.[24] In other cities outside of Judea, Herod constructed temples with images (representations of animals) patterned after the Greeks. The Jews were highly offended by the presence of these structures and images. Herod apologized to the Jews in these cities, stating that the images were placed there upon the commands of others in order to please Caesar and the Romans. He did not place these images in the temple in Jerusalem because of the insurrections it would have caused among the people.

During the 13th year of the reign of Herod, a serious drought hit Judea and surrounding areas, causing much famine. His people were in great distress and he came to their aid by purchasing, with his own money, grain and other essentials from other countries. He also aided Syria during this time of crisis. He was so helpful that many Jewish people who had formerly hated him, now learned to respect him.

At this time he also took another wife. Simon, a citizen of Jerusalem, was the son of Boethus, a priest of great note from Alexandria. Simon had a daughter, named Mariamne, who was famous in Jerusalem because of her beauty. Herod was smitten when he first saw her, and he chose to take her as a wife. Since Simon was of a dignity too inferior to qualify as his father-in-law, Herod deprived Jesus, the son of Phabet, of the high priesthood, and conferred it on Simon, the son of Boethus. By augmenting the dignity of Simon in this manner, and thereby making his family more honorable, he then married his daughter.

---

24 Following the death of his Hasmonean wife Mariamne, Herod married Malthace from Samaria. When this occurred is not specified by Josephus. Herod formed a strong link with Samaria by marrying Malthace the Samaritan. Two sons (Archelaus and Antipas) of great historical importance were the result of this marriage.

When this wedding was over, he built another citadel about 7 miles south of Jerusalem. It was at the place where he conquered the Jews when he was taking his family and others to Masada for protection from Antigonus. He named this citadel Herodium in honor of himself.[25] It was built on a cone shaped hill that had been made higher by the addition of embankments and high walls (with towers) encircling the top. Within the citadel he built royal and very rich apartments for beauty and security. They were reached by descending steps two hundred in number made of polished stones. Since the area was destitute of water it was brought there, at a vast expense, by an aqueduct from a long distance away.

In addition he built a place for horsemen in Galilee, called Gaba. Although justifying the building of these fortresses as national security needs, they were also built to give him personal security from his own people. By encompassing the nation with fortresses he would be able to control any commotion that might occur. The presence of the guards and fortresses would also keep the people in awe. The fortresses would also be places he might escape to, if necessary.

Building of Caesarea

Herod viewed a place near the sea and made the decision to build a magnificent city and seaport there. The place was called Strato's Tower, which he renamed Caesarea in honor of the emperor. Construction began in 22 BC, and it took twelve years to build the city. In order for it to serve as a safe haven for ships, he brought in huge rocks and made leeways out into the sea to serve as breaks against the waves. Because of these breakwaters, Caesarea became a major seaport. He adorned the city with sumptuous palaces and other edifices made of white stone. He built a temple containing statues of Caesar, a theater and an amphitheater capable of holding

---

25   Herodium is the place Herod designated as his burial site.

Chapter 2 Early Years of the Reign of Herod the Great

a vast number of people.[26]

How Caesar Enlarged Herod's Kingdom and the Relationship Among Caesar, Marcus Agrippa, and Herod

The ability of Herod to spend huge sums of money for these monuments affirms the close relationship that existed between him and Caesar. Herod was faithful in sending the required payment to Rome, but after it was paid, he had financial autonomy. Because of this arrangement Herod was capable of accumulating great wealth. Caesar recognized his administrative ability and gave him freedom to rule his kingdom according to his own dictates. Caesar demanded allegiance from all kings and governors throughout the empire, and he also wanted strong leaders who would maintain order in their territories. And indeed, Herod excelled as a ruler. He, in turn, demanded allegiance from those he ruled. He was quick to use tyranny when needed to enforce allegiance, but his administrative skills and tactics eventually produced relative peace and quietness in his kingdom. Because of his ability to rule, **Caesar rewarded him by adding Trachon (Trachonitis), Batanaea, and Auranitis to his kingdom, located east and northeast of the Sea of Galilee. Caesar also gave Herod the privilege of naming the son who should succeed him as king.** This favoritism shown Herod by Caesar often caused jealousy among other rulers of the eastern provinces.

During this period Marcus Agrippa, the powerful Roman authority under Caesar, was sent to administer the countries of the Roman empire east of the Ionian Sea. He chose Mitylene (Lesbos), a Greek island in the Aegean Sea off the coast of Greece, as his headquarters. Herod went to pay homage to Agrippa and also to

---

26   Caesarea became the seat of the Roman government of Judea in 6 AD. Pontius Pilate resided there and after the destruction of Jerusalem in 70 AD, Caesarea became the most important city in Palestine. By the 6th century its population may have reached 100,000. It was abandoned in 1265 AD. Remnants of an aqueduct and a theater from Herod's time are still standing. Investigations by underwater archeologists have confirmed the presence of the harbor with its two massive breakwaters described by Josephus.

request that he make arrangements for his two Hasmonean sons Alexander and Aristobulus to be educated in Rome and to enjoy the company of Caesar. Herod was to name one of these sons to succeed him and he wanted them to experience the benefits of Rome and to associate with Caesar in his own palace. Marcus Agrippa helped pave the way and Alexander and Aristobulus were sent to Rome, where they were lodged in the house of Pollio. They were received graciously by Caesar, who gave them special benefits.[27]

Caesar then made the decision to visit Syria and he recalled Marcus Agrippa from Mytilene to handle the affairs of Rome in his absence. Herod traveled to Syria to be there when Caesar arrived. Also waiting to meet Caesar were inhabitants of Gadara (city southeast of the Sea of Galilee) who brought charges against Herod who had been named by Caesar to rule the territory including their city, in addition to neighboring territories. They were encouraged by the former ruler Zenodorus who was distressed because some of his territory had been taken away from him and given to Herod. He was also jealous of Herod's success in restoring order to the area, which did not exist when he was the ruler. Zenodorus wanted the kingdom taken away from Herod and joined to another province, and hopefully to his province. After listening to the charges, Caesar ruled quickly in favor of Herod. The power of Herod concerning this matter was then manifested by Caesar's announcement, to the alarm of the Gadarens:

> *"There are two men who govern the Roman empire, first Caesar and then Marcus Agrippa, who was his principal favorite. But Caesar favored no one better than Herod except Marcus Agrippa, and Marcus Agrippa had no greater friend than Herod other than Caesar."*

---

27 This arrangement was repugnant to the Jews of Jerusalem, who did not want their future king being educated in Rome by pagan gentiles.

Chapter 2 Early Years of the Reign of Herod the Great

With this announcement, and fearing what Herod would now do to them because they had spoken against him in front of Caesar, many of the Gadarens committed suicide by cutting their own throats, throwing themselves down precipices, or casting themselves into the river. **And then when Zenodorus died unexpectedly, Caesar added the remainder of his country to Herod's kingdom. These were the lands between Galilee and Trachon (Trachonitis) and contained Ulatha and Paneas and the surrounding countries. These new large territories extended Herod's kingdom north and northeast of the Sea of Galilee.** Caesar also made Herod one of the procurators of Syria and demanded that everything should be done with his approbation.

Herod then begged Caesar that part of his large kingdom be given to his brother Pheroras to rule. This request was granted and Pheroras became tetrarch over Perea, the country east of Jerusalem across the Jordan river. Herod reasoned that under this arrangement, his dear brother Pheroras would be independent of one of his sons who would eventually replace him as king.[28] Herod then escorted Caesar to the sea from which Caesar returned to Rome, and Herod returned to Jerusalem.

Rebuilding of the Temple in Jerusalem

"And now Herod, in the eighteenth year of his reign [20-19 BC], and after the acts already mentioned, undertook a very great work, that is, to build of himself the temple of God, and make it larger in compass, and to raise it to a most magnificent altitude, as esteeming it to be the most glorious of all his actions."

The people were greatly concerned with the announcement that a new temple would replace the existing temple, fearing that he would demolish the existing temple and replace it with an edifice

---

28 A tetrarchy is about one-fourth of a country or kingdom, and a tetrarch is the ruler of that tetrarchy.

to honor Rome. Sensing their concerns, Herod announced that the existing temple would not be torn down until the materials for the new one had been obtained and were in place and ready to be used. And so it was done. Over 1,000 wagons brought in the stones, and when all the materials were in place, the existing temple was torn down. The old foundations were removed, replaced by others, and then construction was begun using 10,000 skilled workmen, and sparing no expense. By building this temple (known throughout later history as Herod's Temple and also The Second Temple), Herod was constructing a lasting memorial to himself. About 1,000 priests were assigned to build key structures of the temple. Some of these priests were taught to be masons and others were taught to be carpenters.[29] The temple itself was built in one year and six months.[30] It was also reported that it did not rain during the day time when the temple was being built-- but showers fell at night, so that the work was not hindered.

Because he was not a priest Herod did not enter the inner rooms of the temple while they were being constructed. These rooms contained the altar upon which sacrifices and burnt-offerings were offered to God. However, Herod paid attention to the construction of the cloisters and outer enclosures, which took eight years to build.

During the building of the temple, additions were made to the Tower of Antonia (which previously had served as Herod's palace-fortress) in order to better secure and guard the temple. The

---

[29] Priests were used to build key structures of the temple because Jewish law would not allow laymen to enter inner rooms of the temple.

[30] Even though Josephus says that the temple itself was built in one year and six months and the cloisters and outer enclosures in eight years, the construction of this massive structure was actually ongoing, with outer retaining walls and other structures not being completed for many decades. In *John* 2: 19-20 Jesus was questioned by the Jews how he could raise the temple in three days when it took forty six years to build it. If the actual construction began about 2 years after the announcement by Herod in 20 BC that a new temple was to be built, this interaction with Jesus took place in about 28-30 AD, assuming that the 46 year construction time is correct.

Chapter 2 Early Years of the Reign of Herod the Great

presence of this fortress beside the temple allowed Herod to guard against any sedition which might be made by the people in the temple against him. This tower was first built by the Hasmonians [presumably by John Hyrcanus], and called Baris, the Citadel or the Tower. Vestments of the high priest were kept in this tower, which only the high priest put on when he offered sacrifices during special ceremonies in the temple. Herod also kept the vestments of the high priest in this tower.[31]

It was a day of feasting and celebration when the temple was opened. Herod provided 300 oxen for sacrifice, and many other sacrifices were offered.

> *"The building of the temple in Jerusalem was the most glorious of Herod's actions."*

---

31 The Antonia fortress had corner towers 75 to 100 feet in height and a frontage of about 375 feet.

Josephus

CHAPTER 3

CALUMNIES IN HEROD'S FAMILY LEADING TO THE DEATHS OF ALEXANDER AND ARISTOBULUS

Herod's brothers and sister:

Phasaelus: Taken captive by the Parthians. He committed suicide by beating his head against a wall.

Joseph: Killed in a battle against Antigonus.

Pheroras Made tetrarch of Perea by Caesar at the request of Herod. Perea was located east of the Jordan River and the Dead Sea.

Salome: Married to Joseph who was Herod's uncle (He was killed by Herod).
Married to Costobarus (He was killed by Herod.)
Married to Alexas at the insistence of Herod.

Herod's Wives and Children:

Doris was Herod's first wife. She was an Idumean who was born in Jerusalem. Her son, and Herod's oldest son, was Antipater. When Herod married Mariamne, Doris was put aside, and Antipater was removed from Jerusalem. He was allowed to return to Jerusalem on festival days.

Mariamne was Herod's second wife. She was a Hasmonean who was the daughter of Alexandra and Alexander, and the granddaughter of Hyrcanus. She had 3 sons and 2 daughters. Her oldest son was

63

Alexander. Her second son was **Aristobulus**. Her third son died young while living in Rome. Her daughters were **Salampsio** and **Cypros**.

Malthace, the Samaritan, had two sons (**Archelaus** and **Antipas**) and one daughter (**Olympias**).

Mariamne II was the daughter of Simon the high priest. She had one son, named **Herod [Philip]**[32].

Cleopatra had two sons (**Herod** and **Philip**). The son Philip is often not distinguished in the historical literature from Philip the son of Mariamne II.

Pallas had one son (**Phasaelus**).

Phedra had one daughter (**Roxana**).

Elpis had one daughter (**Salome**).

Herod's niece (Name not given) had no offspring.

Herod's niece (Name not given) had no offspring.

By these 10 wives Herod had a total of 15 children.

Herod's sons Alexander and Aristobulus had been living in Rome for several years to obtain an education. They completed their studies in the sciences and were now ready to return to Jerusalem. Herod traveled to Rome to meet with Caesar and to bring them home. Upon returning home the people in Jerusalem took great interest in them. They were the sons of Mariamne the Hasmonean

---

[32] Herod [Philip], the son of Mariamne II, is often not distinguished in the literature from Philip, the son of Cleopatra. In Mark 6:17 this son of Mariamne II is called Philip.

Chapter 3 Calumnies in Herod's Family

and in the eyes and minds of the people they had regal stature. It was also said that they had countenances of persons of royal dignity. In the minds of the people, Alexander the older, was the heir to the throne. This was also the intent of Herod, even though Alexander was not Herod's oldest son. The oldest son was Antipater, who was born to Herod's first wife (Doris). When Herod married Mariamne, he put Doris aside and forced Antipater to move out of Jerusalem so he would not be a hindrance to the regal grooming of the sons of Mariamne, who were born after he was named king by the Romans.

Because of their destiny, Alexander and Aristobulus were the object of envy of Salome, the king's sister. Salome was greatly concerned that once they achieved power at the death of Herod, they would punish those who had engineered the death of their mother. Her mother Cypros, and others responsible for Mariamne's death, were also greatly concerned. In order to protect themselves, they began to raise calumnies against Alexander and Aristobulus. They planted the story that Alexander and Aristobulus were not pleased with their father because he had put their mother to death, and in fact, it was not even proper for them to converse with the murderer of their mother. This story was never told directly to Herod, but by telling it to many other persons, it eventually reached Herod's ears. He was greatly concerned because he noticed that his two sons did tend to distance themselves from him, giving support to the calumny. In the beginning he tended to ignore the calumny because of the love and admiration he had for these two sons. Soon after their arrival from Rome he selected wives for them: Alexander married Glaphyra (daughter of Archelaus, the King of Cappadocia) and Aristobulus married Bernice (daughter of Salome, Herod's sister).

The Meeting Between Herod and Marcus Agrippa

When Herod learned that Marcus Agrippa was returning once again to Mytilene to administer the affairs of the eastern countries, Herod made haste to invite him to Judea. Marcus Agrippa accepted this invitation and upon arriving in Judea, Herod omitted nothing that might please him. Herod gave him a tour of many parts of his kingdom and entertained him and those accompanying him in a magnificent manner. He showed him the edifices he had built at Caesarea and Sebaste, and the fortresses at Alexandrium, Herodium and Hyrcania. At Jerusalem the people greeted him in festival garments and received him with acclamations. At the temple Marcus Agrippa offered sacrifices to God and feasted all those in attendance. He tarried many days in Jerusalem where Herod held banquets in his honor and bestowed many presents on him. It was also a time when Herod and Marcus Agrippa cemented even further their friendship. He wished to remain longer, but since the season for sailing was almost over and he needed to return to Ionia (on the western coast of Asia Minor), he was forced to depart from Judea.

The following spring Marcus Agrippa was involved in an uprising in Bosphorous [kingdom on the Black Sea], and Herod went to assist him with his fleet. After a long journey by sea Herod finally reached Marcus Agrippa at Pontus in Asia Minor on the Black Sea. His arrival with his fleet was unexpected by Marcus Agrippa and he greeted Herod with great joy, expressing that Herod had manifested the greatest possible act of kindness by leaving his kingdom and coming such a great distance to assist him. He viewed Herod as a consultant in the management of war, an advisor in civil affairs, and a pleasant companion with whom he could relax. Next to the emperor, Marcus Agrippa considered Herod to be his closest friend. When the affair at Pontus was finished Marcus Agrippa and Herod chose to travel together along the coast of western Asia Minor.

When Marcus Agrippa and Herod arrived in Ionia, a great multitude of Jews came to them and brought grievances that they were being discriminated against in many ways. Whereas in the past the Roman government had permitted them to live according to their own laws, the local governors were now ruling otherwise. They were not allowing them to obey the Sabbath day or to worship

Chapter 3 Calumnies in Herod's Family

on holy days. They were also depriving them of the money they normally sent to the temple in Jerusalem, and forcing them to serve in the army with obligatory duties on the Sabbath. Upon hearing their complaints, Herod requested one of his advisors, Nicolaus of Damascus, to plead for privileges.[33] Accordingly, Marcus Agrippa called a meeting of the principal Romans of the area to listen to Nicolaus speak on behalf of the Jews. When he had made the case for the Jews, Marcus Agrippa stated that on account of Herod's good will and friendship, he was ready to grant the Jews what they should ask of him because their requests seemed just. And any future requests would also be honored as long as they were not a detriment to the Roman government. He then dismissed the assembly. At that time Herod stood and saluted him and gave him thanks for the kind disposition he showed the Jewish people from that area. In return Agrippa saluted Herod and embraced him as a sign of their great friendship. Herod then sailed for Caesarea [13 BC] and a few days after landing there he arrived in Jerusalem. There he informed the multitude that because of his friendship with Marcus Agrippa, the Jews of all of Asia had been benefited. And because he was joyful, Herod excused the people from paying the fourth part of their taxes for the year. The people were pleased and wished Herod all manner of happiness.

How Disturbances in His Family Caused Herod to Name His Eldest Son Antipater as His Successor

The situation became tense in Herod's family when Alexander and Aristobulus confronted Salome (Herod's sister) and Pheroras

---

33   The chief advisors in Herod's court tended to be Greeks. An influential member of this court was Nicolaus of Damascus who was either a Greek or a Hellenistic-Syrian. Nicolaus served as Herod's secretary, advisor, and also tutored him on Greek philosophy and rhetoric. He had served as tutor to the children of Antony and Cleopatra, and upon the death of these former employers, he became an advisor to Herod. He ranked high as a scholar and wrote philosophical essays, tragedies and comedies, in addition to musical compositions. He traveled extensively with Herod, and because of his skills in oratory, he often represented Herod at delicate negotiations. There was a mutual respect between Herod and Nicolaus, and Nicolaus was always totally loyal to Herod. Caesar and other members of his court in Rome held Nicolaus in high esteem.

(Herod's brother) concerning their role in the events leading to the death of their mother. Salome and Pheroras responded by planting further calumnies, hoping that they might incite Alexander and Aristobulus to break with their father. They also hoped that Alexander and Aristobulus would become so provoked that they might attempt to seek vengeance on their father, knowing that under that circumstance Herod would take vengeance on them. They planted the calumny that Alexander and Aristobulus planned to use the King of Cappadocia (Alexander's father-in-law) as a means of punishing their father for his crime. The King of Cappadocia was to seek an audience with Caesar so that Alexander and Aristobulus could officially accuse their father. When this calumny reached the ears of Herod from different sources, he was greatly disturbed and depressed. He was also concerned that the mental illness that befell him following the death of Mariamne, whom he loved dearly, might return. He lamented the misfortunes that seemed to be ongoing in his own home since Alexander and Aristobulus had returned from Rome.

As a means of teaching his insolent sons a lesson, he made a bold decision. He ordered that his eldest son Antipater should be returned to the palace, and he let it be known that he was elevating Antipater above Alexander and Aristobulus as the heir to his throne. The purpose was to deflate their pride. Herod went out of his way to favor Antipater in their presence and in the court, hoping that this behavior might cause them to have a better disposition towards him and to honor him properly. It was his strategy that when they had learned their lessons and demonstrated the proper humility, they would be restored to their former prime positions in the palace and in the court.

The situation then became more tense. Alexander and Aristobulus let it be known that their father had done them a grave injury by elevating Antipater above them. They were the sons of Mariamne, of Hasmonean blood, who were born after Herod was

Chapter 3 Calumnies in Herod's Family

named king; hence, they were of royal dignity and the heirs to the government. They had also been brought up with the understanding that they would eventually receive the government, and had been sent to Rome to receive the training and education required for their future positions. But Antipater proved to be a clever and vicious antagonist, and Alexander and Aristobulus were no match for his devious mind. Indeed, he was a master of intrigue. In order to cement his position with Herod, he continued to cause nervous tension in his half-brothers by not yielding to their pre-eminence, and by continuing to plant calumnies about them through assistants and influential persons living abroad. He used others to do his damage, and made every effort to remain unsuspected. Using persuasive powers, he convinced Herod to return his mother Doris to the palace, who had been put aside when Herod married Mariamne. He was also able in time to introduce Doris once again into Herod's bed.

It was difficult for Alexander and Aristobulus to combat Salome, Pheroras, and Antipater, who used every opportunity to demote them in the eyes of Herod. On one occasion Alexander and Aristobulus were observed shedding tears when discussing the death of their mother and their present situation. In the company of supposedly trusted friends they reproached their father for not acting justly concerning them. When Herod learned that they were castigating him publicly, he was very angry and chose to humble them further. He increased the honors bestowed on Antipater, wrote to Caesar in favor of Antipater, and asked that Antipater be received in Rome so that he might become Caesar's friend. At this time Marcus Agrippa was completing ten years as administrator of the eastern countries, and was departing for Rome from Mytilene. Herod sailed with Antipater to Myteline, met with Marcus Agrippa, gave him many presents, and requested that he take Antipater with him to Rome.

Antipater arrived in Rome laden with many gifts for Caesar

and others, and he was well received. Herod had also sent good recommendations to his friends in Rome concerning him. Antipater made a good impression in Rome, but because he was absent from Jerusalem he knew that he was missing opportunities of eliminating the threat of his half-brothers. Fearful that Herod might have a change of heart and become favorably impressed once again with the sons of Mariamne, he took every opportunity to send from Rome any stories that might grieve and irritate his father against them. He was able to have his friends circulate the major calumny that his half-brothers planned to poison their father and then make a claim to the throne since they were Hasmoneans and the first to be born after Herod was named king. Antipater continued his ways, with the aid of others, until Herod was very ill-disposed towards his two sons, and contemplated having them killed. Desiring not to be too blameworthy or too impulsive, Herod decided to take them to Rome and accuse them before Caesar. He requested an audience with Caesar concerning this matter, and Herod, his sons, and others, then made the long journey to Rome.

In front of Caesar and his court in Rome, Herod accused Alexander and Aristobulus:

> *"They were enemies to him. . . and by all means they showed their hatred of him. They would take away his life and therefore obtain the kingdom in a most barbarous manner. He had hitherto given them all that they needed as sons of the king and had married them into illustrious families. Although he had the authority to punish them for their crimes, he had chosen not to do so, but to bring them before Caesar, their common benefactor."*

The sons knew they were innocent, but how to respond to the charges of their father without offending his honor? When they noticed a kindly disposition towards them from Caesar and

Chapter 3 Calumnies in Herod's Family

from certain others in the audience, Alexander stood up and, gave an eloquent review of their situation, claiming their innocence and devotion to their father. He concluded by saying that if their father believed they were guilty, it was in his power to put them to death. Alexander was so effective with his words that the audience began to weep, and even Caesar was touched. Caesar then expressed correctly that although they were innocent of the great calumny, nevertheless they were guilty of not being humble and demeaning in their relationship with their father. They were also guilty of not expressing devotion to him as a means of preventing the suspicions that had been spread abroad concerning them. He also exhorted Herod to lay all such suspicions aside and to be reconciled to his sons. Caesar then embraced Alexander and Aristobulus, and all in attendance were deeply affected by what they observed.

Herod, Alexander, and Aristobulus gave thanks to Caesar and departed with Antipater who in a hypocritical way rejoiced at the reconciliation.

Caesar had previously told Herod that he had the authority to appoint his successor, or to distribute the kingdom in parts to any or all of his sons and others, so that all would have dignity. When Herod returned to Jerusalem with Antipater, Alexander, and Aristobulus, he went to the temple and made a speech to the assembled persons reviewing his experiences in Rome and the kindness of Caesar. He then concluded by announcing that his sons were to reign after him: **Antipater first, and then Alexander and Aristobulus.** He said that all three would eventually be kings; the age of one of them (Antipater) and the nobility of the other two, warrant that all should be rulers. Indeed, the kingdom is large and is sufficient for several kings, but in the meantime they should all honor him as king since he was not yet hindered by old age. He then dismissed the assembly.

The announcement caused contention among the three sons. Alexander and Aristobulus were grieved that the privilege of the first-born was again given to Antipater who was not a Hasmonean and who was born before Herod was named King. Antipater was angry that his brothers would succeed him as king and not his own sons.

About this time the amphitheater at Caesarea was finished, the 28th year of Herod's reign. It was also the year of the 192 Olympiad, and sumptuous preparations were made for the festivals. Herod sent all sorts of ornaments to adorn the furniture, and Caesar's wife Julia[34] sent a great part of her most valuable furniture from Rome so that the structure lacked nothing. Games were scheduled in honor of Caesar, which were to be repeated every fifth year also in honor of Caesar. Many ambassadors came to Caesarea to see the shows, and they were all entertained extravagantly by Herod. And it was reported that Caesar and Marcus Agrippa often said that "the dominions of Herod were too little for the greatness of his soul; and that he deserved to have both the kingdoms of Syria and Egypt also."

Being the major port for Judea, Caesarea was located a moderate distance from Jerusalem, and a place about mid-distance between these two cities was needed for travelers to rest and spend time. When the festivities at Caesarea were over, Herod chose a site known as Capharsaba as a fit place for the new city. It was in the plain between Jerusalem and Caesarea and noted for its good soil and water. He built a city there and named it Antipatris, in honor of his father Antipater. He also built a city above Jericho and named it Cypros in honor of his mother. In addition he built a city in the valley of Jericho and named it Phasaelis for his beloved brother who had been captured by the Parthinians. He also bestowed financial benefits on Syria, Greece, and many other places he visited. He built public works in Syria, erected Apollo's temple at Rhodes, and public edifices at Actium. The costs to Herod for these constructions were immense.

---

34   Caesar's wife was named Livia Drusilla, but after the death of Caesar Augustus, she assumed the name Julia Augusta. In his writings Josephus uses the name Julia.

Chapter 3 Calumnies in Herod's Family

Psychological Profile of Herod, According to Josephus
"Herod was a man of contrast. On one hand he would bestow magnificent benefits on mankind. On the other hand he was brutal and would even inflict great harm on nearest relatives. I am of the opinion... and imagine that both sorts of actions were one and the same. For being a man ambitious of honor, and quite overcome by that passion, he was induced to be magnificent in order to enhance his reputation, or whenever there appeared to be any hopes of a future memorial. Because his expenses were often beyond his abilities (to pay), he was forced to be harsh on his subjects by raising taxes. His gifts and edifices were many and he had to be a stern procurer. He was hated by those under him because of the injuries he did to them. As to his court, if anyone was not obsequious to him, and would not confess to being his slave, or to think of any new innovations in his government (or to suggest another plan), he was not able to contain himself and would prosecute even his own family and friends. He did this wickedness because of his desire that only he alone would be honored. The respects he paid to his superiors (in Rome) he expected to be paid to him by those of his nation, including family and friends. His behavior was contrary to Jewish law that preferred righteousness over glory, and for this reason the nation was not agreeable to him. It was not their way to flatter his ambition with statues and temples, or by any other means."

Herod was in need of additional resources after he had spent huge sums of money building cities and edifices both within and beyond his own kingdom. In desperation, he opened David's sepulcher hoping to find riches. Herod did this at night in the company of his most faithful friends. He found gold furniture, which he removed. Then, in the interest of doing a very careful search, he approached the area containing the bodies of David and Solomon, where, legend says, two of Herod's guards were killed by a burst of flame that came out from where they attempted to go in. Herod was terribly frightened and later built a propitiatory monument, of white stone, at the entrance to the sepulcher.

His problems with his family increased in viciousness following his intrusions into the sacred tomb. The tumult was so great that it was almost as if a civil war had broken out in his palace. Being very cunning, Antipater knew how to be solicitous to his brothers in their presence, and how to connive against them in their absence; thus, he was able to conceal his hatred towards them. To their detriment, his brothers, depending on the nobility of their birth and their self-righteousness, often expressed with their tongues what they had on their minds, without considering the consequences. Many spying friends would provoke them into making statements, and what they heard was then told to Antipater, who managed to have it reported to Herod, with additions or distortions. Great imputations were forged from the smallest events. Antipater would continually set up situations that would provoke them to speak so that the lies he was spreading would have some foundation of truth. If any of the many stories being circulated could be shown to be true, the rest could be assumed to be true as well. Most of Antipater's attacks were leveled at Alexander, since he was older and thereby next in line. He corrupted Alexander's friends and servants with money, flattery, or promises, and brought them to betray him. But while doing so, Antipater was quick to defend Alexander when in his presence. He would pretend to be on his side, and to show dismay at the stories, which, in fact, he had initiated. Antipater's main objective was to make it generally believed that Alexander and Aristobulus intended to kill Herod, and to have Herod become possessed with this intention.

Chapter 3 Calumnies in Herod's Family

The situation was wearing on Herod, who was showing diminishing affection for Alexander and Aristobulus. As his affection decreased for them, it increased for Antipater. The members of the court, the king's family and friends, some by their own inclination and some by the king's injunction, were also showing diminishing respect for Alexander and Aristobulus. All members of the court paid homage to Antipater, and it was upon the command of Herod, given even to his closest friends, that they should not go near Alexander or pay any regard to him and his friends.

Alexander and Aristobulus sensed the gravity of the situation and especially because of the coldness of their father, but they were unaware of the calumnies raised against them, and therefore they were not in a position to defend themselves. The wives of Alexander and Aristobulus complicated the situation even further. Glaphyra (Alexander's wife) was the daughter of a king (Archelaus, king of Cappadocia) who also had nobility on her mother's side. In a haughty manner she pretended to be more noble than any of the daughters, or daughter-in-laws of Herod. Glaphyra claimed that Herod's wives had been chosen for their beauty rather than for their family. These women grew to hate Glaphyra and Alexander, and were therefore quick to accept any calumny against Alexander. Bernice (Aristobulus's wife) took offense to the charge made by Glaphyra that she and her mother Salome were commoners. Aristobulus, who was angry at Salome for the damage she had done to him and his brother by her calumnies, upbraided his wife for the meanness of her family, and complained that he had married a woman from a low family while his brother had married one of royal blood. Bernice responded by weeping and confiding with her mother, who, by using persuasion and sedition, began to turn her daughter against her husband. Salome urged her daughter to confide in her if Aristobulus ever said anything in private concerning Herod. She would then take this information, distort its meaning to suit her favor, and use it against the brothers. Following a quarrel with her husband, and to please her mother, Bernice reported that Alexander and Aristobulus often talked about the crime that was done to their mother. They admitted that they hated their father because of his criminal actions, and if they received the kingdom they would make Herod's other sons country school masters, for their education and diligence in learning fitted them for such an occupation. They would also make the mothers of their other brothers weave with their maidens, for they had been trained for such employment. This story was carried by Salome to Herod, who was greatly concerned upon hearing it. Another rumor brought to Herod's attention concerned the clothes that had been worn by Mariamne, which Herod would often distribute to his other wives. Herod heard the rumor that Alexander had announced that when he assumed the throne that these wives would no longer wear royal garments, but would be clothed instead in hair-cloth. Herod finally challenged Alexander and Aristobulus concerning these charges. After hearing their claims of complete innocence, he apologized for paying any attention to the calumnies.

An irksome situation then befell Herod. Pheroras went to Alexander and said that he had heard from Salome that Herod was enamored with Glaphyra and his passion was incurable. Alexander became inflamed at this information, and went directly to Herod and informed him what Pheroras had said. Herod was furious and demanded an explanation from Pheroras, who said that he had only passed on information told him by Salome. Salome, who was present, denied ever making such a statement, and in tears announced her total loyalty to the king. Although he considered taking hard measures against Salome and Pheroras [such as having them killed] because of their malicious crime against him, Herod only dismissed them from his sight, and eventually let the matter pass. Thus, one of Salome's calumnies came home to haunt her.

The Affair Between Salome and Sylleus
Previous to this time, Malchus, king of Arabia had died, and Caesar appointed his son Obodas to replace him. King Obodos was elderly, inactive and slothful in nature. Because of his ineptness,

Chapter 3 Calumnies in Herod's Family

most of the affairs of his kingdom were managed by Sylleus, who was a handsome young man, but shrewd and calculating. One time when Sylleus was visiting Herod, he met Salome, and learning that she was a widow, he took an interest in her, believing that such a marriage would be politically advantageous for him. Because Salome at this time was not in good favor with her brother Herod, she looked with favor on Sylleus, believing that it would be to her benefit to be married to him. During the following days, it became obvious to many in the palace that an amorous relationship was developing between Sylleus and Salome. The rumor then reached Herod that Salome and Sylleus were in love. Sylleus soon departed but returned to Jerusalem a few months later and requested of Herod that Salome be given to him as his wife. Sylleus suggested that the proposed marriage would benefit Herod since Arabia was already mostly under Herod's power, and would likely be given to Herod by Caesar at a later time. The marriage might make the transition more logical. When Herod discussed this matter with Salome, she immediately agreed to the marriage. Herod then approached Sylleus and informed him that he would give Salome to him in marriage, if he would first convert to the Jewish religion and become circumcised. Sylleus was adamant in his refusal to do so, stating that he would be stoned to death by the Arabs if he became a Jew. He then departed hurriedly for Arabia. After his departure, Salome was reproached by her brother Pheroras for having become Sylleus's mistress. Various women in the palace expressed the same concern, stating that that Sylleus had debauched her by his actions.

Although still in love with Sylleus, Salome was then compelled by Herod to marry Alexas, who was Herod's good friend. Salome was reluctant to do so, and conferred with Julia, who was Caesar's wife, about this matter. Julia insisted that she follow Herod's mandate since Herod had sworn that he would never be friends with Salome, even though she was his sister, if she refused to marry Alexas. Julia also announced that she would also be her enemy if she did not comply with what Herod requested. Julia advised her that it would be to her advantage to agree with Herod concerning this proposed marriage. With this pressure Salome agreed to marry Alexas.

Further Problems Facing Alexander and Aristobulus

Any advantage acquired by Alexander and Aristobulus because of the fallout between Herod and his siblings Salome and Pheroras, soon disappeared with an event involving three eunuchs who were held in high esteem by Herod. One eunuch was appointed to be his butler, another brought him his supper, and the third would put him to bed and also managed certain affairs of state. The rumor reached Herod that Alexander had corrupted them with great sums of money for illicit purposes. Herod had the eunuchs tortured and when the tormenters, complying with orders from Antipater, stretched the rack to the very utmost, they said that Alexander had confessed that he hated his father, and often said disparaging things about him, such as, " persons of power in the kingdom ought not to fix their hopes upon Herod, an old man who colors his hair to make himself look young again. Instead, they ought to fix their hopes on him who was to be his successor in the kingdom, and who would avenge himself of his enemies and make his friends happy and blessed." The eunuchs also said that Alexander had also confessed "that men of power in the kingdom were already paying respects to him privately, and captains of the soldiery and the officers did secretly come to him."

These confessions terrified Herod. He sent spies privately by night and by day looking for persons of power in the kingdom, in the army and elsewhere, who might be paying homage to Alexander, and when he found some suspected of such treason he put them to death. As a result, the palace was full of turmoil and unjust proceedings. Many took advantage of his rage to forge calumnies against innocent persons in order to improve their own status. Antipater especially made gain of this situation. Lies were easily believed by Herod and punishments were inflicted quickly. In some cases, he who had just accused a person, was accused by someone else, and he and the person whom he had accused were led to their executions together.

By using torture Herod attempted to obtain confessions from some of Alexander's friends, and many died from this ordeal. Most would reveal nothing, because there was nothing that they knew. Others spoke falsely about Alexander in order to save themselves. One man said that Alexander was proud of his tallness and marksmanship and other physical attributes, which nature had given him, and he knew that his father envied him for them. When he walked with his father he would depress himself so he would not appear to be tall, and in marksmanship games with his father, he would purposely miss the target in order not to demonstrate that he was more skilled than his father. The man also said that Alexander and Aristobulus planned to lay in wait for their father when he was on a hunting trip, kill him, and then travel to Rome and claim command of the kingdom. These statements were often believed by Herod, but then his mind would enter a state of not knowing whom to trust because he continually heard conflicting information. Antipater was the main instigator of these calumnies against Alexander and his brother.

At this time Archelaus, Alexander's father-in-law (the king of Cappadocia), came to see Herod because of his great concern about the fate of his daughter Glaphyra and his son-on-law Alexander. He approached Herod carefully, commiserating with him over the problems he faced with his son. Using good psychology he was able to calm the seas, and before he left he was able to deliver his son-in-law out of the dangers he faced.

How Sylleus Caused Caesar to Become Angry at Herod and How this Precarious Situation was Resolved

Herod soon found himself in an alleged war against the Arabians without the knowledge of Caesar. This situation had serious consequences because Caesar demanded total allegiance and subservience from the rulers of the territories and it was expected that no ruler would go to war against the ruler of another territory unless told to do so by Caesar. The country of Trachonitis (northeast of the Sea of Galilee) had been added by Caesar to the territory governed by Herod. The inhabitants of Trachonitis resisted this change and the tactics used by Herod to keep them under control. Herod wanted them to realize the agricultural potential of the land, and to be peaceful, but they resented his dominion over them. At the time when Herod was in Rome with Alexander and Aristobulus to bring charges against his sons in front of Caesar, the Trachonites spread the rumor that Herod was dead, and many of them began to revolt. Herod's commanders put down the revolt, but about 40 of the principal leaders of the insurrection managed to escape into Arabia, where Sylleus gave them sanctuary. Sylleus, who was still smarting because he had not been allowed to marry Salome unless he became a circumcised Jew, entertained these fugitives, allowed them to raid neighboring areas in Judea and Celesyria, and then to retreat into Arabia where they were given protection. When Herod returned from Rome and learned of this event, he was greatly concerned because he was unable to get at those responsible for the revolt because of the protection they were receiving in Arabia. Determined to punish them for their deeds, he sought out their relatives in Trachonitis and had them slain. This infuriated the Trachonites, and added to the number fleeing to Arabia for protection. The fugitives in Arabia, now numbering about 1,000, increased their terrorism in Herod's kingdom and elsewhere.

Herod had previously loaned King Obodas of Arabia sixty talents, and since the time of payment had already passed, he demanded that the money be paid immediately. Because of the ineffectiveness of King Obodas, Sylleus had been able to take control of the kingdom. Sylleus denied that any of the fugitives from Trachonitis were being given sanctuary in Arabia, and he put off payment of the money. To seek amends, Herod then sought council with Saturninus and Volumnius, who were presidents of Syria. At a hearing before Saturninus and Volumnius, with Sylleus

Chapter 3 Calumnies in Herod's Family

being present, it was agreed that Sylleus would make payment of the money owed Herod within 30 days and Sylleus would give up the fugitives.

Before the 30 days had passed, Sylleus departed for Rome without making any payment or delivering any of the fugitives. After consulting with Saturninus and Volumnius, and with their permission, Herod made the decision to seek justice. He marched into Arabia with a band of soldiers and when he came to the garrison housing the robbers from Trachonitis, he took them all and demolished the place, but did no harm to others. When the Arabians came to the assistance of the Trachonites, a battle ensued, resulting in the death of a few of Herod's soldiers and about 20 of the Arabians including Nacebus, the leader of the Arabians. The remaining Arabians, knowing they were defeated, took flight. After Herod had punished those responsible for the rebellion, he placed 3,000 Idumeans in Trachonitis to maintain order. He also sent an account of this affair to various captains in Phoenicia, stating that he had done nothing but what he should have done to punish the refractory Arabians. When they made inquiries, they agreed that what he said was true.

Messengers from Arabia were then sent to Sylleus in Rome, informing him of what had transpired, and as is usually the case, the events were exaggerated by these messengers. At this time Sylleus had been able to ingratiate himself with Caesar and others in the palace. With the news from his country, he dressed in black and told Caesar that his country Arabia was involved in a war, and his kingdom was in great confusion because Herod and his army had made it a waste land. With tears in his eyes he said that 2,500 of the principal men among the Arabians had been killed. In addition, general Nacebus, who was his close friend had also been slain. Furthermore, the riches of Raepta had been carried off. He also claimed that King Obodas, who was despised by the people, was unfit for war because of the feeble state of his body, and as a result he had not raised an army to oppose Herod. Sylleus then announced that if he had remained in Arabia he would have taken steps to ensure that Herod would not have had the advantage in this war. Caesar was provoked at what he heard and then asked only one question of Herod's friends in the court. The question was, "Did Herod lead an army into Arabia?" When they all confessed that such was the case, without saying why he did it and how it was done, Caesar expressed great anger at Herod and wrote him an epistle with the strongly worded theme that *whereas in the past he had treated him as a friend, he would now treat him only as a subject.*[35]

Sylleus wrote an account of this meeting to the Arabians, who were so delighted with what they read that they did not deliver the fugitives whom they were protecting. Nor did they pay Herod what they owed him. They also stopped paying rent on pastures that had been leased from Herod, believing, and hoping, that Caesar would soon take Herod's kingdom away from him, and therefore nothing would be owed to Herod. The inhabitants of Trachonitis also rose up against the Idumean garrison placed there by Herod. Herod was distraught by all that had happened, and was cast into sadness and fear when Caesar would not accept ambassadors from him to explain why he had led soldiers into Arabia and the consequences of that invasion. Of even greater concern was Sylleus's continuing presence in Rome, where he had access to Caesar and was able to improve the potential of his political future, to the detriment of Herod's future.

Events then occurred in Arabia that had an impact on Sylleus's charges against Herod. King Obodas died and his brother Aretas took over the government without first conferring with Caesar. Caesar was angry with Aretas because of this unwise act, and Sylleus took advantage of this opportunity. By using calumnies and bribes,

---

35   This statement was a bad omen for Herod, who up until this time had been Caesars's favored client-king. With the ire of Caesar, Herod's kingdom and future were now in great jeopardy.

Chapter 3 Calumnies in Herod's Family

and promising much money to Caesar, Sylleus attempted to have the kingdom denied to Aretas and have himself named king. In the meantime Aretas sent an epistle, presents, and a golden crown to Caesar, with the epistle accusing Sylleus of being a wicked servant and having killed King Obodas by poison. Aretas also claimed that while King Obodas was alive, Sylleus had controlled him and therefore had ruled the country. Aretas also accused Sylleus of debauching the wives of the Arabians and borrowing money for bribes in order to obtain the government for himself. Caesar paid no attention to these accusations because of his anger towards Aretas, and sent the ambassadors away without accepting any of the gifts.

Anarchy then began to reign in Judea and Arabia because it was sensed that neither king had power to govern. Aretas had not been confirmed as king of Arabia by Caesar, and Herod's future as king was precarious because it became known that Caesar was angry at him. In an effort to bring an end to the madness and mischievous acts occurring in Judea and to resolve his relationship with Caesar, Herod sent Nicolaus of Damascus to Rome as his ambassador. Upon arriving in Rome, Nicolaus found that he had important allies among certain Arabians, who informed Nicolaus of all the wicked things that Sylleus had done in order to obtain the government for himself. These Arabians, who had broken away from Sylleus's party, presented evidence in the form of testimonies and documents to support their charges. Nicolaus made the decision to defend Herod by attacking Sylleus. At the hearing in Rome in front of Caesar, with Sylleus and Areta's ambassadors being present, Nicolaus accused Sylleus, as follows: There were robbers in Trachonitis, and to escape punishment from Herod they escaped into Arabia where Sylleus received them, gave them food, and protected them. Sylleus also encouraged them to continue stealing from those in neighboring countries, and he profited from their robberies. He orchestrated the destruction of Obodas and other prominent Arabians. He borrowed large sums of money for no good design. He was guilty of adultery, not only with Arabians, but also with Romans. He had alienated Caesar from Herod, and all that he had said about Herod was false. At this point Caesar interrupted Nicolaus and instructed him to speak on whether Herod had led an army into Arabia, killed 2,500 Arabians, taken prisoners, and pillaged the country. Nicolaus replied by stating that if these accusations were true, then Caesar would be justified in being very angry at Herod, but none or very little of the accusations were true. Nicolaus then said a debt of 500 talents was due Herod, and a bond (agreement) had been written when the loan was granted that if the money had not been repaid by the allotted time that it would be lawful to make a seizure out of any part of the country. As for the pretended army, Nicolaus asserted that it was not an army but a band of soldiers sent to obtain payment of the loan. Prior to that time Sylleus had met with Saturninus and Volumnius (the presidents of Syria) at Berytus and made an oath that he would pay the money within 30 days and deliver the fugitives from Trachonitis that were in his dominion. When Sylleus had not abided by this oath, Herod appeared before the presidents and obtained their permission to lead a band of soldiers into Arabian to seize what was owed him. Nicolaus, then asked of Caesar, "How can this be called a war? It was permitted by your presidents, allowed by your covenants, and it was not executed until thy name, O Caesar, as well as that of other gods, had been profaned." When the Arabians came to the rescue of the fugitives, Herod and his soldiers defended themselves, and in this battle Nacebus, the general of the Arabian soldiers and 25 other Arabians were killed, but no more than 25. Nicolaus then accused Sylleus of increasing each casualty to 100 to obtain his fictitious number of 2,500.

This last statement provoked Caesar, who in a rage turned to Sylleus and asked him how many Arabians were killed. Sylleus, hesitated, and then said that he had been told incorrectly by others. Nicolaus then read covenants about the money Sylleus had borrowed, letters from the presidents of Syria defending the actions taken by Herod, and complaints from the residents of several cities who

Chapter 3 Calumnies in Herod's Family

had been injured by the robbers protected by Sylleus. Caesar then castigated Sylleus for his calumnies and the misery he had caused, and sent him away to repay the debt he owed Herod, after which he was to be punished by death. Caesar then reconciled himself with Herod and apologized for the things he had written to him.

Caesar was still offended by Aretas who had assumed the Arabian government without obtaining consent. He was inclined to abide by his earlier decision to add all of Arabia to Herod's kingdom, but then he received letters from Syria outlining the problems Herod was having with his sons. After reading these letters Caesar reached the conclusion that it would not be wise to add another large kingdom to Herod's domain because Herod was getting old and he had such an ill relationship with his sons. Accordingly, he summoned Areta's ambassadors before him, and after reproving Aretas for his rashness for assuming the government without first conferring with him, he accepted the presents from Aretas offered to him previously and confirmed the kingdom on him.

Events Leading to the Deaths of Alexander and Aristobulus, the Sons of Mariamne

The discord in Herod's family grew worse because of the mischievous ways of Antipater, who promised rewards to various persons of importance who would make charges against Alexander and Aristobulus. One was Eurycles, a Lacedemonian who had been a companion to Mark Antony when he had power in the Roman Empire. He was a corrupt man, but because of his previous relationship to Antony, he was welcome in the palace in Jerusalem where he had close contact with Antipater, Alexander, and Aristobulus. With bribes from Antipater, Eurycles praised Antipater in front of Herod and reported that both Alexander and Aristobulus were committed to the premise that bloodshed was necessary to appease the ghosts of Mariamne and Hyrcanus, their mother and grandfather. Antipater had other persons appear before Herod and make similar statements about his half-brothers. Some said that they had conversed with two persons who had served as Herod's guards until they were dismissed, and these former guards had received large gifts from Alexander. Because Herod was suspicious of them, he had them tortured, and finally one confessed that Alexander had persuaded them to kill Herod while they were hunting, and have it appear as if he had fallen off a horse and onto his own spear. Another person informed Herod that money had been deposited at the garrison at Alexandria for the use of Alexander and Aristobulus after Herod had been killed. The commander of the garrison was then caught and tortured. The commander could not reveal anything about this plot, but his son came in and delivered a letter allegedly written by Alexander stating that they expected to be received in the fortress. Upon reading this letter Herod had no doubt about the designs of his sons against him, even though Alexander responded that the letter was a forgery, written by Herod's scribe at Antipater's request. (At a later time this scribe was shown to be a forger and was put to death by Herod.)

Herod then had all these persons whom he suspected put before the multitude at Jericho, where their guilt was proclaimed, and they were stoned to death. The multitude would also have stoned Alexander and Aristobulus, but Herod would not permit it. Alexander and Aristobulus were then put under guard, kept in custody in different quarters, ordered to put in writing all the ills they had against their father, and to bring the writings to him. They wrote that they had no treacherous designs, nor had made any preparations against their father, but that they had intended to fly away [to Cappadocia] because of the distress they were in and because their lives were uncertain and tedious.

Herod was greatly concerned to read that they intended to escape to Cappadocia where they would be protected by Alexander's father-in-law, Archelaus, the king of Cappadocia. It would be a crime against him if king Archelaus intended to take them to Rome secretively and defend them in front of Caesar. About this time an

Chapter 3 Calumnies in Herod's Family

ambassador came from Cappadocia. Since Herod was suspicious that king Archelaus was not acting in good faith, he had Alexander brought before him and the ambassador. He asked Alexander questions about his proposed flight to Cappadocia. In front of the ambassador Alexander replied that king Archelaus had promised to send them to Rome for their safety, but that they had no wicked nor mischievous designs against their father, and that nothing of that nature which their adversaries had charged against them was true. They had hoped that he would have questioned (certain) accusers more strictly before they had been suddenly slain by the means of Antipater, who had put his own friends among the multitude for that purpose.

Herod then had Alexander and the ambassador taken to Glaphyra, who was asked if she knew anything about Alexander's treacherous designs against him. When she saw Alexander in bonds, she beat her head and fell into tears. Her comment was, "There was no such wickedness . . .but . . . they . . . had resolved to fly to king Archelaus, and from thence to Rome."

When Glaphyra's statements were brought to the attention of her father king Archelaus, he replied that he had not done any ill-will to Herod. He confirmed, however, that he had promised to receive the young men, because it was to their advantage, and to Herod's advantage, that he do so because too severe procedures might be carried out against them in Jerusalem because of the anger and disorder that was present. But even though he promised to receive them in Cappadocia, he had not promised to send them to Caesar. The conflict between Glaphyra's statement and her father's statement concerning sending them to Rome made Herod believe that Archelaus was involved in a conspiracy against him.

When Caesar had been fully informed of the latest events he wrote to Herod and said, ". . . he was grieved for him on account of his sons. . . in case his sons had been guilty of any profane and insolent crimes against him, it would behoove him to put them to death (as parricides). . . for which he gave him power accordingly. . .but if they had only contrived to fly away, he should only give them an admonition, and not proceed to any extremity with them." Caesar also advised him to get an assembly together consisting of governors of nearby provinces (governors of Syria and the king of Cappadocia), others known to be friendly to him, and members of his own kindred, to listen to the evidence and to advise him as to the outcome. Caesar recommended that this assembly meet at Berytus.[36]

Herod asked 150 persons to assemble at Berytus, including the principal leaders of Syria and his own friends and kinsmen (including Salome and Pheroras). A notable person not invited was Archelaus (king of Cappadocia and Alexander's father-in-law). He was not invited because of Herod's present hatred for him for agreeing to receive his sons when they escaped from Jerusalem, and because he was conceived as a possible obstacle to his designs. Alexander and Aristobulus were also not invited to attend. Instead, they were kept at a village near Sidon, where they could be called to meet before the assembly if demanded by the occasion. It was apparent that Herod did not want them to be able to respond to the charges. They were comely young men and Alexander was a man of words who in an eloquent manner could likely have influenced the members of the assembly by showing the flimsiness of the charges against them. Herod stood before the assembly and by himself accused his sons. No witnesses were called for or against the charges, and he asserted the charges to be true only by his own authority. In essence, he charged that his sons had plotted to kill him and then fly away to Cappadocia, and then to Rome. He read the writings that confessed to the proposed flight. Evidence for the plot was exaggerated, and he expressed it in a vehement manner as if they had actually confessed to designing it. He concluded by saying that "he had sufficient authority by nature and by Caesar's grant to do what he

---

36   The city of Berytus is now named Beirut, located on the coast of Lebanon.

Chapter 3 Calumnies in Herod's Family

thought fit." He also added a law of the country: "That if parents laid their hands on the head of him that was accused, the (onlookers) were obliged to cast stones at him, and thereby slay him."

By Herod's design, the members of the assembly were not there to serve as judges, but as persons to declare how unworthy it would be if such treacherous acts were not punished. When he had finished his pronouncements and his sons had not been given any opportunity for a defense, the members of the assembly perceived there was no room for equity or reconciliation. Consequently, they confirmed his authority to do what he wanted to do. However, several persons argued that his sons, although guilty, should not be put to death.

Herod departed with his sons and went to Tyre and then to Caesarea, all along debating what sort of death the young men should suffer. All of Judea and Syria at this time were waiting for the last act of this tragedy.

At Caesarea an old soldier named Tero, who had served valiantly in Herod's army, was publicly proclaiming that "justice was being trampled underfoot, and truth had perished while lies and ill-will prevailed." Tero had been influenced by his son who was loyal to Alexander. Tero eventually went to Herod and lamented that a king could kill those who are dearest to him. He also pointed out that at one time Herod resolved to put Salome and Pheroras (his own siblings) to death, yet now he believed them rather than his own sons. He also proclaimed that killing his sons would leave all to Antipater who was hated by the soldiers. He told Herod that certain officers in the army commiserate with Alexander and Aristobulus, and many captains show great indignation at what was about to occur. He then made the grievous mistake of naming the persons in the army who showed such indignation. Herod then gave orders that Tero and those whom he had named should be put in prison.

Trypho, who was one of the king's barbers, then came forward in a moment of madness, not foreseeing the consequences for him personally, and informed Herod that Tero had encouraged him to cut Herod's throat with his razor when he trimmed him, promising that Alexander would reward him for doing so. Upon hearing this information Herod ordered that Tero, Tero's son, and Trypho should be tortured to obtain additional information. When Tero and his son denied the barber's accusation, Herod ordered that Tero should be tortured severely. Tero's son then promised to proclaim the truth if his father would no longer be tortured. He said that his father, at the persuasion of Alexander, had made plans to have Herod killed. Some said that the son made this statement only to free his father from further torture, but others said that it was true.

The testimony of Tero's son was the final blow. In a rage Herod ordered that Tero, Tero's son, Trypho (the barber) and 300 army officers (who had been named or suspected as favoring Alexander) should be killed. Alexander and Aristobulus were then taken to Sebaste, where, following Herod's orders, they were strangled. This event ended the troubled lives of Alexander and Aristobulus, the sons of Herod and Mariamne. At night time their bodies were taken to Alexandrium, where many of their relatives on their mother's side had been buried.

Chapter 4

THE DOWNFALL OF ANTIPATER, HEROD'S ELDEST SON

At the death of his half-brothers Alexander and Aristobulus, Antipater governed the nation jointly with his father. Although now free of the fear that Alexander and Aristobulus might wrest the power from him, his life was not a pleasant one. The hatred of the nation was intense against him because of his assumed role in the deaths of his two half-brothers. And as predicted by Tero, the soldiery was alienated from him.

Complicating his life was the fear that eventually Herod might realize the truth concerning his role in the demise of his half-brothers, and if so, he would never achieve his objective of being the sole ruler of the nation. The hatred he had for his half-brothers was now directed toward his father. The longer Herod lived the more likely it would become that he would discover the truth. And once the truth was known, they would be enemies. So he began to make plans for the death of his father.

He sent great presents to his friends in Rome and to the ruler of Syria. He also gave presents to Salome, the king's sister, hoping to have her favor. But Salome was well aware of his wickedness and what he was capable of doing, so she was wary of him. Even though they had been partners in the crime leading to the deaths of Alexander and Aristobulus, she did not trust him, and in fact, she hated him.

At the deaths of Alexander and Aristobulus, Herod sent Alexander's wife (Glaphyra) back to her father in Cappadocia. He also returned all portions of her estate so there would be no dispute between him and the king of Cappadocia. However, he kept her children and brought them up with care. Alexander and Glaphyra had two sons. Aristobulus and Bernice (Salome's daughter) had three sons and two daughters. Herod presented these children to his relatives in the palace. Deploring the misfortune of his own sons, he prayed that no such ill fortune would befall them, and that they would increase in virtue. To insure their future he betrothed them to members of his family, so they would marry well when they reached the proper age. One notable arrangement was betrothing Alexander's oldest son to Pheroras's daughter.

Antipater's jealousy of his former half-brothers now extended to their sons, and he was especially concerned with his father's plan that these grandsons would be given special advantages. Antipater was fearful that at some future time these children would be favored over him. Even if he were named king when Herod died, he feared that the succession might go to Alexander's sons, because they were Hasmoneans, and not to his own sons. A special concern was Alexander's eldest son. His grandfather was king of Cappadocia, and now he had been betrothed by Herod to Pheroras's daughter. Since Pheroras was the tetrarch of Perea, this Hasmonean son would have the support of both a king and a tetrarch, which would make him a worthy adversary. He lamented the problem he might face, knowing the feelings of the multitude against him and the affection they had for the children of his deceased brothers. And now to compound the issue, Herod himself was showing great affection for these children. After pondering how to resolve this problem he decided to go directly to Herod and to explain that he had been placed in a difficult position. Even though he would have the name of king, the espousals placed the future power in the hands of Alexander's eldest son because he would have a king and a tetrarch in his lineage. When Herod heard his concerns he became very angry and then suspicious. He began to wonder if his sons had been put to death because of the false tales of Antipater. He gave Antipater a curt

Chapter 4 The Downfall of Antipater, Herod's Eldest Son

answer and told him to be gone. Later he succumbed to Antipater's flatteries, and reversed himself. He betrothed Pheroras's daughter to Antipater's son, instead of to Alexander's oldest son, which pacified Antipater.

Antipater Becomes Intolerable and Friction Arises Between Herod and Pheroras

A new problem for Herod began to surface in the palace. Pheroras was married to a former servant from a low family.[37] At one time Herod urged him to put this wife away and marry one of Mariamne's daughters, but Pheroras refused to do so because of his love for his wife. Pheroras's wife, her mother, her sister, and Antipater's mother Doris, as a group of four women, became very impudent and domineering in the palace. They, and especially Pheroras's wife, became insolent towards the king's unmarried daughters, Salome and Roxanne. The four women met secretly and gossiped incessantly about these daughters and other events occurring in the palace. Herod became incensed at the trouble they were causing and especially the unhappiness felt by his unmarried daughters because of their actions. He also sensed that one of their goals was to do him mischief. His sister Salome was his spy and he instructed her to make an effort to learn what transpired in their clandestine meetings, and then to relay the information to him.

An active group of Pharisees, for their own advantage, inveigled themselves into the confidence of this group of women. They listened to their gossip about what transpired in the palace, prodded them for new information, and used them for political purposes. For many years the Pharisees had been trouble-makers for kings, and they had become especially quarrelsome at this time. Although the Jews in Judea had given their assurance of goodwill to Caesar and to king Herod, this group consisting of about 6,000

---

37   Even though Pheroras was tetrarch of Perea, he and his wife preferred to spend most of their time in Jerusalem, living in Herod's palace where major political activities (and intrigues) took place.

persons did not give this goodwill. When Herod imposed a fine on them, Pheroras's wife secretly paid the fine for them from her own money. Many members of this sect had the reputation of being able to predict the future, and after Pheroras's wife had paid their fines, they prophesied that Herod's government would soon cease, his posterity would be deprived of it, and the kingdom would come to her and Pheroras and their children. These predictions of the Pharisees became known to Salome, who told them to Herod. Even though Herod knew that the predictions were contrived to please Pheroras's wife and others, they concerned him because many persons believed them and some of the believers might take steps to make them come true. Herod took actions to quell the effect of the predictions. He slew the Pharisees responsible for the predictions, and he also slew members of the palace, including certain family members, who believed what the Pharisees foretold. Herod also killed Bagoas the eunuch who had been puffed up by the Pharisees, and was led to believe by the predictions that he would be favored by the newly appointed king, who would have great powers and enable him to marry and have children begotten by him.

Because the predictions foretold that Pheroras, his beloved brother, would succeed him as king, Herod now had to look askance at Pheroras who could become his enemy. He also had to take action against Pheroras's wife, who had been the main instigator of the troublesome affair. Herod gathered an assembly consisting of family members and friends. In their presence he chastised Pheroras's wife for dishonoring his two daughters Salome and Roxanne, for introducing a quarrel between him and his brother, and for allowing the fines he had levied against the Pharisees not to be paid, which allowed certain offenders to escape his punishment. He then turned to his brother and said that if he values his relation with him, he would put this wife away. Pheroras replied that he would never renounce his brotherly love, but would rather die than to be deprived of a wife who was so dear to him. Because of his show of emotion towards his wife, Herod became soft-hearted, but as punishment he

Chapter 4 The Downfall of Antipater, Herod's Eldest Son

informed Antipater and his mother Doris that they could not have any further conversations with Pheroras or with Pheroras's wife. To seal this agreement with Antipater, he gave him 100 talents, an amount of money that only the two of them knew about. Herod also ordered that the troublesome women must stop holding their meetings. Even though all parties agreed to follow his orders in his presence, they were quick to defy him. The troublesome women still had their secret meetings, and Antipater sometimes met with them. Antipater and Pheroras also had secret meetings. It was also reported that Antipater had "criminal conversations" with Pheroras's wife, and that they had been brought together by Antipater's mother.

Antipater now became very concerned that his secret meetings with Pheroras and Pheroras's wife might be learned by Salome, or someone else, and reported to his father. To remove himself from the scene, he made the decision to leave Judea and go to Rome. But the main reason Antipater was anxious to be in Rome, away from Judea, was that he had engineered a plot to kill his father by poison, and he wanted to be away from Judea when it happened so that he would not be suspected. Because of their secret meetings with Antipater, the troublesome women of the palace became aware of the plot. They were also aware of the "criminal conversations" between Antipater and Pheroras's wife, during which the details of the plot were discussed. Certain others living in the palace and elsewhere were also knowledgeable of the plot. It was planned that when Herod was poisoned Antipater would return from Rome as king, with the full support of Caesar. In order to justify going to Rome, Antipater wrote to his friends in Rome and urged them to write to Herod and say that "Antipater should be sent to Caesar for a given period of time." Herod responded favorably to these letters and sent Antipater to Rome laden with expensive gifts. **He also sent him with a testament for Caesar stating that Antipater would succeed him as king, but if Antipater should die first, his successor would be Herod [Philip], the son of Mariamne II.**

This testimony was of great concern to Antipater because it meant that his sons were excluded from the line of succession. He had to take actions to insure that his sons would succeed him as king, and not Herod [Philip] or the sons of Herod [Philip].

The Death of Pheroras

After the departure of Antipater to Rome, Herod ordered Pheroras to retire to his tetrarchy, and to remain there because he was so obstinate in his affection for his wife. In essence, this order meant that Pheroras had been banished from his presence. With this affront, Pheroras took an oath that he would never return to Jerusalem until he heard that his brother was dead. Soon after the departure of Pheroras from Jerusalem, Herod became ill and thought that he might die. He requested that Pheroras come and see him, but Pheroras stood by his oath and refused to go to his bedside. Herod soon recovered from this illness. At a later time Pheroras became gravely ill, and was not expected to live. Upon hearing this news Herod went to see him, without being sent for, and expressed great brotherly love for him. When Pheroras died, Herod took care of the funeral and had him buried in Jerusalem. Herod was greatly saddened with the death of his brother and proclaimed a period of mourning for him.

Curiously, the death of Pheroras ushered in a bizarre event that resulted eventually in the demise of Antipater. When the funeral was over, two of Pheroras's freedmen[38] came to Herod and pleaded with him to avenge the murder of his brother. They told him that Pheroras had dined with his wife the day before he became ill, and during the dinner a certain potion was brought for him to eat, which was described as a love-potion, but in reality it was a deadly poison. The potion was brought out of Arabia by a woman renowned for

---

38   A freedman and a freedwoman was a person who had been freed from slavery. Freedmen and freedwomen often earned their release from slavery because of their hard work and dedication to their owners. It was also common for them to remain as employees of their previous owners. This was likely the situation for the freedmen and freedwomen residing in the household of the tetrarch Pheroras.

Chapter 4 The Downfall of Antipater, Herod's Eldest Son

making love-potions. Both the mother and sister of Pheroras's wife had been at the place where the woman lived, and they had persuaded the woman to sell them the potion, which they gave to Pheroras's wife the day before the supper. The freedmen believed that Pheroras was murdered by his wife, her mother, and her sister.

Herod was provoked by this story and had some of Pheroras's wife's maid servants and freedwomen questioned and then tortured. One, under extreme agony, said, "She prayed that God would send the like agonies upon Antipater's mother, who had been the occasion of these miseries to all of them." Herod was astonished to learn that Doris, his first wife and Antipater's mother was mentioned. This suggested that all four of the troublesome women were somehow involved in the seditious act to poison Pheroras. Herod increased the torture of the maid servants and freedwomen until other things were discovered. These women had overheard many of conversations of the troublesome women in Herod's palace. Herod learned about the secret meetings of these women, which he had forbidden, and he also heard what he had said alone to Antipater, and what he had charged Antipater to conceal, which was the gift of 100 talents as part of the agreement that he would not have any conversations with Pheroras or Pheroras's wife. Herod also learned from the maid servants and freedwomen that Antipater hated his father, and had complained to his mother how very long his father was living. Antipater had said to his mother that because he himself was almost an old man (as evidenced by the growing number of gray hairs upon his head), the pleasure of being king would only be for a short period of time. Herod also learned that Antipater had lamented that he had many half-brothers, in addition to the sons of Alexander and Aristobulus, who had hopes for the kingdom, and the hopes of these persons made his own hopes uncertain. Antipater had also been quoted as being bitter that Herod had decreed that he would be succeeded as king by his brother Herod [Philip] and not by his own son.

Herod was astounded at what he had learned from these

women. The statements verified what his sister Salome had reported when she warned him about the secret meetings held in the palace by the troublesome women. Since the maid servants and freed-women knew about the 100 talents given to Antipater in secrecy, it was also apparent that Antipater had betrayed him by talking with Pheroras's wife.

Based upon the statements made by the maid servants and the freedwomen and the warnings of Salome concerning the troublesome women, Herod also reached the conclusion that his wife Doris had malicious intentions towards him. Hence, he deprived her of all her fine ornaments which were extremely valuable and banished her from the palace for the second time.[39]

By sending Doris away, Herod was also expressing his displeasure with Antipater. To learn more about Antipater's involvement with the troublesome women, Herod tortured Antipater's steward who handled Antipater's governmental financial affairs, and learned that Antipater had obtained a deadly potion, which was to be administered to Herod while he was in Rome. By being away, Antipater would not be blamed for participating in the murder of his father. The potion was given to Antipater by one of his friends named Antiphilus, who had brought it out of Egypt. Antipater gave the potion to Theudion, who was Doris's brother. Theudion then gave it to Pheroras's wife who, at the instructions of Pheroras, was to keep it until it was ready to be used.

Herod then confronted Pheroras's wife with the evidence, who confessed everything. Herod demanded that she produce the potion, and when she went to fetch it she jumped from a housetop attempting to kill herself. Instead of landing on her head, she landed on her feet and was not badly hurt. Herod comforted her and promised her that she would be pardoned, and her domestic help would also be pardoned, if she told the complete truth.

---

39   The first time Doris was banished was when Herod married Mariamne.

Chapter 4 The Downfall of Antipater, Herod's Eldest Son

However, if she failed to do so, she would suffer utmost miseries by torture. With this promise of a pardon, she said that the poison was obtained by Antipater for the sole purpose of killing his father. It was brought out of Egypt by Antiphilus and given to her brother Theudion, who, in turn, gave it to her. Pheroras had instructed her to keep it hidden until an opportunity presented itself for its use. When Pheroras took sick and Herod came from Jerusalem "to take care of him," Pheroras observed the many kindnesses and brotherly love that Herod extended to him. He was overcome with grief, stating that he did not expect to live very long, and he could not defile his forefathers by murdering his beloved brother. He then announced that he could not participate any further in the murderous plot designed by Antipater. So, he instructed her to burn the potion in his presence, which she did, but secretly retained a small portion that she might use to commit suicide in case Herod should treat her miserably after the death of her husband. Upon admitting all of this, she produced the box containing the potion, for all to see.[40]

To his further dismay Herod learned that his wife Mariamne II was accused in the confessions of being aware of the murderous plot and concealing it. Her brothers, under torture, declared it to be true. **In his latest testament to Caesar, Herod had named her son Herod [Philip] to be next in line behind Antipater to received the government. Herod then divorced Mariamne II and blotted her son's name from the testament.** Herod also took the high priest position away from her father Simon and appointed Matthias the son of Theophilus, who was born in Jerusalem, to be high-priest.

---

40   Although Pheroras's freedmen concluded that Pheroras had been poisoned by his wife, such was not the case. The poison was meant for Herod, and it was given to Pheroras's wife for her to keep until Pheroras had the opportunity to use it to kill Herod. The freedmen learned that the poison was in the house, and when Pheroras died, they supposed that it had been given to him as a love-potion by his wife at dinner. It is of historical significance, however, that their error had far reaching circumstances, affecting the lives of Antipater and many others.

At this time, Bathyllus, who was Antipater's freedman, came from Rome. While being tortured he confessed that he had brought another potion with him (the poison of asps and the juices of other serpents) which he was to deliver to Doris, with instructions that she was to give it to Pheroras in case the first potion was not successful. Bathyllus also brought letters from Rome containing false statements made by Archelaus and Philip. Archelaus was the son of Malthace (the Samaritan) and Philip was the son of Cleopatra. For educational reasons, Archelaus and Philip had been in Rome along with Antipas (also the son of Malthace), and Archelaus and Philip had just been recalled to Jerusalem by the order of Herod. The letters had been written by Herod's friends in Rome, but at the suggestion of Antipater who paid heavily for them. The letters stated that Archelaus and Philip commiserated the deaths of Alexander and Aristobulus at the hands of their father, and they feared that they had been ordered to return to Jerusalem to be destroyed in turn by him. Antipater had also written to his father about the letters and urged Herod to excuse them of their guilt because they were still youthful.

Many charges were now being levied against Antipater, but being in Rome he was unaware of them. His enemies in Jerusalem did not contact him out of principle. His friends in Jerusalem, who now believed that he was doomed, did not dare contact him for fear of retribution from Herod.

The Imprisonment of Antipater

Antipater, not knowing what was happening in Jerusalem concerning him, wrote to his father and friends in Jerusalem stating that he had accomplished all his goals in Rome, and he had been dismissed with honor by Caesar. Thus, he would soon return to Jerusalem. In his reply Herod urged him not to delay his journey. Herod wished to have this "plotter against him" in his own hands. He feared that Antipater might learn what would befall him upon his arrival in Jerusalem and therefore decide to remain in Rome, where he could continue his calumnious acts and bias influential persons

Chapter 4 The Downfall of Antipater, Herod's Eldest Son

concerning the situation. As a consequence, Herod expressed affection for Antipater in his letter, hoping to convince him that all was well between them. In the letter, however, Herod commented that he had a complaint against his mother, but if he made haste and returned quickly, he would put aside those complaints. The letter reached Antipater in Cilicia [in Asia Minor], after he had left Rome. Prior to receiving this letter he had received a letter in Tarentum [Grecian city in Italy] giving an account of Pheroras's death. The news about Pheroras affected him deeply; not out of any affection for his uncle, but because he had died without having murdered Herod, which he had promised to do. He shed false tears for Pheroras in front of his companions, while being greatly concerned that the plot to murder Herod, as well as the poison obtained for that purpose, might be discovered. When he learned in Cilicia that Herod had a complaint about his mother, he worried about what other events, unknown to him, might have occurred in Jerusalem, and he debated whether he should continue his journey. Some of his traveling companions urged him to tarry somewhere until he had received further information about the events concerning his mother, suggesting that he could be a victim of the calumnies involving her. Other traveling companions, who were anxious to see their native country once again, advised him to sail home without delay, arguing that he was the chosen son, with a royal future, and upon arriving in Jerusalem he could put an end to all accusations against his mother. Furthermore, nothing benefited the accusers more than his absence from the palace. Being influenced by the latter advice, he sailed on towards the haven of Caesarea.

He became alarmed and feared the worst when he arrived in Caesarea. Although he had been given a magnificent farewell, fitting of a future ruler, when he departed from Caesarea for Rome, he was now met with complete ignominy upon his return from Rome to Caesarea. The contrast was ominous. No one greeted him when he docked, and everybody avoided him when he went into the city. The rumors circulating in Jerusalem concerning him had reached

Caesarea, and out of fear of the consequences of befriending him, persons chose not to approach him. Because of this reception in Caesarea, Antipater realized that misfortunes would greet him when he arrived in Jerusalem, but he was able to disguise his suspicions and to proceed in a bold manner. Besides, after considering alternatives, he had no reason to go any place other than Jerusalem without dire consequences. He hoped that nothing had been discovered concerning his role in the plot to poison his father. He also anticipated that by cunningness and artful tricks, which he had used successfully in the past, he would be able to deliver himself from any adversity that might await him. So he journeyed onward to Jerusalem.

When he reached the palace in Jerusalem, his friends who accompanied him were turned away, and he was escorted by porters to meet Herod. At the palace at that time visiting with Herod was Varus, who was the newly appointed president of Syria. Varus had been invited to Jerusalem by Herod to serve as his adviser on present affairs. Antipater entered the room where Herod and Varus were meeting, put on a bold face, approached his father and attempted to salute and embrace him. Herod turned his head away from Antipater and cried out, "Even this is an indication of a parricide, to be desirous to get me into his arms, when he is under such heinous accusations. God confound thee, thou vile wretch. Do not thou touch me till thou has cleared thyself of these crimes that are charged against thee. I appoint thee a court where thou are to be judged, and Varus, who is here, is to be thy judge." Herod then told him that he would be judged the next day and he should prepare his defense. With this reception Antipater learned of his dire situation, and upon being dismissed, details were supplied by his wife, who was the daughter of Antigonus, king of the Jews before he was deposed by Herod and Sosius, the Roman general. Antipater was then left to prepare for his trial to take place the following day.

Invited to the trial were Varus, friends of Herod, relatives of

Chapter 4 The Downfall of Antipater, Herod's Eldest Son

Herod, including Herod's sister Salome, and those, including some who had been tortured, who had information about the case. The first event was to bring forward some slaves of Antipater's mother. They produced a letter written by Antipater's mother, which was to have been sent to Antipater. The letter said that he should not come back, because Herod had full knowledge, and that Caesar was the only refuge he had left to prevent him and her from being delivered into his father's hands. Antipater than fell at his father's feet, and pleaded that he should not be judged until he had been heard.

Herod then gave a long and emotional lamentation about the troubles he had experienced with his children. He had suffered great misfortunes concerning them, and now Antipater had caused him great misfortune when he was in his old age. He then recounted all the privileges he had given his sons, including maintenance and education. Yet none of these favors had hindered them from contriving against him, and bringing his own life into danger. He grieved that even though Antipater had been named in his testament as his successor, and had been given wealth and opportunities, Antipater had plotted to take away his life before nature had run its course. He then took up the case of Alexander and Aristobulus (sons of Mariamne) who had been accused by Antipater. If they were guilty, as charged by Antipater, then he had imitated their example, but if they were not guilty, then Antipater was their parricide by bringing forth groundless accusations against them. Herod then fell weeping, and could say no more.

At Herod's request, Nicholas of Damascus, being the king's friend, then began speaking. Nicholas was fully knowledgeable of the circumstances of the case and marshaled all the evidence against Antipater. Antipater, in his defense, turned towards his father, expressed the great love and affection he had for him, and how he had always served him faithfully and loyally, and with great honor. Hence, it was impossible that he could be guilty of the treacherous contrivances laid against him. Had he not come to his father's aid by informing him of the murderous plot against him by his brothers Alexander and Aristobulus? He argued that his enemies had plotted against him when he was in Rome, where he could not defend himself in person. Caesar was a witness of his loyalty to his father, and Caesar's opinions expressed in letters should take priority over any calumnies conjured by his enemies. He argued that the evidence against him was false and obtained by torture, and the distress caused by torture naturally obliges those being tortured to say things to please those who torture them. In an effort to learn the truth, Antipater offered himself to be tortured.

The assembly was moved by Antipater's words of innocence. His weeping and expressions of love for his father made them commiserate with him, and even some of his enemies were moved to compassion. Herod was also affected, although he did not let it be known by his mannerisms or expressions. Nicholas then began a vigorous prosecution, and with great bitterness, summarized all the evidence contained in the testimonies or obtained by torture. He commented that he was not too surprised by the behavior of Herod's former sons (Alexander and Aristobulus) because they were young and had been corrupted by wicked counselors, but he was amazed at the horrid wickedness of Antipater, who had great benefits bestowed upon him by his father, who loved him, had been his benefactor, had made him in reality his partner in the kingdom, and had openly declared him to be his successor. Nicholas then summarized the many wickedness attributed to Antipater, stating that his brothers Alexander and Aristobulus had died because of the calumnies he had raised against them. After their death, he then laid designs against those brothers who were still alive, as if they might be challenging him for the throne. Nicholas then proceeded to convict Antipater for the plot to poison Herod, relating in detail how Antipater had enticed Pheroras to murder his brother, and by so doing, had corrupted those that were dearest to the king. In conclusion, he said that Antipater had filled the whole palace with his wickedness.

Chapter 4 The Downfall of Antipater, Herod's Eldest Son

When Nicholas finished his long and incriminating presentation, Varus invited Antipater to defend himself. Antipater was unable to respond to the charges, other than by saying, "God is my witness that I am entirely innocent." Varus then brought forth the poison that had been meant for Herod, and upon his command had it administered to a prisoner who had been condemned to die. The prisoner died quickly, showing the potency of the poison and demonstrating what would have happened to Herod if Antipater's heinous plot against his father had succeeded. The assembly was then dismissed by Herod.

Varus then had a private discourse with Herod about the guilt of Antipater, prepared a written account of what had transpired, and departed the next day for his residence in Antioch. Herod had Antipater bound in prison, and then sent a written report to Caesar informing him of this new misfortune. He also sent messengers to inform Caesar by word of mouth of Antipater's wickedness.

At this very time a new calumny orchestrated by Antipater came to light, which was a plot to undermine Salome (Herod's sister). Julia (Caesar's wife) was sent a letter with Salome's signature, but composed by Antipater. This forgery contained bitter accusations against Herod. Antipater then bribed Julia's maid-servant (Acme) to send a copy of the letter to Herod. Acme was a Jew living in Rome who had been corrupted by Antipater with a large sum of money to assist in his pernicious designs against his aunt Salome. Acme's letter to Herod read as follows: "Acme to King Herod. I have done my endeavor that nothing that is done against thee should be concealed from thee. So, upon my finding a letter written to my lady against thee, I have written out a copy, and sent it to thee; with hazard to myself, but for thou advantage. . . Do thou therefore tear this letter in pieces, that I may not come into danger of my life." Antipater's role in this calumny was discovered when two letters, meant for Antipater, being carried by Antiphilis's slave were intercepted. The first letter from Antiphilis to Antipater (written in

Egypt) said that he was sending a copy of Acme's letter to him, noting that he (Antiphilis) would be in grave danger if his role in this affair is discovered. The second letter was incriminating: "Acme to Antipater. I have written such a letter to thy father as thou desired me to do. I have also taken a copy and sent it, as if it came from Salome, to my lady. (When read) I know that Herod will punish Salome for plotting against him."

Herod was so amazed at the prodigious wickedness of Antipater that he considered having him slain immediately as a turbulent person who plotted not only against him, but also against his sister, and by so doing had even corrupted Caesar's domestic help. Salome was distraught at the evilness of Antipater towards her, and when Herod informed her of what had occurred, she beat her breasts and bid him to kill her if he could produce any credible testimony that she was the author of that letter. Herod had Antipater brought before him and ordered him to defend himself concerning this matter. But Antipater, when faced with the letters, had not one word to say on his behalf. Herod also considered sending Antipater to Rome so that Caesar could have an account of his wickedness, but Herod soon became afraid that once there, Antipater, with the assistance of his friends, might escape the danger he was in. So he kept him bound in prison, and sent more letters and ambassadors to Rome to accuse his son. He also gave an account of the assistance Acme had given Antipater in his wicked designs against Salome, with copies of the incriminating letters.

Thus, Herod's eldest son, bound in prison, awaited his fate.

Chapter 5

THE LAST DAYS OF HEROD THE GREAT

Herod was about 70 years old when he had his eldest son Antipater bound in prison. The calamities involving his children and other family members had taken their toll on him. He became ill and melancholic, manifesting no pleasure in life even on days when he was seemingly in good health. **Fearing that his days were numbered, he sent for his testament and altered it, naming Antipas (son of Malthace) to succeed him as king**. He willed money to Caesar, Caesar's wife, Caesar's children, and to friends and freed-men. He also distributed his money, his revenues, and his lands among his sons and their sons. In this new testament he also made Salome (his sister) very rich because he believed that she had always remained faithful to him under all circumstances.

Stricken with poor health Herod manifested fierceness in his interactions with people when dealing with troublesome matters. He also became possessed with the idea that he was despised by the people throughout the nation who, he believed, took great pleasure in his misfortunes with his family and looked forward to his death. The fact that Antipater was still alive aggravated his illness. Herod did not want to have Antipater put to death privately. He resolved to have him slain in a public manner when improved health allowed him to do so.

A sedition then arose that angered him. Two men named Judas and Matthias were revered by the people because of their abilities in interpreting Jewish law. They were known as the two most eloquent men among the Jews, and their lectures on Jewish law were attended by large numbers of young scholars. When these men learned that Herod was ill and might not recover, they decided that now was the time to remove all those works which Herod had erected that were contrary to Jewish law, and they encouraged young men to do so. A major target was a large golden eagle that King Herod had erected over the great gate of the temple. Jewish law forbids the worship of idols or representations of any living creature, and although this eagle was not worshipped, its prominent position over the main gate of their house of worship was viewed as an anathema by the Jewish people, and contrary to Jewish law. Judas and Matthias insisted that it should be torn down, and if they were to die because of their actions, they would have died for a virtuous cause. These discourses by Judas and Matthias excited the young men to action. A further stimulus was a report that the king was dead and therefore now was the time to make the needed changes. So in the middle of the day, while a great number of people were in the temple and others were watching, the young men pulled the eagle down and cut it into pieces with axes.

The king's captain, upon hearing about the undertaking, arrived on the scene with a large number of soldiers. They captured Judas and Matthias and about forty others of the young men who had the courage to remain at the scene. Many others who had participated in the removal of the eagle ran away when the soldiers arrived. The captured persons were then taken to the king, who asked them if they had been so bold as to pull down what he had dedicated to God. They all replied, "Yes," and justified their actions by the laws of Moses which were taught them by God. They said that they were willing to undergo death for their actions because of their love for their religion. Following this response, Herod had them bound and sent to Jericho.

Herod then called together the principal men among the Jews (including Matthias the high priest) and had them assemble in the theater. Because he was too ill to stand, he spoke to them from a couch. He reminded them of the many labors he had undertaken on their account, including the rebuilding of the temple, which was a

Chapter 5 The Last Days of Herod The Great

major and vast project. He mentioned that he had done more works for God than the Hasmoneans who had ruled for 125 years. He then cried out against those who had pulled down in the daytime, in view of the multitudes, what he had dedicated.

The influential Jewish men in attendance, who feared that Herod would inflict punishment on them, said that the destruction of the golden eagle had been done without their approbation, and it seemed to them that the perpetrators should be punished. Herod treated the members of this assembly mildly, but did deprive Matthias of the high priesthood because of his failure to stop the sedition. He bestowed the high priest position upon Joazer the son of Boethus, who was the brother of Matthias's wife. But he took no pity on the men (including Judas and Matthias) who destroyed the golden eagle. He ordered that they should be burned alive, which was done. ***And that very night there was an eclipse of the moon.***[41]

Herod's illness then became much worse:

> *"The chief violence of his pain lay in his colon; an aqueous and transparent liquor also had settled itself about his feet, and a like matter afflicted him at the bottom of his belly. Nay, further, his privy member was putrefied, and produced worms; and when he sat upright, he had a difficulty of breathing, which was very loathsome, on account of the stench of his breath. . . he also had convulsions in all parts of his body. It was said by those who pretended to divine, and who endued with wisdom to foretell such things, that God inflicted this punishment on him the king on account of his great impiety.*[42]*"*

---

41   Astronomical calculations indicate that this eclipse occurred on March 13th in 4 BC.

42   These dramatic descriptions of his illness are typical expressions for that time of history of what befalls evil men.

Herod went to Jericho where he grew more choleric. Believing that he was near death, he designed a wicked scheme. He commanded that all the principle men of the entire Jewish nation, wherever, they lived, should come to him in Jericho. A great many came because death was the penalty for those who disregarded the epistle that was sent to them. Upon their arrival they were all locked up in the hippodrome (a place for horse races). He then sent for his sister Salome and her husband Alexas, and spoke the following to them: He would die in a little time, so great were his pains, and death under such situations ought to be welcomed by all men. But what principally troubled him was that he would die without being lamented, and without such mourning as usually occurs at a king's death. He knew that the Jewish people would celebrate his death because during his lifetime they reviled him and were willing to revolt against him. It was his intention to have a great national mourning at the time of his funeral, such as no king ever had before, and it would be a true mourning and not one done falsely, as is often done. He then gave the following orders to Salome and Alexas. As soon as they could see that he had died, they should place soldiers around the hippodrome and give the order that they should kill all those in custody with their darts. And it should be done before the soldiers knew that he was dead so that they would assume that they acted upon the orders of the king. The slaughter of those in the hippodrome would insure that the whole nation would be in mourning, and give him the honor of having a memorable mourning at his funeral. With tears in his eyes, he made Salome and Alexas promise that they would do as he asked. They assured him that they would not transgress his commands.

This order to Salome and Alexas reveals vividly the demented temperament of Herod's mind, who thought so little of human life that he would put the whole nation into mourning by slaying a prominent member of Judean families, innocent men, who had committed no crime. And it would be done only to insure a national mourning at the time of his funeral.

Chapter 5 The Last Days of Herod The Great

As he was giving these commands to Salome and her husband, letters were received from his ambassadors who had been sent to Rome to inform Caesar about the deceit of Antipater. The letters said that Acme had been slain by Caesar out of indignation for the role she played in Antipater's wicked plot against Salome. Caesar also left it to Herod to act as a father and king, and either to banish Antipater or to have him slain. This news improved Herod's spirits, who was given the power by Caesar to do what he pleased with Antipater.

He soon became very ill again and asked for an apple and a knife to peel it. When he was given the knife, he made a motion to kill himself with it, but was prevented from doing so by his first cousin Achiabus, who held his hand and cried out loudly. The shouting caused a woeful lamentation throughout the palace [in Jericho], and many assumed that the king was dead. The news reached Antipater that Herod had died, and hoping to be released from his bonds and given the government, he urged the jailer to set him free, promising him great rewards now and later. The jailer refused to do so and informed Herod of Antipater's solicitation, and of other solicitations that had occurred in the past. When Herod heard what the jailer had said, he cried out, raised himself up on one elbow, called for his guards and commanded them to kill Antipater immediately and to bury him in an ignoble manner in Hyrcania. This was done, and so ended the life of Antipater.

Herod then altered his testament once again and granted his kingdom to Archelaus.[43] He named Antipas (who had been named to succeed him as king in the previous testament) as tetrarch of Galilee and Perea. Both Archelaus and Antipas were

---

43   If approved by Caesar, Archelaus would inherit the kingdom formerly controlled by his father and have the royal title of king. His brothers Antipas and Philip, with titles of tetrarch, would govern territories within the kingdom, but would be subservient to king Archelaus. This was the model that existed when king Herod's brother Pheroras served as tetrarch of Perea.

sons of Malthace the Samaritan. Herod named Philip (son of Cleopatra) as tetrarch of Gaulonitis, Trachonitis, and Paneas, and he bequeathed Jamnia, Ashdod, and Phasaelis to Salome. He made provisions for his other kindred members, making them all wealthy. As in the previous testament, he also bequeathed large sums of money to Caesar and his wife Julia, and to other persons.

Herod died after completing this new testament. His death in Jericho occurred five days after he had ordered his son Antipater to be slain. The death of Herod occurred 37 years after he had been named king of Judea by the Romans and 34 years after he wrested the kingdom away from Antigonus.[44]

Before Herod's death was known, Salome and Alexas dismissed the persons who were locked up in the Hippodrome, telling them that the king had ordered them to go away to their own lands and to take care of their own affairs. When this was done the king's death was made public. Salome and Alexas gathered the soldiery and others together in the amphitheater at Jericho and read a letter from Herod thanking them for their fidelity and good-will to him, and exhorting them to give his son Archelaus, whom he had named to be king, similar fidelity and good-will. Ptolemy[45] then read the king's testament, *which he said needed to be confirmed by Caesar*. There was an acclamation made to Archelaus as king, and the soldiers and their commanders marched by Archelaus and promised the same good will to him, and readiness to serve him, as they had given Herod. They also prayed that God would be of assistance to him and bless the government.

Plans were then made for his funeral, and Archelaus took care that the procession to his father's sepulcher would be sumptuous.

---

44   Herod died not too long after the eclipse of the moon which occurred on March 13, 4 BC.

45   Ptolemy was a long time public administrator under Herod.

Chapter 5 The Last Days of Herod The Great

Herod was carried upon a golden bier, embroidered with precious stones. He had a diadem upon his head, a scepter in his right hand, and a golden crown was mounted on top of the bier. Both Herod and the bier were draped in purple. Next to the bier in the procession were his sons and his numerous relatives. They were followed by his guards and other units of his soldiery, and behind them was an army dressed as if they were going to war. These groups were followed by 500 of his domestics carrying spices. The procession went from Jericho (northeast of Jerusalem), where Herod died, to Herodium (southeast of Jerusalem), where he was buried.[46]

---

46   Herodium is about 7 miles southeast of Jerusalem. This is the locality where Herod was victorious over the Jewish forces loyal to Antigonus in a battle that occurred in 40 BC when Herod and his army and members of his family, including his mother, sister and future spouse Mariamne, were fleeing to the safety of Masada. Just before the battle occurred, Herod's mother was almost killed when the wagon in which she was riding turned over because of the haste of the journey and the rocky terrain. To celebrate her survival and the success of the battle, Herod chose a small mountain at that locality, rising about 300 feet above the desert, as the place for his tomb. He named the location (Herodium) for himself. Over a period of many years he built a fortress and a magnificent palace on the top of the mountain. He also built a small city at the base of the mountain with a theater that would seat 450 spectators. Water was brought to Herodium from springs three and one-half miles away via an aqueduct. A distinctive feature of Herodium is the unusual appearance of the upper portion of the small mountain. Herod ordered workers to transport massive amounts of sand, gravel and rocks to the summit, and then to place the materials around the periphery in locations that would increase the height of the mountain an additional 65 feet. The placement of the added materials, and the raking and smoothing of the sand and rocks caused the mountain, from a distance, to resemble an inactive symmetrical volcano with a smooth upper region. The royal palace, cisterns, bath houses and other structures on top were surrounded by high double walls, which made it a relatively formidable fortress.

Josephus

Chapter 6

THE DEBATE OVER WHO SHOULD REPLACE HEROD AS KING AND THE BEGINNING OF THE RULE OF ROMAN PROCURATORS IN JUDEA, SAMARIA, AND IDUMEA

At the end of the required mourning period of 7 days (by Jewish law) Archelaus sponsored a feast for the multitude. He put on a white garment and went into the temple where he received acclamations from the people. He went to a high elevation in the temple and took a seat on a golden throne which had been prepared for him. From that seat he spoke kindly to the multitude. He thanked them for their acclamations, for honoring him, and for the goodwill they had extended to him. He thanked them for not reminding him of the injuries his father had done to them. He promised to make amends and to serve them well. However, he could not at present take on the authority of king until Caesar had confirmed the succession. He said that even though the soldiers at Jericho had tried to place a diadem on his head, and honor him as king, he would not accept it. Archelaus spoke civilly to them and the multitude obtained the impression that he would be a gentler king than his father. Sensing that a new era was beginning, various persons spoke in favor of reform, and urged him to ease them of some of their annual payments, release from prison those who had been put there by Herod, and remove those taxes laid upon goods which are publicly sold and bought. In order to obtain their good will and because of the euphoria of the occasion, Archelaus did not contradict them. His mannerisms gave great hope to the people, and they sensed that at last they would be relieved of the heavy burdens imposed on them by his father. Archelaus then departed from them, offered sacrifices to God, and attended a feast with his friends.

The Beginning of Seditions Against Archelaus

Seizing upon the opportunity that a new government would soon be formed, some of the influential Jewish men got together and decided to push for immediate reforms. To begin with, they took up the case of the golden eagle. They lamented that no proper mourning had been carried out for Judas and Matthias and the others who were slain by Herod over the removal of the golden eagle from the entrance to the temple. They demanded that Archelaus punish those who had sided with Herod over the golden eagle affair. Furthermore, he should remove the high priest (Joazar the son of Boethus) appointed by Herod, and replace him with one having greater purity and the required credentials. Archelaus was greatly offended by the demands. The people were asking him to do things that he could not do because he had yet to be appointed king by Caesar.

Instead of confronting the people himself, Archelaus sent his general to meet with them. The general relayed the following messages: The deaths inflicted on their friends because of the golden eagle affair was according to law. Archelaus was offended by the magnitude of their petitions, and this was not the time for such actions because he had yet to be named king by Caesar. After he has been given the government he will consider their petitions, but in the meantime they should restrain themselves and not appear as rebellious persons. The people would not let the general speak, and even made threats on his life. Archelaus sent others to speak with the people, but the outcome was the same. The situation became tense and Archelaus feared that the sedition could rise to a high level and threaten the security of the government.

This was the time of the feast of the unleavened bread (Passover). Many people from all over the nation came to Jerusalem to participate in this feast. They resided within the walls of the city

Chapter 6 The Debate Over Who Should Replace Herod as King

and camped in neighboring regions. Many of the activists took the opportunity to gather in the temple and lament the deaths of Judas and Matthias (renowned as noble Jewish teachers) and others who had been killed by the tyranny of Herod. They stressed the need for justice. They remained in the temple, received food from others, and encouraged the people to unite with them and demand needed changes. Archelaus became fearful of what was being said in the temple and sent a regiment of armed men to suppress what was happening there. The people resented this intrusion and threw stones at the armed men, forcing them to flee. Archelaus then reached the decision that the only way to preserve the government was to take drastic actions against those who opposed him. He sent a whole army against the activists in the temple, and also against those in tents outside the temple, to prevent them from assisting those being attacked in the temple. Over three thousand persons participating in this sacred feast were killed. Many escaped by fleeing Jerusalem and hiding in nearby mountains. Archelaus then ordered that all others should return to their homes, which ended the festival. The Jewish people who witnessed this carnage reached the conclusion that Archelaus was as brutal as his father.

Archelaus then went to Caesarea to begin the voyage to Rome to meet with Caesar for the purpose, hopefully, of being named king. He left his brother Philip (son of Cleopatra) in charge of the government. He took with him Nicolaus and Ptolemy, and many others who were his friends and supporters. Also accompanying him were Salome (Herod's sister) and many members of her family, who went in the pretense of supporting him, but actually to oppose him in front of Caesar because of what he had done in the temple during the Passover festival.

At Caesarea, before he boarded the ship for Rome, Archelaus met with Sabinus, who was Caesar's steward for Syrian affairs. Sabinus was traveling hastily to Judea with the announced objective of preserving Herod's treasures for Caesar, believing that during the time following the death of Herod and the appointment of his successor by Caesar, the treasures of Judea might be hidden by Archelaus and others. Varus (president of Syria) also came to Caesarea at that time and prevailed upon Sabinus not to seize any of the treasures, but to allow Archelaus to remain in charge until Caesar had made a decision about Herod's testament concerning who was to succeed him as king. Sabinus agreed to do so, but after Archelaus sailed for Rome and Varus had returned to Antioch, Sabinus went to Jerusalem and seized the king's palace. He also sent for those who had charge of Herod's treasures, demanding that they give him an accounting of what was in their possession. However, those loyal to Archelaus refused to cooperate, stating that they were keeping all things for Caesar.

Also going to Rome was Antipas, brother of Archelaus, who was accompanied by his mother Malthace. Antipas went to Rome with the objective of contesting Herod's testament and convincing Caesar that he should be named king rather than his brother. He was supported by Salome (Herod's sister) who believed that he was more honest and more qualified to be king than Archelaus. Antipas also had the support of most of the family members, not out of great good will towards him, but because of their dislike of Archelaus. If a king was to be named, they preferred that Antipas should be given that distinction. Sabinus, who was in Judea, also wrote letters to Caesar, stating that Archelaus was not fit to be named king based upon what he had learned about him.

With two brothers contending for the throne, Caesar called together a group of his friends in order to obtain their opinions. Antipater, Salome's son, was the first to appear before the group. Antipater was an able orator and spoke against Archelaus. In an eloquent manner he stated that it was ridiculous for Archelaus to plead for the throne, because he had already assumed it before Caesar had granted it to him. He argued that Archelaus insulted Caesar by acting as king, before being authorized to do so. This was

Chapter 6 The Debate Over Who Should Replace Herod as King

done by sitting on the king's golden throne in the temple, by making determinations about law-suits, by giving orders to kill many Jews at the Passover festival, and by listening to petitions and making concessions. Antipater also stated that Archelaus had released the prisoners in the Hippodrome after the death of his father. Thus, he acted as king by overruling an order made by his father.[47] Antipater also charged Archelaus with the neglect of proper mourning for his father, which began with merry meetings the night his father died. Although he shed tears for him during the daytime (as an actor), he celebrated in the evenings with his friends for his good fortune of obtaining the government (as specified in Herod's testament). The nightly celebrations (singing and dancing) during the period of mourning were as if an enemy had fallen, while in actuality, they were held because of the death of his father. Antipater argued that Archelaus would behave towards Caesar in the way he had behaved towards his own father (i.e., in a two faced manner), and therefore Archelaus could not be trusted by Caesar. The slaughter in the temple during the Passover was heinous, and it was done by a person who pretended to be king. Antipater argued further that Herod was well aware that Archelaus was not fit to be king. In the earlier testament (when he was sound of mind) Herod rightfully overlooked Archelaus and named Antipas as king, even though Archelaus was the elder brother. In the last testament, when Herod was in a dying condition, both physically and mentally, he named Archelaus as king only because he was elder. Antipater urged Caesar to consider the earlier testament, the one written when Herod was sound in mind.

When Antipater sat down, Nicolaus rose and spoke for Archelaus, stating that what happened in the temple during the Passover should be blamed on the persons who had been killed, rather than on Archelaus, because in actuality those persons were

---

47   The fact that Salome's son made this claim suggests that Salome and her husband Alexas conferred with Archelaus about the problem of the prisoners in the Hippodrome, and it was Archelaus's decision to release them rather than to have them killed as ordered by Herod. The earlier account in Josephus states that Salome and Alexas had them released.

119

rebelling against Caesar, and Archelaus only acted to defend Caesar. He also argued that Herod was of sound mind when he wrote his final testament, and that Caesar and Herod had always been friends and confederates, and it is fitting that Caesar, in his great wisdom and understanding, should consider the testament of his longtime friend, rather than listen to wicked persons, who out of jealousy and hatred, would bring seditions against the person named by Herod in his last testament.

Now when Nicolaus had ended his plea on behalf of Archelaus, Caesar raised Archelaus up (from where he had cast himself down at his feet), and said that Archelaus well deserved the kingdom and so far he was moved in his favor, but he was not ready to make a decision. After those in attendance had departed, Caesar pondered whether he should give the entire kingdom to Archelaus, or divide it among Herod's posterity because they were all in need of assistance.

Before things could be brought to a settlement, letters came from Varus, the president of Syria, stating that the nation of Jews began to revolt after Archelaus sailed for Rome. Varus reported that he had punished many who were part of the sedition, and before returning to Antioch he had left one legion of his army to maintain peace. The seditions continued, however, mainly because of the actions of Sabinus who made use of Varus's army to seize citadels in his search for Herod's money and other treasures. On the approach of the Pentecost [Jewish festival which begins the 50th day after the Passover], tens of thousands of the Jewish people congregated to celebrate the festival and also to express their indignation towards Sabinus because of his injuries towards them. People came from Galilee, Idumea, Jericho and other regions, and plots were made to assault Sabinus and the Roman soldiers who were encamped there. In alarm Sabinus sent a letter to Varus asking for assistance, noting that the soldiers were outnumbered and would be cut to pieces. Sabinus hid away in the fortress Phasaelus, built in honor of Herod's brother, and gave the order for the Romans to attack the

Chapter 6 The Debate Over Who Should Replace Herod as King

Jews. A great battle then ensued, with casualties on both sides. Part of the temple was burned during these skirmishes, and although the Romans were temporarily victorious in Jerusalem, many sieges broke out throughout Judea, with bands of men fighting against the king's troops (Herod's old army) and other supporters of the Romans.

A person known as Judas of Galilee then rose to great prominence in Judea and Galilee. He attracted many followers because of his declarations and actions. He declared that the Jewish people should revolt against the heinous actions of Sabinus and the Romans, declaring that God alone should be their ruler. He got together a band of men and attacked the city of Sepphoris in Galilee. He and his men seized the palace and took away all the weapons that had been stored there. They also carried away all the money that had been deposited in the palace. A man named Simon, who had been one of Herod's slaves, put a diadem on his own head and declared that he was as worthy to be named king as anyone else. He and his supporters burned the palace at Jericho and plundered what was in it. He also set fire to many other houses of the former king Herod in several places in the country. Eventually he was overpowered by Roman soldiers and beheaded. Similar seditions occurred throughout Judea and surrounding areas, with Jews fighting Romans and Herod's old army, and some members of Herod's old army joining forces with the Jews who were revolting. Judea was also full of robbers who took advantage of the seditions to gain profit. They did mischief to the Romans and also to their own people, committing many murders.

When Varus became informed of these events occurring in Judea and Galilee, he became concerned for the legion that he had left in Jerusalem. He took two legions, four troops of horsemen and several auxiliary forces, and made haste for Ptolemais. As he passed through Berytus he gained 1,500 other soldiers. Out of hatred for Herod, and to gain the favor of the Romans, Aretas, the king of

Arabia also gave him footmen and horsemen. Varus committed part of these forces to his son, and sent them into Galilee. These forces attacked Sepphoris, made slaves of the inhabitants, and burned the city [4 BC]. Varus and his army then traveled through Samara on their way to Jerusalem, burning various villages on the way. When he arrived at Jerusalem he reproached the Jews for what they had done. Varus sent a part of his army into the country to seek out those who had been responsible for the revolt. Some were punished, and some were dismissed; the number crucified was 2,000. Varus was told by the Jews in Jerusalem that Sabinus was primarily responsible for the revolt because of his cruel and rash actions. Sabinus avoided meeting Varus and stole out of the city secretively. When Varus had settled all the affairs, he placed the Roman legion once again in Jerusalem and returned to Antioch.

A new problem now faced Archelaus in Rome. With the permission of Varus a delegation of 50 Jews arrived in Rome from Judea with a petition stating that they be allowed to live according to their own laws, that they be delivered from a kingly form of government, and that they be added to Syria under the authority of a president named by Caesar.[48] They stated that they would be an orderly people if allowed to live according to their own laws and if governed in a moderate manner. Siding with the 50 Jewish ambassadors were 8,000 Jews residing in Rome.

Also arriving in Rome at this time (with the encouragement of Varus) was Philip (son of Cleopatra), the brother of Archelaus and Antipas. The professed purpose was to assist his brother Archelaus obtain the kingdom, but since Varus suspected that a change would

---

48 It is likely that these Jewish people would not have opposed a kingly form of government if the king were a Hasmonean. Archelaus had strikes against him. His father Herod was part Idumean and his mother Malthace was a Samaritan. Idumeans and Samaritans were considered to be foreigners by the Jews of Judea. Furthermore, Archelaus had been educated in Rome by gentiles. The ambassadors believed that a hellenized person with his heritage was not qualified to be king. The same criticisms applied to his brother Antipas.

Chapter 6 The Debate Over Who Should Replace Herod as King

be made in the government (i.e., different than proposed in Herod's testament), he persuaded Philip to be in Rome in order to increase the likelihood that he might be named to prominence. Caesar scheduled a meeting in the temple of Apollo. In attendance were the 50 Jewish ambassadors and the 8,000 Jewish residents of Rome, Archelaus and his followers, including Philip, and the opponents of Archelaus, who stood separately from the others. The Jewish ambassadors spoke about all the atrocities under Herod, and that when he died they hoped that Archelaus would rule in a moderate and civil manner and honor the Jewish laws. In the beginning they were optimistic, but in his first major action he slaughtered 3,000 Jews in the temple, demonstrating that his kingship would be no different than Herod's kingship. Thus, they petitioned Caesar to deliver them from a kingly form of government, and to enact a form of government under Syria, with a presidency, that would allow them to live according to their own laws.

As soon as the ambassadors had presented their case, Nicolaus arose and defended Herod's long years of service to Caesar and Rome, stating that Archelaus's actions were precipitated by Jewish injuries to Caesar. He also accused the Jews of taking pleasure in their seditions against Archelaus, and failing to learn to submit to justice according to the laws.

After Caesar had listened to the pleadings he dismissed the assembly and a few days later made the following announcement:

Archelaus (son of Malthace) was denied the title of king and instead was appointed ethnarch of about half of the kingdom ruled by Herod,[49] with the promise to make him king at a later

---

49   Caesar divided Herod's kingdom into three different territories with none of the rulers having the royal title as king. Each ruler reported to Caesar in Rome. Being named ruler of about half of his father's kingdom, with the title of ethnarch, was a huge disappointment for Archelaus who expected to inherit the entire kingdom and the royal title of king, as stated in Herod's last testament. However, his territory was larger than the territories ruled by Antipas and Philip, and was of greater historical, religious and economic

time if he rendered himself worthy of that distinction. His half of the kingdom contained Judea, Samaria, and Idumea. The following cities were also made subject to Archelaus: Jerusalem, Strato's Tower [i.e. Caesarea], Sebaste, and Joppa. (The Grecian cities Gaza, Gadara, and Hippos were cut off from the kingdom and added to Syria.)

The other half of the kingdom was given to Antipas (son of Malthace) and Philip (son of Cleopatra). When divided between them, each had about one-fourth (i.e., a tetrarchy) of the former kingdom ruled by Herod. Antipas was made tetrarch over Galilee and Perea.[50] Philip was made tetrarch over Batanea, Trachonitis, Auranitis, and part of an area in Syria, (north of Paneas) near Mt. Hermon and known as the House (or possession) of Zenodorus, or the possession of Lysanius, the tetrarch of Abilene.

Salome was granted what Herod gave her in his testament: Ashdod, Jamnia and Phasaelis. She was also given the royal habitation at Ascalon.

---

significance because it contained the major seaports (such as Caesarea) and the city of Jerusalem with the temple. The regional capital of Antipas's tetrarchy was Sepphoris, located about 4 miles from Nazareth in Galilee. Antipas rebuilt this city into a major cultural center, and Jesus of Nazareth and his father Joseph may have used their carpentry skills in the construction of this city. Another palace was at the fortress in Macherus in Perea. This major fortress was originally built by the Hasmonean king Alexander Janneus, but was rebuilt by Herod to guard the southeast territory of his kingdom from the Arabs. The major city of Philip's tetrarchy was Paneas, which Philip renamed Caesarea Phillippi to honor Caesar and himself.

50 Because the large territory of Decapolis extended across the Jordan River south of the Sea of Galilee, the tetrarchy governed by Antipas was split into two regions (Galilee and Perea) that were separated geographically. Decapolis was established by Pompey in 63 B.C. when he took territories away from the Jewish people and annexed them administratively to Syria. The northern boundary of Decapolis had changed with time as additional territories were given to Herod the Great. The northern boundary of Decapolis east of the Jordan River was also altered when king Herod's kingdom was split into three territories by Caesar and given to Archelaus, Antipas, and Philip. Christ attracted large crowds when he visited regions in Decapolis southeast of the Sea of Galilee and east of the Jordan River (see Mark 5:1, Mark 7:31 1, Matthew 4:25).

Chapter 6 The Debate Over Who Should Replace Herod as King

The rest of Herod's offspring were bequeathed what Herod had stated in his testament. Caesar also gave Herod's virgin daughters large sums of money and gave them in marriage to the sons of Pheroras.

The Case of the Spurious Alexander

A curious event then occurred that demonstrated the longing the Jewish people had for Hasmonean leaders and the high respect they had for Mariamne and her two sons who were put to death by Herod. A young man of Jewish birth was brought up by a Roman freedman in Sidon (seaport in Phoenicia). He bore a remarkable resemblance to Alexander and many persons who encountered him attested to that fact. For the purposes of economic gain, a plan was contrived that he would pose as the true Alexander. This required the services of a Jewish man who was fully informed of the affairs of the palace. This Jewish man served as his mentor, and instructed him on how to act and what to say, if he indeed were Herod's son. After extensive coaching the spurious Alexander declared himself to be Alexander, stating that he and his brother Aristobulus were not put to death at the command of their father. Instead, one of the men who was supposed to strangle them, stole them away, and slew two other men instead, who were now buried at Alexandrium. He traveled to Crete and was so well versed on life in the palace that when Jews came to discourse with him, he was able to convince them that he was Alexander. The Jews were elated that the proper heir to the throne, one with royal Hasmonean blood, was alive and they gave him vast sums of money, hoping that he would acquire the throne and reward them. He next traveled to Melos where he and his mentor received even more money. The news that Alexander was still alive was spread far and wide. He was then taken to Rome by enthusiastic supporters. Upon landing at Dicearchia he carried out the masquerade brilliantly, and those who had known Alexander as a youth confirmed that he was Alexander. As he approached Rome the whole multitude of Jews residing there met him and ascribed

125

to Divine Providence that a Hasmonean, and rightful heir to the throne had been returned to them. Many persons who had known Alexander took oaths that the man was truly Alexander. In Rome he was carried through the streets in a royal sedan with all the ornaments of a king, with the expense being borne by those who accepted him. The multitude flocked around him and made acclamations to him.

When these events were told to Caesar, he expressed disbelief that the command of Herod to strangle his sons would have been thwarted, but having some suspicion that it might have happened, he ordered that the man be brought to him. Caesar was not deceived and although the man bore a remarkable resemblance to Alexander, he realized immediately that the man was an impostor. This spurious Alexander had the rough hands and muscled body of a laborer (which is the life he had led), in contrast to the soft hands and body of Alexander, resulting from his pampered existence as the son of Herod. Playing along with the masquerade, Caesar asked him why Aristobulus did not accompany him to Rome in order to obtain the dominion that was also due him. The spurious Alexander replied that Aristobulus had remained at Crete out of concern that some accident at sea might cause both of them to drown, resulting in the demise of both sons of Mariamne. It was planned that as the elder son he would travel by himself, and if any accident by treacherous design happened to him on his journey to Rome, Aristobulus would come forth, punish the responsible persons, and claim the throne. Caesar was astounded at the extent and cleverness of the lying, and the boldness of the young man. He assessed quickly that this spurious Alexander had been well coached, and therefore he alone was not to blame for this masquerade that had so successfully convinced multitudes of Jews in Crete, Melos, and Rome, and even persons in his own palace.

Caesar took the young man aside and in private informed him that he would preserve his life if he would inform him who had been bold enough to contrive such a fraud as this, for such a contrivance was too villainy to be undertaken by a person of his age. Realizing that he had no other recourse, the spurious Alexander exposed his mentor and explained the manner in which the contrivance had been put together. Honoring his word to preserve his life, Caesar placed the spurious Alexander among those who row as mariners, sensing that his musculature was well designed for such strenuous activity; but he had the mentor put to death for his involvement in the contrivance. That ended the case of the spurious Alexander.

The Banishment of Archelaus to Vienna, Gaul

When Caesar gave Archelaus the title of ethnarch he admonished him to rule virtuously, with the promise that he would be given the title of king when he earned it. But when Archelaus took possession of his ethnarchy he began to rule in a barbaric manner, taking steps to punish those that had prevented him from obtaining the title of king. He also made decisions that infuriated the Jews of Judea and Samaria. He took the high priesthood from Joazar the son of Boethus, accusing him of assisting in the sedition, and named Eleazar the son of Boethus as high priest.[51] He rebuilt the royal palace at Jericho in a magnificent manner and diverted half the water needed by the village to water palm trees that he had planted in a large area. He also built a new city near the Jordan River and named it after himself. He pursued Jews of Judea and Samaria whom he accused of being involved in seditions against him, and treated them in a barbaric manner. He also transgressed Jewish law by marrying Glaphyra (the daughter of the king of Cappadocia), who had been married to his Hasmonean brother Alexander, by whom she had 3 children. Following the death of Alexander by order of Herod, Glaphyra had married Juba, king of Libya. After his death, she returned home and lived as a widow with her father. Archelaus fell in love with her, divorced his wife, and married her. It was detestable to the Jews that he would do such a thing because

---

51   The Jews were displeased with this appointment, because Eleazar was as poorly qualified for this most honored position as his brother Joazar.

Jewish law stated that it is forbidden to marry your brother's wife. Following this marriage, Archelaus took the high priest position away from Eleazar son of Boethus and gave it to Jesus son of Sie.

During the tenth year of Archelaus's government, principal men from Judea and Samaria accused Archelaus in front of Caesar for his tyrannical behavior. Whereupon, Caesar became very angry and ordered that Archelaus appear before him in Rome and respond to the accusations against him. After listening to his defense, Caesar banished him to Vienna, Gaul (area in France), and took all his money away from him, making it part of Caesar's treasure.

That ended the career of Archelaus after serving as ethnarch from 4 BC to 6 AD, a period of ten years.

The Beginning of the Rule of Roman Procurators

With the banishment of Archelaus, his ethnarchy was reduced to a province and Caesar appointed Coponius (a Roman) as procurator (governor) over the province, and to have supreme power over the Jews living there.

The daily welfare of each inhabitant of the province was now in the hands of a Roman procurator. The province (Judea, Samaria, and Idumea) governed by Coponius was attached administratively to Syria. Cyrenius, a distinguished Roman Senator, was designated by Caesar to travel to the greater territory of Syria, to judge that nation, and to take an account of their substance. Moreover, Cyrenius arrived in Judea with Coponius to dispose of Archelaus's money and also to take an account of the substance of the province added to Syria.[52]

---

52 Taking account of their substance is defined as assessing the financial resources of the people and extracting appropriate taxes. According to Josephus, Cyrenius traveled to Judea in 6 AD, about 10 years after the death of Herod, to dispose of Archelaus's money and to take account of the substance of the province (Judea, Samaria, and Idumea) formerly ruled by Archelaus. Luke (1:5-31 and 2:1-2) gives a different scenario of these events, which he states occurred during the reign of Herod. Luke (2:1-2) refers to Cyrenius as the

Chapter 6 The Debate Over Who Should Replace Herod as King

The Jews in this province reacted negatively to the new Roman authority, viewing it as heinous.[53]

Events Occurring in Judea and in the Territories Ruled by Antipas and Philip

When Cyrenius had accounted for Archelaus's money, and taxation had been concluded (37th year of Caesar's victory over Antony at Actium), Cyrenius deprived Jesus, the son of Sie, of the high priesthood, who was honored by the multitude, and appointed Ananus, the son of Seth, as high priest. The year was 7 AD.

During this period of time, Herod Antipas and Philip (both tetrarchs) settled their own affairs. Herod Antipas built a wall around Sepphoris [adjacent to Nazareth] and made it the metropolis of Galilee. Herod Antipas also built a wall around Betharamphtha, which was a city, and called it Julias (in honor of Caesar's wife). Philip enlarged Paneas, a city at the fountains of the Jordan, and named it Caesarea Philippi in honor of Caesar and himself. He also built a city situated near the Lake of Gennesareth [Sea of Galilee], and named it Julias (in honor of Caesar's daughter.)

Coponius (procurator) returned to Rome, and was replaced as procurator by Marcus Ambivius [9AD]. During his term as procurator, Salome (sister of king Herod) died. She left her kingdom to Julia (Caesar's wife).

---

governor of Syria, but Josephus names him as a distinguished Roman Senator who was given a special assignment by Caesar Augustus.

53 The arrival of Coponius as the procurator (governor) began a new era of hatred of the Romans by the Jewish people living in the ethnarchy formerly ruled by Archelaus. Antipas and Philip continued to rule their territories as Herod had been allowed by Caesar Augustus to rule his kingdom. As rulers they were responsible for collecting taxes in their territories and sending the required funds to Rome. The people living in Judea, Samaria, and Idumea, however, were now governed and taxed by the Roman procurator. The ominous presence of the reigning Romans and direct taxation by the Romans led to massive discontent throughout the new province.

Death of Caesar Augustus

Marchus Ambivius was replaced as procurator by Annius Rufus [12 AD]. During his time as procurator Caesar Augustus died [14 AD] at age 77 after ruling the Roman empire for 57 years. He was succeeded as emperor by Tiberius, who was his wife's son.[54]

---

54   Tiberius's father, named Tiberius Claudius Nero, was a high priest, magistrate and a former fleet captain for Julius Caesar. His mother, the beautiful Livia Drusilla, was her husband's cousin and may have been only 13 when Tiberius was born. In 39 B.C. Augustus became attracted to Livia, divorced his wife who was pregnant, and forced the elder Tiberius to give up Livia, who was also pregnant, and married her. It was commonly believed that Augustus was the father of the expected child. After the death of Caesar Augustus she took the name Julia Augusta, which is the name (Julia) used by Josephus in his writings. As noted by Josephus, Julia was a devoted and influential wife who counseled Caesar Augustus on governmental affairs. Tiberius and his younger brother Drusus lived with their father until his death when Tiberius was 9 years old. Then he and his younger brother went to live with Julia and the emperor. Tiberius soon married, but when Caesar's daughter Julia (by his first wife) became a widow for the second time, Caesar ordered Tiberius to divorce his wife and marry her. The marriage was not a happy one, mainly because Tiberius still loved his former wife, and Julia was not loyal to Tiberius, much to his embarrassment and consternation. Caesar and Tiberius had a strained personal relationship resulting from the trauma brought on by the unhappy marriage. After about 6 years of marriage, Tiberius went into self-imposed exile on the island of Rhodes, leaving his wife in Rome. Eventually Caesar was made aware of his daughter's infidelities, and exiled her for life to a small island. Tiberius remained on the island of Rhodes for a decade until called back to Rome by Caesar in 4 AD. At one time Caesar favored 3 of his grandsons (sons of his daughter Julia, by former husbands) as his future heir. One eventually fell into disfavor with Caesar and was sent into exile with his mother. The other two were prime candidates, but with the death of both of them, Caesar Augustus adopted Tiberius as his son and named him heir to the throne. Upon the death of Augustus Caesar in 14 AD, Tiberius succeeded him as emperor. At the time Tiberius was 56 years old. During the early years as emperor Tiberius was a wise and just leader. He did not attempt great conquests, or change governors of provinces without good reason. He also brought about many reforms. In 23 A.D. his son Drusus (by his first wife) died. The death of Drusus, who was the apparent heir to the throne, greatly saddened Tiberius. Tiberius would not allow the friends of his deceased son to come into his sight, because upon seeing them he thought of his son and his grief was revived. From that time on he spent less and less time governing, and delegated much authority to Sejanus, whom he had appointed to command the Praetorian Guard. The Praetorian Guard was established in the second century BC to act as bodyguards for Roman generals. In 27 B.C. Caesar Augustus created a permanent guard, stationing them around Rome as bodyguards for the emperor, with two prefects to command them. In 23 A.D Tiberius appointed Sejanus as the sole commander. Sejanus concentrated them in barracks outside the walls of Rome, and they acquired significant political influence. With the passage time Sejanus assumed great political power. Golden statues were erected

Chapter 6 The Debate Over Who Should Replace Herod as King

Early in his tenure as emperor (about 15 AD), Tiberius sent Valerius Gratus to Judea to succeed Annius Rufus as procurator. Valerius Gratus deprived Ananus, the son of Seth of the high priesthood and appointed Ismael, the son of Phabi to be high priest. In a short period of time he deprived Ismael of this position, and gave it to Eleazar, the son of Ananus. In a year, Gratus deprived Eleazar of the position, and gave it to Simon, the son of Camithus. After Simon had the position for no longer than a year, Gratus deprived him of it and gave it to Joseph Caiaphas who was the son-in-law of Ananus.[55]

---

to honor Sejanus, and his birthday was declared a holiday. In 29 A.D., at the age of 67, Tiberius visited some of the southern parts of Italy, stopped at the island of Capri, and never returned to Rome. There he built villas, collected treasures, and led a sumptuous life. In these villas he received and entertained visitors from throughout his empire, and was attended by servants, guards, musicians, philosophers, astrologers, and persons seeking favors. He also built prisons, underground dungeons, torture chambers, and places for execution. It seems likely that during this period of his life that he was showing signs of mental instability. He was quick to denounce, torture and execute persons for various suspected offenses. Tiberius finally realized that Sejanus had become too powerful and was a major threat to him. He was also given evidence that Sejanus had murdered his son Drusus (with the compliance of Drusus's wife), and furthermore, that Sejanus was plotting against him with the goal of taking over the empire. Tiberius sent a letter to the Senate denouncing Sejanus and calling for his execution. Disturbed by this action and the charges, and perhaps out of fear of the strength of the Praetorian Guard now commanded by Marco who was loyal to Tiberius, the Senate complied and Sejanus was immediately put to death. With Sejanus out of the way, Tiberius then became concerned who would rule when he was gone. There were few successors with any real claim, and it became a matter of choosing a person who was the least offensive. One candidate was his grandson (son of Drusus), but Tiberius finally chose Gaius (called Caius by Josephus), usually known historically by his nickname Caligula. Caius (i.e., Gaius) was a great-grandson of Caesar Augustus through his daughter Julia (married to Tiberius) and her daughter. In 37 A.D. Tiberius took part in a ceremonial game in which he threw a javelin. He hurt his shoulder, went to bed, became very ill, and lapsed into coma. His physicians declared that his death was imminent. With this prognosis, his chosen successor Caius was summoned. Members of the Praetorian Guard declared their support for the new emperor, and the news was proclaimed throughout the empire. But then to the consternation of those who made the proclamation, Tiberius recovered, sat up, and asked for food. Marco, the commander of the Praetorian Guard, then took charge of the situation. He went to Tiberius's bed, took blankets, put them over Tiberius head and smothered him to death.

55   Caiaphas was the high-priest who helped orchestrate the death of Jesus Christ. Although Caiaphas was high priest, his father-in-law Ananus, the former high priest, was still an influential person who was involved in the sentence imposed on Jesus (John, 18: 12-14, 24, 28).

Valerius Gratus served as procurator for 11 years. When he returned to Rome he was replaced by Pontius Pilate [26 AD].[56]

Sedition of the Jews Against Pontius Pilate

Pontius Pilate made his headquarters in Caesarea, but one of his first acts as procurator was to order his army to take winter quarters in Jerusalem instead of Caesarea. He intended to abolish Jewish laws, and the presence of the army in Jerusalem would be a show of force that would enable him to meet his goal. Ensigns were brought into the city bearing effigies of the emperor. This was done covertly during the darkness of night. Although these effigies were present in Caesarea and certain other cities, Pilate was the first to introduce them into Jerusalem. The people of Jerusalem were alarmed because Jewish law forbids the making and worshiping of images. Multitudes of people went to Pilate in Caesarea and pleaded with him to remove the images from Jerusalem. He refused stating that it would be an insult to the emperor to do so. The people persevered and when they reappeared on the sixth day and petitioned him again to remove the images, he ordered soldiers to surround them and threaten them with immediate death unless they stopped disturbing him and returned to their homes. The people threw themselves on the ground and laid their necks bare, stating that they would take death willingly, rather than to have their laws transgressed. Pilate was deeply moved by this act and ordered that the images should be removed from Jerusalem and returned to Caesarea.

Pilate then proceeded to bring water (via a canal) to Jerusalem from a distance of 25 miles, using sacred money to pay for the project. The Jews were not happy with this project or the use of sacred money to finance it, so they protested. Many thousands clamored against

---

56   Pontius Pilate was appointed procurator by Tiberius, but the appointment was made through the influence of Sejanus who at that time in history had acquired great political power in the Roman empire (See Footnote 11.

Pilate, and abused him vocally. Pilate then ordered soldiers with daggers under their garments to mingle with the crowds. When the people began to protest, Pilate gave a signal and the soldiers used their daggers to kill the protesters in addition to many who were merely silent observers of the protests. Many people were slain and many others ran away wounded. That was the end of the sedition.

Mention of Jesus the Christ
<u>Book XVIII, Chapter III, Paragraph 3 of *Antiquities of the Jews*</u>
"Now there was about this time Jesus, a wise man; if it be lawful to call him a man; for he was a doer of wonderful works, a teacher of such men as receive the truth with pleasure. He drew over to him both many of the Jews and many of the Gentiles. He was [the] Christ. And when Pilate, at the suggestion of the principal men amongst us, had condemned him to the cross, those that loved him at first did not forsake him; for he appeared to them alive again on the third day; as the divine prophets had foretold these and ten thousand other wonderful things concerning him. And the tribe of Christians, so named from him, are not extinct at this day." [57]

---

[57] This paragraph has been used by some Christian writers as evidence that Josephus testified to the divinity of Jesus. Although the exact wordings of the phrases in the paragraph vary in different translations of Josephus, the meaning is similar in all of them, and if each is taken literally, it might be concluded that Josephus was indeed attesting that Jesus was divine. However, based upon all his writings, it is evident that Josephus was a devout Jew and a strong defender of the Jewish faith. If Josephus truly believed that Jesus was divine, he would not have limited his presentation of Jesus to only a single paragraph. Some scholars have proposed that this paragraph was not written by Josephus and instead it was written by an early Christian copyist who inserted the paragraph at a later time in history into the section dealing with Pontius Pilate. Because the paragraph was referred to by Eusebius in his *Ecclesiastical History*, published in about 325 AD, the proposed insertion was done prior to that time. A more likely explanation is that Josephus presented a brief statement about Jesus, which was then embellished by a copyist with the insertion of additional phrases in an effort to present a divine description of Jesus. As a resident of Jerusalem and Galilee during the early years of his life and later as a Jewish historian in Rome, it is certain that Josephus would have encountered followers of Jesus or heard stories about him. He would have known about Nero's attempts to blame the Christians

About this time another sad calamity put the Jews into disorder. A Jew living in Rome professed to instruct men on the wisdom of Moses, but being a wicked man, he and three other men who were similarly wicked persuaded a woman of dignity who had embraced the Jewish religion to send gold to the temple in Jerusalem. The men then spent the money themselves. When Tiberius learned of this event from the husband of the woman, he ordered all Jews to be banished from Rome. Four thousand were sent to Sardinia, and others were punished who refused to serve in the army because of the laws of their forefathers. These events happened because of the wickedness of four men.

A man living in Samaria, who thought lying to be of little consequence, urged the people to get together upon Mount Gerizzim where he would show them sacred vessels put there by Moses. The man was believed because Mount Gerizzim was viewed by the Samaritans as a sacred mountain. A large number of people gathered at a village called Tirathaba, with the plan that they would all ascend the mountain together, as one large group. Since many were armed, Pontius Pilate was alarmed at this gathering, and fearing that a revolt was brewing, he prevented them from going up the mountain. His horsemen and footmen seized the roads and attacked those assembled in the village, resulting in the death of many who

---

for the fire that ravaged Rome in 64 AD. Because of the notoriety given to the Christians living in Rome during that period of time, it would be expected that Josephus would have mentioned Jesus when writing about the career of Pilate in Judea. Josephus's commentary about Jesus could have been brief and in the following form: "A wise man known as Jesus, called Christ by his followers, was condemned to the cross by Pilate at the suggestion of principle Jewish men, and the followers of this man claimed that he appeared to them alive on the third day." Although most of the words and phrases found in the paragraph appear elsewhere in the works of Josephus, the word "tribe" is atypical for a description of the "followers" of Jesus, and the expression , "if it be lawful to call him a man" seems to be contrived. It was also wrong to say that "many of the gentiles" were drawn to him, because the missionary work of Jesus had been primarily among Jews. However, when Josephus wrote this section of *Antiquities* many gentiles living in Rome and elsewhere had been drawn to Jesus Christ. The word Christ also appears in Antiquities when Josephus mentions James, the brother of Jesus, who was called Christ.

Chapter 6 The Debate Over Who Should Replace Herod as King

had assembled for the trek up the mountain. Pilate tracked down those who were able to escape. He selected among them those he believed were the leaders, and ordered them to be slain.

At the conclusion of this tumultuous event, the Samaritan senate sent ambassadors to Vitellius, the president of Syria, and accused Pilate of the murder of innocent people. In response, Vitellius sent Marcellus, a friend of his to handle the affairs of Judea, and he ordered Pilate [36 AD] to return to Rome and answer to the accusations of the Jews before the emperor. So after serving as governor for 10 years, Pilate left for Rome in obedience to the orders of Vitellius.[58]

Vitellius then traveled to Jerusalem at the time of the Passover Festival, where he was received magnificently. As an act of goodwill he released the inhabitants of Jerusalem from all taxes on fruits that were bought and sold, and returned to the priests of the temple the high priest vestments which had previously been taken from them by the Romans. He did this as an act of kindness and to oblige the nation to him. He also deprived Caiaphas of the high priesthood, and appointed Jonathan son of Ananus to succeed him. After making this appointment, Vitellius journeyed back to Antioch.

Because of the wisdom and actions of Vitellius, temporary peace occurred in Jerusalem and surrounding areas.

The Three Major Sects of Jewish Philosophy

The three major sects of Jewish philosophy [described in Josephus] are the Pharisees, Sadducees and the Essenes [spelled Essens in Josephus].

---

58   Pilate did not dare repudiate this order because Sejanus was deceased and Pilate was lacking any major political support in Rome. Tiberius, who had appointed him as procurator, was dead before Pilate arrived in Rome.

The Pharisees are skillful in interpreting their laws. They perform their worship, prayers, and sacrifices according to their interpretations. They ascribe all to fate (providence) and God, yet persons have the right to do what is right, or to do what is wrong (act the way they think fit), even though the will of God prevails in the end. The Pharisees say that some actions are the work of fate, and some of them are in our own power, but the Essenes affirm that fate governs all things, and nothing befalls men but what is according to its determination. The Sadducees take away fate, and say there is no such thing. They propose that all our actions are our own, and that we ourselves are the causes of what is good. Thus, we receive what is evil from our own folly.

The Pharisees believe that souls are immortal, and there will be rewards or punishments according to whether persons live virtuously or viciously. Those that live viciously will be detained in an everlasting prison. Those that live virtuously will have the power to live again, while the souls of bad men are subject to eternal punishment. The Essenes also taught that the souls are immortal-- whereas bodies are corruptible, souls continue forever. Souls come out of the most subtle air and unite with bodies as drawn by a certain natural enticement. When they are set free from the bonds of the flesh, they, as released from a long bondage, rejoice and mount upward. As contrasted with both the Pharisees and the Essenes, the Sadducees promote the philosophy that souls die with the bodies.

The Pharisees teach some practices and observances that are not contained in the Laws of Moses, but have been passed from generation to generation by tradition (oral transmission). These practices and observances are all rejected by the Sadducees, stating that the people should observe only what is written. This difference causes many disputes between the Pharisees and Sadducees.

Because of their doctrines the Pharisees have influence on the masses. The Pharisees are friendly to one another and strive for accord. They have great influence over the multitudes, and when they say anything against the king, or against the high priest, they are presently believed.

The Sadducees teach that it is man's choice to do what is good or what is evil, and in all cases only the written law should be followed. The Sadducees believe it virtuous to debate philosophical issues. Many dignified persons are numbered among them, even though the overall number is relatively small. When they become magistrates, as they are often forced to do, they tend to adhere to the teaching of the Pharisees; otherwise they have no influence on the multitudes.

The Essenes teach that all things are best described to God, and that the rewards of righteousness should be earnestly striven for. They lead simple lives, adhering to dietary codes. Although they send what they have dedicated to God into the temple, they do not offer sacrifices there or attend Jewish festivals in Jerusalem. There are about four thousand men that live this way, and most do not marry or keep servants. They live by themselves (in all cities) and minister one to another. They are also despisers of riches. Nor is there any one to be found among them who hath more than another, for it is a law among them that those who come to them must let what they have be common to the whole order, resulting in patrimony among all the brethren. These Essenes reject pleasures as evil, and esteem the conquest over our passions to be virtue. They guard against the lascivious behavior of women. Although they do not absolutely deny the fitness of marriage, which is necessary for the succession of mankind, they prefer to choose other person's children to be their kindred, and form them according to their own manners.

There are those among the Essenes who foretell things to come. By reading the holy books, and using several sorts of purifications, and by being perpetually conversant in the discourses of the prophets, it is seldom that they miss in their predictions.

The Essenes dispense their anger in a just manner, restrain their passion, and are ministers of peace. Swearing is avoided by them--they say that he who cannot be believed without swearing (by God) is already condemned. He who wishes to join the sect goes through an initiation period of over a year, carrying a hatchet and wearing a girdle and white garment. If he appears worthy after this period of time, by living a Spartan and exemplary life of virtue and righteousness, and sacrificing for the good of the sect, he is then tested for two more years before being admitted into the society.[59]

In addition to the Pharisees, the Sadducees and the Essenes, a fourth sect of Jewish philosophy began to grow in prominence in Judea as discontent fermented with the administration by Roman procurators. A major author of this philosophy was Judas the Galilean,[60] [61] who proclaimed that the taxation by the Romans is no better than an introduction to slavery, and exhorted the nation to assert their liberty. His proclamations were effective, and he had

---

59   A small group of Essenes occupied a settlement known as Qumran located southeast of Jerusalem near the Dead Sea not far from the desert caves where the Dead Sea Scrolls were found. This settlement may have been a retreat where Essenes would come from the cities for special communions and training. Because of the proximity of these caves to Qumran it was originally assumed that the Dead Sea Scrolls were written by the Essenes. The scrolls consist of 972 texts written in Hebrew, Aramaic, and Greek. Because of the life style of the Essenes, with many members of this sect living by themselves in different cities, it seems unlikely that they were the authors of the scrolls. Even though they took great pride in studying the writings of the ancients, and preserving the books of their sect, there is no indication from the writings of Josephus that the Essenes had the scholarly training or commitment to be the authors of the Dead Sea Scrolls, and especially those scrolls written in Greek. Many current scholars favor the hypothesis that the scrolls were written by priests in Jerusalem, and when the massive Roman army was preparing to attack Jerusalem following the Jewish revolt against Rome (see Chapters 9 and 10), the scrolls were removed from the library in the temple in Jerusalem, and then hidden in the isolated desert caves near Qumran. It was apparently hoped that these caves would provide protection for the scrolls if Jerusalem was destroyed by the Romans.
60   See Acts 5: 37.

61   Judas the Galilean was also known as Judas the Gaulonite.

Chapter 6 The Debate Over Who Should Replace Herod as King

many followers. The members of this sect follow all the tenets of the Pharisees, but in addition they ascribe to the inviolable belief in liberty, and that God alone is to be their Ruler. In pursuit of their immovable belief in freedom from any kind of political domination, they are willing to give up their lives, as well as the lives of their relations and friends.

Josephus

Chapter 7

AN ACCOUNT OF JOHN THE BAPTIST, THE EXILE OF HEROD ANTIPAS, AND THE RISE TO POWER OF AGRIPPA

Out of respect for his father, Antipas the tetrarch took his name and was known as Herod Antipas. He was esteemed highly by Tiberius, and early in the reign of Tiberius he built a city in the best part of Galilee, at the lake of Gennesareth [Sea of Galilee], and named it Tiberius in honor of the emperor. At a later time, Herod Antipas had a quarrel with Aretas the king of Arabia [with a palace at Petra, south of the Dead Sea]. Herod Antipas was married to the daughter of King Aretas, but on a visit to Rome he had lodged with his half-brother Herod [Philip], the son of Mariamne II. Herod [Philip] was living in Rome with his wife Herodias, the daughter of Aristobulus (son of king Herod and Mariamne) and Bernice (daughter of Salome). Herod Antipas became infatuated with Herodias and proposed that she divorce Herod [Philip] and marry him. She agreed to this matrimonial arrangement, which would remain secret until the necessary divorces were arranged.

Even though Herod Antipas thought that his wife was unsuspecting of his plan regarding Herodias, she became aware of it. Without letting him know that she knew his intentions, she requested that he send her to Macherus [east of the Dead Sea], which is a place that borders the dominions ruled by Antipas and her father Aretas. Herod Antipas agreed to send her there. She had planned carefully, and upon arriving in Macherus she was met by several generals of Areta's army, who then escorted her to her father in Arabia, whom she informed of her husband's plans. Aretas became furious with Herod Antipas over this treatment of his daughter. Previously they had quarreled over the boundaries of an adjoining territory, but this insult to his daughter now resulted in declared warfare. Opposing generals and their armies joined in battle and Herod Antipas's army was defeated. Herod Antipas informed Tiberius of this situation, who became very angry at Aretas, and wrote to Vitellius (president of Syria) and instructed him to make war on Aretas. He was ordered to bring Aretas to him in bonds, or to kill him and send his head to him.

So Vitellius prepared to make war against Aretas. He led his army through Judea on his way to Petra to engage Aretas's army. He joined up with Herod Antipas in Judea and they journeyed together with friends to Jerusalem to offer sacrifices to God and to participate in a Jewish festival. He remained there for three days and was honorably entertained by the multitude of Jews. During that time he deprived Jonathan of the high priesthood and gave it to his brother, Theophilus, the son of Ananus.

On the fourth day of his stay in Jerusalem, letters arrived informing him that Tiberius was deceased. Vitellius compelled the multitude to take an oath of fidelity to Caius, the new emperor,[62] and

---

[62] Josephus states that Tiberius was succeeded as Emperor by Caius, which was a variant spelling of Gaius that was used by Josephus. He was named Gaius at birth, but when he was two years old he acquired the affectionate nickname Caligula (Little Boot) by Roman soldiers because of the soldier-like boots (caliga) he was wearing when he was a camp mascot. His father was Germanicus Caesar, a nephew of Tiberius. When named Emperor he adopted his father's name and became known as Gaius Caesar Augustus Germanicus, but he is usually referred to historically as Caligula, a name he did not like when he was Emperor, believing that an Emperor should not be named after a boot. Caius (i.e., Gaius) served as emperor from 37 AD to 41 AD. He was the great-grandson of Augustus Caesar, through his daughter Julia and his granddaughter Agrippina, who was married to Germanicus Caesar. Caius manifested erratic behavior during his short tenure as Emperor, and at times showed great cruelty by executing many individuals, even those who had been close to him, whom he suspected of not supporting him. After becoming Emperor he quickly used up vast amounts of money in the treasury left there by Tiberius, and then resorted to the extortion of wealthy Roman citizens by confiscating their estates to support his extravagances. He showed signs of mental instability during the last two years of his life. The Roman populace became weary of his unpredictable behavior, and conspiracies formed against him. In 41 AD his murder was arranged by officers of the

Chapter 7 An Account of John the Baptist, Herod Antipas, and Agrippa

because he no longer had any authority to make war against Aretas, he recalled his army, and returned to Antioch.

John the Baptist

Now some of the Jews thought that the destruction of Herod Antipas's army in his battle with Aretas was a just act of God as punishment for what Herod Antipas had done to John who was called the *Baptist*. John the Baptist was a good man who commanded that the Jews exercise virtue, both as to righteousness towards one another and piety towards God. He also commanded them to be baptized, for that washing [with water] would be acceptable to him not only for the putting away [remission] of sins, but also for the purification of the body, supposing that the soul was thoroughly purified beforehand by righteousness. Crowds gathered to hear him, and were greatly moved by his words. Herod Antipas became aware of the influence of this man, and feared that he might be able to raise a rebellion against him because the people seemed ready to do anything that he should advise. Herod thought that it best to put him to death as a means of preventing any mischief he might cause. Accordingly he made him a prisoner and sent him to the castle at Macherus in Perea [east of the Dead Sea], where he had him put to death.[63]

Praetorian Guard. He was succeeded as Emperor by Claudius, who was his uncle.

---

[63] In Mark 6:14-28, it is stated that John the Baptist was critical of Herod Antipas because he had married Herodias who was the wife of Philip [Herod]. It was against Jewish law for him to marry his brother's wife. The daughter of Herod [Philip] and Herodias was Salome, and as told in Mark 6:22 she danced for Herod Antipas and his male guests at a supper celebrating his birthday. Her performance (which has been glamorized in stories, operas, and movies) pleased Herod Antipas and his guests so much that he promised (in front of his guests) to give her whatever she requested, even half of his kingdom. At this time, John the Baptist was in prison to appease Herodias. When the damsel Salome asked her mother what she should request, her mother answered that she should demand the head of John the Baptist. Herod Antipas was alarmed at this request, but since he had made an oath, he ordered the executioner to behead John the Baptist. The executioner gave the head to the damsel, who then gave it to her mother. Mark 6: 21 states that Herod Antipas entertained his "lords, high captains, and chief estates of Galilee," but does not say where the celebration took place. Josephus said that John the Baptist was

Philip the tetrarch died [33 AD] after he had been tetrarch for 37 years. He died in Julias, on the shore of the Sea of Galilee, during the twentieth year of the reign of Tiberius. His death ended the life and meritorious career of the son of king Herod and Cleopatra. History is explicit in describing Philip the tetrarch as a successful ruler. He was a person of moderation and quietness in the conduct of his life and government, and he lived constantly in the country that he had been chosen to rule. He was a just leader, who came to the assistance of those who needed it, and who made no delay when it came to making important decisions. After hearing complaints, he convicted those who were guilty and absolved those that had been accused unjustly. He was respected by those whom he ruled. **Since Philip the tetrarch left no sons to succeed him as ruler, Tiberius added his territory to the province of Syria.**

The Early Life of Agrippa

Before the death of king Herod, Agrippa (son of Aristobulus who was the son of king Herod and Mariamne) moved to Rome where he lived for many years. He became a close friend of Drusus, who was Tiberius's son. Drusus died at a young age. He also had a close relationship with Antonia (daughter of Mark Antony and Octavia) who was married to Tiberius's brother Drusus. Because of her long friendship with Bernice, who was Agrippa's mother, Antonia took a special interest in Agrippa. In Rome Agrippa led a sumptuous life, and made magnanimous and generous gifts to his friends and to the emperor's freedmen[64] in order to gain their

---

put to death at Macherus. This would suggest that the guests from Galilee traveled to Macherus for the birthday celebration. The fortress Macherus, located in the tetrarchy ruled by Herod Antipas, contained a luxurious palace which would have been suitable for such a celebration. The damsel Salome later married Philip the tetrarch of Trachonitis. Gaulanitis, and Bataneans. They had no children. After his death, she married her uncle Aristobulus (brother of Herodias and Agrippa I), and they had three sons.

64   Slavery in ancient Rome was not based on race, even though most slaves were prisoners of war, or were purchased from another country. In some cases, desperate Roman citizens sold their children into slavery in order to raise money. Slaves worked in private businesses, households and on farms. They also worked for cities [or the

Chapter 7 An Account of John the Baptist, Herod Antipas, and Agrippa

assistance. A major source of his funds was his mother Bernice, who was anxious that Agrippa would have every advantage. Following her death, Agrippa soon found himself living far beyond his means. Tiberius was of no economic help to him because he forbade the friends of his deceased son Drusus to come into his sight because on seeing them he was reminded of his son and his grief was revived. Agrippa borrowed money from friends and influential persons, and was soon in great debt. With no way of paying back what he owed, he made the decision to escape his creditors by sailing away from Rome to Judea.

Agrippa retired to a tower at Malatha in Idumea, where he experienced such great depression that he threatened suicide. He lamented the loss of the money he once had and the large sums of money he owed many different persons. His wife Cypros perceived his suicidal intentions and tried all sorts of methods to divert him from taking such a course. She sent a letter to his sister Herodias who was then the wife of Herod Antipas, and let her know of her brother's intentions. Cypros requested that she and Herod Antipas come to his aid. Cypros was a close relative of her husband Agrippa. Salampsio and Aristobulus were two of the offspring of King Herod and Mariamne (the Hasmonean). Salampsio was the mother of

---

Roman bureaucracy] on engineering projects, including the building of roads, aqueducts, and buildings. A slave could be killed by his owner, for any reason, without facing any punishment. The Romans had a liberal view concerning the freeing of slaves, and during the height of the Roman empire about 5% of the population of Rome were freedmen. To stabilize this percentage value, a law was passed during the tenure of Caesar Augustus as emperor, that slaves could not be freed until they reached the age of thirty. Some slaves were freed by their owners as a reward for dedicated service. Others were allowed to purchase their freedom, or were freed in wills upon the death of the owner. The possibility of being freed outright by their owner encouraged most slaves to be obedient and hardworking. Well educated and well trained slaves were often given their freedom. Freedmen were given Roman citizenship and the ability to own land, but because of the stigma of being a former slave, they could not run for public office or hold a high rank in the army. Their children, however, were given full citizenship. Some freedmen became very wealthy because of their entrepreneurship or success as land owners. Freedmen often remained in the service of their previous owner (such as the emperor), and in some cases they obtained positions of influence.

Cypros and Aristobulus was the father of Agrippa. Thus, Cypros and Agrippa were first cousins through Salampsio and Aristobulus. They were also related through the spouses of Salampsio and Aristobulus. The father of Cypros was Phasaelus, who was the son of Phasaelus, who was the brother of king Herod. The mother of Agrippa was Bernice who was the daughter of Salome, who was the sister of king Herod. Because of their close relationship, Cypros was hopeful that Herodias and her husband Herod Antipas would be of assistance to them.

Upon receipt of the letter, Herod Antipas sent for Agrippa and Cypros. He allowed them to live in Tiberius, made Agrippa magistrate of that city and gave him an income for his services. The positive relationship between Agrippa and Herod Antipas had a short tenure. Herod Antipas soon began making derogatory remarks about Agrippa, reminding him of his former state of poverty, his indebtedness, and how Agrippa depended on him for his daily subsistence.

The situation became unbearable for Agrippa, so he contacted Flaccus, a man who had been a close associate in Rome, who was now president of Syria. Flaccus invited Agrippa and Cyrpos to live with him, and he received them kindly. Also living with Flaccus was Agrippa's brother Aristobulus. Even though the relationship between the brothers Agrippa and Aristobulus was not pleasant, Flaccus was a considerate and benevolent host for both of them. A difficulty arose, however, when Aristobulus informed Flaccus that Agrippa had involved himself in a land dispute involving the cities of Damascus and Sidon. Agrippa had agreed to influence Flaccus to make a decision in favor of Damascus, and for his services Agrippa was to receive a large sum of money. Flaccus became furious with Agrippa for his actions and dismissed him as a friend. Agrippa then went to Ptolemais, but not knowing how he was to obtain a livelihood, he decided to return to Italy, hoping that life might be better for him there. He did not have the funds for the journey by sea, but with the

Chapter 7 An Account of John the Baptist, Herod Antipas, and Agrippa

aid of his freedman he was able to borrow enough money to pay for the trip. Upon receipt of the money, he went to Anthedon, where he made arrangements for the voyage to Italy. Herennius Capito, the procurator of Jamnia, sent a band of soldiers to detain him and to demand that he pay the three hundred thousand drachmae of silver that he owed Caesar's treasury in Rome. Agrippa agreed to do so, but at night he cut cables and sailed for Alexandria.

At Alexandria he approached Alexander, governor of the Jews there (and brother of Philo the Jewish philosopher) and asked him to loan him money.[65] Alexander refused to do so, but did say that he would loan the money to his wife Cypros because of her virtue and the affection she had for her husband. Upon receiving the money, Agrippa sailed for Italy, and Cypros and their children departed for Judea.

Upon arriving in Italy, Agrippa wrote a letter to Tiberius Caesar, who then lived in Capri, and requested permission to visit him. Tiberius responded that he was glad that his journey had been a safe one, and that he would be glad to welcome him in Capri. Tiberius gave him a warm welcome, but the next day Tiberius received a letter from Herennius Capito, stating that Agrippa had borrowed three hundred thousand drachmae and had not paid it back at the appointed time. When it was demanded of him, he had run away as a fugitive. Tiberius was greatly troubled by this letter and gave the order that Agrippa should be excluded from his presence until he had paid his debt. Agrippa then went to Antonia (mother of Germanicus) and asked her to loan him the three hundred thousand drachmae so that he could remain in the good graces of Tiberius. Antonia complied with his request out of respect for his deceased mother Bernice. Upon paying this debt owed to the treasury, there was nothing to hinder Tiberius from being his friend. Tiberius

---

65 Alexander of Alexandria was a Jewish administrator of great wealth. He held various offices for Rome including general tax administrator in charge of customs. At one time he donated the gold and silver to plate nine gates of the temple in Jerusalem.

received him kindly and encouraged him [which was an order] to remain close to his grandson Tiberius (son of Drusus) and always to accompany him when he went abroad.

Because of the kindness of Antonia, who had loaned him the money, and the respect he had for her, Agrippa also made an effort to become a good friend and companion of her grandson Caius (Caligula) who was held in esteem because of the high reputation of his father Germanicus. Agrippa spent more time with Caius than he did with the grandson of Tiberius, and therefore he was disobeying the order given to him by Tiberius. Agrippa was also able to borrow a million drachmae from a freedman of Caesar. With this sum he repaid his debt to Antonia, and still had ample funds to live in fine style and especially to ingratiate himself with Caius. By doing so Agrippa cemented a long lasting and close relationship with Caius, but he also maintained his very good relationship with Antonia, who was close to Tiberius. Antonia was greatly esteemed by Tiberius. She had been married to his brother Drusus, and did not remarry after his death, even though she was a young woman when he died. She refused all marriage proposals, even though Caesar Augustus encouraged her to remarry. She was widely revered for her chastity and made every effort to keep her reputation free of reproach. Tiberius was especially indebted to her because she alerted him that a dangerous plot had been laid against him by Sejanus, who had enlisted the aid of many senators and key members of the soldiery. It was Sajanus's plan to overthrow Tiberius and assume the government. Antonia discovered his designs, wrote a letter giving an exact account of the whole affair, and gave the letter to her most faithful servant for delivery to Tiberius. When the plot was fully understood by Tiberius, he had Sejanus and his confederates put to death. Because of her loyalty, Tiberius looked upon Antonia with even greater respect, and depended upon her for many things.

The friendship between Agrippa and Caius reached a great height, but one day an event occurred that had a major impact on the

Chapter 7 An Account of John the Baptist, Herod Antipas, and Agrippa

life of Agrippa. Caius and Agrippa were in a chariot together and Agrippa uttered some words concerning Tiberius. He commented that he was praying to God that Tiberius would soon go off the stage [die] and leave the government to Caius, who was in every respect more worthy of it. These words were heard by Eutychus, Agrippa's freedman, who was in the chariot with them. Later when Agrippa accused Eutychus of stealing some garments (which was true), Eutychus ran away. He was soon caught and brought before the governor of the city. When the governor asked him why he had ran away, Eutychus replied that he had something to say about Agrippa to the emperor that affected his security and preservation. So the governor had him bound and sent to Capri. Eventually he was brought before Tiberius, who asked him what he had to say about Agrippa. Eutychus repeated the words he had heard Agrippa speak, and also added that Agrippa had said that when Caius was emperor, Tiberius's grandson (Tiberius, son of Drusus) would be taken off (killed), and when that occurred, the earth and he (Agrippa) would be happy. Tiberius believed the words of the freedman, and he also held a grudge against Agrippa because although he had commanded him to pay his respects to his grandson Tiberius, Agrippa had disobeyed him by transferring most of his attention to Caius. Tiberius then ordered Macro to bind Agrippa. Agrippa attempted to supplicate himself, reminding Tiberius that he had been brought up with his son Drusus, and that he had helped educate his grandson Tiberius, but it was to no avail. He was manacled with chains, coupled with the soldier who was guarding him, and led around, with other prisoners, even in his purple garments.

Agrippa viewed this situation as heinous. Although it was not proper for her to approach Tiberius about this matter, Antonia came to some assistance by encouraging Macro to ensure that the soldiers guarding Agrippa were of a gentle nature, and also that the centurion who was over all the prisoners was of a similar disposition. She also encouraged Macro to allow Agrippa to bathe himself each day, and to allow his freedmen to bring extra food and garments to use as bed clothing at night. Macro honored her requests. Agrippa remained under these conditions for six months.

Tiberius then became very ill. Fearing that his days were numbered he instructed his freedman Euodus to bring Caius and his grandson Tiberius to him the next morning. He gave this order because a decision had to made about who would succeed him as emperor. Because his only son Drusus was deceased, he had no sons to succeed him. His grandson was a likely successor to the throne, but Tiberius knew that consideration must also be given to Caius. Caius was now grown-up with a liberal education and was held in high esteem by the people, mainly on account of the excellent reputation of his father Germanicus, who had attained the highest honor among members of the senate and influential persons from nations who were subject to the Romans. Germanicus was at ease with people, and treated all persons whom he contacted as his equal. Upon his death, there was great lamentation throughout the Roman Empire, and the high esteem felt for him was transferred to his son Caius. Principal men of the army and prominent and influential persons such as Macro, prefect of the Praetorian Guard, hoped that Caius would attain the government solely out of his respect for Germanicus.

When Tiberius ordered Euodus to bring Caius and his grandson to him in the morning, he prayed to his gods for a manifestation as to which one he should select to succeed him. He was very desirous to name his grandson as his successor, but nevertheless he felt obligated to leave the matter in the hands of his gods. Therefore, he made the decision to appoint the one who arrived first in the morning. To increase the likelihood that his grandson would arrive first, he ordered his grandson's tutor to bring his grandson to his quarters early in the morning. But his attempt to influence the result failed, which he attributed to fate and therefore to an act of his gods. When morning came, Tiberius told Euodus to call in the one who was outside the door. Euodus opened the door and found Caius

Chapter 7 An Account of John the Baptist, Herod Antipas, and Agrippa

standing there. His grandson was still in his quarters waiting for his breakfast.

Tiberius reflected on the power of his gods, and how the ability to appoint his successor was taken out of his hands. He lamented that his grandson was going to lose the Roman empire, and he also feared that his grandson would lose his life by the actions of the new emperor who would view his grandson as a possible threat. He informed Caius that he was to succeed him as emperor, and urged him to take special care of his grandson, suggesting that he would be of great benefit to him. Tiberius was unable to persuade Caius concerning the future of his grandson. Caius had Tiberius's grandson killed during his tenure as emperor.

A few days after Caius was named by Tiberius to succeed him, it was reported that Tiberius had died. There was great rejoicing among the Romans at this news because Tiberius had brought a vast number of miseries on the best families of the Romans. He was easily inflamed, had a vicious temper, was fierce in all the sentences he gave, and made the death the penalty for even light offenses. With the report of Tiberius's death, Agrippa's freedman came running to Agrippa to tell him the good news, and there was a happy celebration. Even the centurion who was guarding him joined in the festivity. The joy was short lived, because it was then reported that Tiberius was still alive. The centurion, believing that a trick had been played on him, furiously ordered that Agrippa should be bound again (because he had previously removed the chains), and was fearful that he would be punished for the joy he had expressed at the announcement of Tiberius's death, and for removing the chains from the prisoner. He placed a severe guard over Agrippa, but the next day it was confirmed that Tiberius was truly deceased. Caius was acclaimed as the new emperor, and one of his first acts was to return the body of Tiberius to Rome for a sumptuous funeral, according to the laws of his country. Tiberius had held the government for 22 years, 5 months, and 3 days.

Although Caius had every intention of releasing his good friend Agrippa from his bonds immediately, he was advised not to act in haste by Antonia. She feared that an immediate release would make some men believe that he received Tiberius's death with pleasure, and disagreed with the decision made by Tiberius to have Agrippa placed in chains. She urged Caius to move slowly. However, after several days had passed, Caius sent for Agrippa, made him a guest in his home, had him shaved, and gave him a change of clothes. **He then placed a diadem on his head and appointed him king of the tetrarchy formerly ruled by Philip, and also gave him the tetrarchy formerly ruled by Lysanias.**[66] As a good-will compensation for Agrippa's past six months as a prisoner, he changed his iron chain (with which he had been bound) for a gold chain of equal weight. Caius also sent Marullus to be procurator of Judea, replacing Pontius Pilate who arrived in Rome after the death of Tiberius.[67]

In the second year of the reign of Caius, Agrippa desired to sail for home and settle the affairs of his government, but he promised Caius that he would return to Rome when everything was in order. So with the emperor's permission, he arrived in his own country as king, with all the authority, wealth and trappings of a king. Thus, Agrippa became a king because of his friendship with Caius.

---

66   This small territory, with Abila apparently being the major city, was located at the base of Mount Hermon in Syria. It had formerly been ruled by Lysanias, a cousin of Antagonus, who had fought against Herod for the control of Judea. Lysanias was a contemporary of Mark Antony and Cleopatra, and it is evident that the territory had great value because Cleopatra coveted it. Because Lysanias was a supporter of the Parthinians who were opposing the advances of the Romans, Antony eventually had Lysanias assassinated. It is of historic interest that the tetrarchy of Lysanias was owned for a short period of time by Cleopatra.

67   In 36 AD, Vitellius, president of Syria, ordered Pontius Pilate back to Rome because of his transgressions in Samaria and sent his friend Marcellus to handle the affairs of Judea. This was a temporary assignment because only emperors could appoint procurators. In 37 AD Caius appointed Marullus as procurator replacing Pontius Pilate.

Chapter 7 An Account of John the Baptist, Herod Antipas, and Agrippa

The Banishment of Herod Antipas

Herodias, Agrippa's sister and wife of Herod Antipas, tetrarch of Galilee and Perea, was exceedingly envious of the good fortune of her brother king Agrippa, and especially because he now had more dignity than her husband. She became distraught when she saw him marching among the multitudes with the usual ensigns of royalty. She recalled that he had come to them in extreme poverty, depended upon them for the basic necessities of living, which were supplied him by them, and then eventually fled from his creditors by sea. Now he was a king, with the authority and fortunes of a king, while her husband was only a tetrarch. She was grieved at this turn of events, and she was not able to conceal the envy that possessed her. She complained bitterly to her husband that he should not be content with this shameful situation. She urged him to go to Rome, no matter what the expense, either of gold or silver, and acquire a kingdom and the title of king, so they would have the dignity that they deserved.

Herod Antipas opposed her request. He was now getting older, and preferred a leisurely and private life. He was content with his present circumstance, and he sensed that the trip to Rome could cause unwanted trouble. However, the more he drew back, the harder she pressed him, arguing that he should leave no stone unturned in order to be a king. Her persistence finally won, and he gave in to her. He made the necessary preparations, and traveled to Rome to meet with the emperor, taking Herodias with him.

When king Agrippa became aware of their intentions, he sent one of his freedmen to Rome with presents for Caius and letters against Antipas, stating that Antipas had been in confederacy with Sejanus against Tiberius, and that he was now a confederate of the king of Parthia who was in opposition to Caius's government. As evidence of the latter, he stated in the letter that Antipas had armor sufficient for seventy thousand men in his armory. The freedman followed Herod Antipas to Rome but had such a successful journey that he arrived with his letters at the exact time when Antipas was having an audience with Caius. While Caius and Antipas were in conversation, Caius read the letters Agrippa had sent him, and was moved at the information. He asked Antipas whether he actually had in his armory enough armor for seventy thousand men. Antipas could not deny the existence of such armor, because the truth of it could be readily verified, so he confessed that it was there. Caius took that confession as evidence that Antipas intended to join with the king of Parthia and revolt against his government. **He responded by taking away his tetrarchy and adding it to king Agrippa's kingdom.**[68] He gave Antipas's money to king Agrippa, and banished Antipas permanently to Lyons, Gaul. He made Herodias a present of the money that was her own, and told her that because she was a sister of king Agrippa, she did not face the same calamity that was facing her husband. She replied that even though the emperor acts in a magnificent manner, the kindness which she had for her husband hindered her from partaking of the favor of the gift, and since she was a partner in his prosperity, she would not forsake him in his misfortune. Caius was angry with this response, sent her with Antipas into banishment, and gave her estate to king Agrippa.

> *"And thus did God punish Herodias for her envy of her Brother, and Herod Antipas for giving ear to the vain discourses of a woman."*

The Reign of Caius (Caligula)

Caius managed public affairs with great magnanimity during the first and second years of his reign, and behaved with such moderation that he gained the good-will of the Romans and his other subjects, but with the passage of time he went well beyond the bounds of human nature in conceit of himself by making himself

---

68   Because of the actions taken by the emperor Caius, Agrippa was now the ruler of the tetrarchies previously held by his uncles Philip and Antipas, making him king of about half the territory held by his grandfather Herod the Great.

Chapter 7 An Account of John the Baptist, Herod Antipas, and Agrippa

a god and acting otherwise in a bizarre manner. He demonstrated his madness to the Jews in Jerusalem, and to all peoples under the jurisdiction of Rome. The citizens of Rome soon felt the dismal effects of his ten thousand mischiefs. He plundered the wealthy, including wealthy senators, by seizing their riches. He asserted his own divinity and insisted that great honors should be paid to him. He frequently visited the temple of Jupiter, the most holy of temples and had the boldness to call himself the brother of Jupiter. When his daughter was born, he carried her to the temple and put her on the knees of the statue. He then announced that the child was common to him and to Jupiter, and therefore the child had two fathers, but he left undetermined which of these fathers was the greater. He allowed slaves to accuse their masters of any crimes whatsoever, and many accusations by them were made at his suggestion. These charges were then used as an excuse to plunder the riches of the accused, or to have them killed. He built a bridge about 3.75 miles in length across a bay, at great expense, because it gave him pleasure to ride his chariot across the bay rather to row across it in a small ship. He thought that as a god, it was fitting for him to travel on such roads. He began an incestuous relationship with his sister Drusilla, and it was rumored that he was involved in such relationships with his other sisters as well. In all nations subject to Rome, he had temples and statues built to honor him, and respect was paid to these statues as if he were one of the gods.

The Uprising Against Caius by the Jewish People Over His Decision to Place His Statue in the Temple at Jerusalem

Because of a tumult that had arisen in Alexandria, a group consisting of Jews and Greeks came to see Caius. The spokesperson for the Greeks was Apion, who stated that Jews in Alexandria uttered blasphemies against Caius. Among other things, Apion stated that even though temples and altars were rightfully being built to honor Caius throughout the empire, the Jews thought it dishonorable to erect statures in honor of him and being forced to receive him as they would receive their God. Apion hoped to provoke Caius to be angry against the Jews. The spokesperson for the Jews was Philo, the Jewish scholar.[69] He was prepared to defend the Jewish people of these accusations, but Caius prohibited him from speaking, because of what he had heard from Apion.

Learning therefore that he was despised by the Jews, Caius sent Petronius to be president of Syria as a replacement for Vitellius, and gave him orders to invade Judea with a great body of troops for the purpose of forcing the erection of a statue of himself in the temple in Jerusalem. If the Jewish people opposed this action, he was to conquer them by war and then erect the stature. Accordingly, Petronius assumed the government of Syria, and then made preparations to march towards Jerusalem. He went as far as Ptolemais, where he wintered with the intention on continuing the march in the spring. He wrote to Caius and informed him of his plans. Caius commended him for his alacrity, and once again encouraged him to make war against the Jews if they refused to obey his commands. A large group of Jews came to Ptolemais and urged him not to compel them to violate the laws of their forefathers. They stated that if he was resolved to erect this statue in their temple, he should first kill them, because as long as they were alive they could not tolerate a violation of their sacred laws. Petronius informed them firmly that even though he was in sympathy with their petition, he could not disobey the emperor's decree. They responded that they likewise could not disobey the laws of their forefathers. Petronius then realized that an attempt to erect the stature in the temple would result in a great deal of bloodshed.

Being greatly concerned, Petronius took his friends and servants and went to Tiberius [on the shore of the Sea of Galilee], hoping to obtain additional information from the Jews about this matter. At Tiberius he was met by ten thousand Jews. When Petronius asked

---

69   Philo, the famed Jewish philosopher, was the brother of Alexander of Alexandria, who was the Jewish administrator of great wealth who loaned money to the wife of Agrippa when she and her husband were financially destitute.

Chapter 7 An Account of John the Baptist, Herod Antipas, and Agrippa

them if they would make war against Caesar, considering his great strength and their weakness, they replied that they would not make war against him, but they would die before allowing their laws to be transgressed. They then threw themselves prostrate on the ground, stretched out their necks, and said that they were ready to be slain. And they did this for 40 days, staying away from the fields even though it was the season to till the ground and plant seeds.

Petronius was then approached by Aristobulus (king Agrippa's brother) and other principal men of that family. They argued that Petronius should petition Caius to reconsider placing the statue in the temple because of the resolve of the Jewish people. Fulfilling Caesar's decree would result in massive bloodshed, the destruction of the Jewish nation, and the loss of revenues normally expected by Caesar. From what he had heard and seen, Petronius knew that it was a horrible thing for him to be a slave to the madness of Caius, and be forced to kill thousands of Jews because of their religious commitment to their God. He decided to write to Caius and attempt to persuade him to reconsider his decree, realizing that he was placing himself in great jeopardy. He was prepared to begin the war, however, if told to do so by the emperor.

Petronius then met with the ten thousand Jews in Tiberius, and placed his army opposite them. He announced that he was prepared to execute anyone who disobeyed what had been commanded, and he would do it immediately, for it was proper for him not to contradict the emperor in any thing. Yet, he said, he did not think it just for him to sacrifice so many who are only trying to preserve the laws which have come down from their forefathers. Nor did he want to see their temple fall into contempt by means of the imperial authority. He announced that he was going to write to Caius and inform him of their resolutions, and petition Caius on their behalf. He hoped that God would be their assistant.

He then dismissed the assembly of Jews and encouraged them

to return to their homes, till the soil, plant seeds, and go about their occupations. As he finished his speech, the heavens opened and it began it rain, which was beyond the expectations of the people, for there had been an extensive period of drought, and the appearance of the sky gave no indication of rain. The amount of rain that fell was extensive, and the Jews hoped that this was a sign that Petronius would not fail in his petition for them. Petronius himself was greatly surprised and perceived that God evidently took care of the Jews. He then wrote his letter to Caius, urging him not to have thousands of Jews slain. By causing this slaughter he would lose the revenue they paid him, and he would be publicly cursed by them for all future ages. Moreover God, who was their governor, had shown his power most evidently on their account by the occurrence of the needed rain.

At this time king Agrippa was living in Rome, and he and the emperor had a very close and friendly relationship. He invited Caius to a supper and went to a great effort to make it a feast that would exceed all others, both in expense and in preparation. Caius was greatly pleased that his loyal friend would entertain him in such an extravagant manner, and he was desirous to show that he was equally generous. After drinking plentiful wine and following an eloquent toast given by Agrippa, Caius proclaimed that he knew how much respect Agrippa had for him. He also said that he was fully aware of how much suffering Agrippa had experienced at the hands of Tiberius on his account. To show his thankfulness, he announced that he wished to do anything that would contribute to Agrippa's happiness. Caius assumed that Agrippa would respond by asking for the rule of some large country or the revenues of certain cities, which he was prepared to give him. Agrippa had planned carefully, and replied that it was not out of any expectation of gain that he had paid his respects to him, for the gifts that he had already received were great and beyond the hopes of any craving man. What he had done in the past and present was out of great respect. Hence, he expected and wanted nothing more. Caius was astonished at this

Chapter 7 An Account of John the Baptist, Herod Antipas, and Agrippa

response and pressed him to make a request for something that he might give him, out of gratification for their special relationship. King Agrippa then replied that he wanted nothing for himself, but did desire something that would benefit Caius by making Divinity an assistant in all of his future governmental affairs. What he desired was that Caius would no longer think of installing his statue in the temple at Jerusalem, as he had ordered Petronius to do.

King Agrippa knew that he had gambled personally by making this dangerous request, because if Caius did not approve of it, his life was in great danger. He also knew that the problem of the stature, if not resolved, would have terrible consequences among his people in his own country. Caius was taken back by the request, but out of respect and admiration for Agrippa, and also because not granting the request would be viewed by witnesses that he does not follow his own word, he granted Agrippa what he requested. He wrote to Petronius and told him, "If thou hast already erected my statue, let it stand; but if thou has not yet dedicated it, do not trouble thyself further about it. . . for I have now no occasion for the erection of that statue. This I have granted as a favor to Agrippa, a man whom I honor so very greatly, that I am not able to contradict what he would have, or what he desired me to do for him."

Soon after sending this letter to Petronius, Caius received the letter from Petronius informing him that the Jews were ready to revolt about the statue, and war and great bloodshed were imminent. The letter also contained his petition to Caius concerning this affair. Caius was displeased that any attempt should be made against his government, and being a vicious person who received much pleasure by indulging his anger, he wrote to Petronius and accused him of being insolent and subservient to the Jews, and valuing presents from the Jews over his commands. He said that he would make him an example to the present and future ages, as what happens when one dares contradict the commands of the emperor. He then charged him to be his own judge as to what he should do. In essence, he was informing Petronius that because he was now under his displeasure, he expected him to kill himself with his own hands.

Petronius received this letter after other letters had arrived informing him that Caius was dead. The ship containing the letter that he was expected to commit suicide sailed so slowly that the other letters announcing the death of Caius arrived first. Petronius rejoiced at God's providence by delaying the ship and thereby allowing him to escape death, which he viewed as his reward for attempting to assist the Jews in their predicament and for his regard for the sanctity of the temple.

There were several conspiracies against Caius during the third and fourth years of his reign as emperor because of his bizarre behavior and extreme cruelty, with seemingly no regard for human life. With the assistance of others he was finally assassinated by Cherea, a tribune of the Praetorian Guard. Because of his hatred of Caius, Cherea also ordered Lupus to kill Caius's wife and his young daughter, and this was done soon after Caius had been killed. Caius had been emperor for four years and was only 28 years old when he was assassinated [41 AD].

Chapter 8

EVENTS OCCURRING IN JUDEA WHEN CLADIUS AND NERO WERE EMPERORS OF THE ROMAN EMPIRE

Claudius, the uncle of Caius, was a private man who spent his early life in academic pursuits. He was content with his life and fortune and stayed away from political intrigues. However, he had noteworthy credentials. He was a person of moderation who was respected for his high learning, and he was the brother of Germanicus, a person who would have been popularly acclaimed by the multitude to succeed Tiberius as emperor if he had lived long enough.

At the time of Caius's assassination and the killing of his wife and daughter, the palace was in disarray. Forces loyal to the emperor were seeking to punish those who had murdered him, and there was chaos in the palace because of the fear that the conspiracy against Caius, which had extended to his wife and daughter, might involve other family members or close associates. The palace was full of soldiers and distrust was rampant. Claudius was caught up in this frenzy, and he feared for his life. In great distress and trying to save himself, he hid in a narrow dark place in the palace. He was discovered there by one of the soldiers belonging to the palace guard, who then announced to the soldiers accompanying him, "This is a Germanicus; come, let us choose him for our emperor." The soldier then said to Claudius, "Go to, therefore, and accept the throne of thy ancestors." He was then carried to a large court in the palace where he was treated with dignity by many soldiers who, because of their respect for his brother Germanicus, thought it right to make him emperor.

He was not acclaimed, however, by most senators who favored a democratic form of government. Allowing the senators to choose the emperor would give more dignity and power to them, but they were also of the conviction that it would free the Roman Empire of the tyrannical rule of emperors such as Tiberius and Caius. They also believed that such a procedure would increase the likelihood that the chosen person would be worthy of the position. Now was the time to form a government with the ruler chosen by a vote of the senate members. Two well respected ambassadors from the senate went to Claudius and urged him not to seize the government by force, but to abide by the decision of the senate. They informed him that if he decided to live foolishly and try to claim the government, having learned nothing by the death of Caius, he would be opposed by the senate which would be able to muster a sizable army against him. Claudius behaved moderately towards these ambassadors even though they treated him in an insolent manner.

What King Agrippa did for Claudius

King Agrippa had remained loyal to his long time friend Caius, and after Caius had been mortally wounded, he embraced his body, laid him upon a bed, and covered him as well as he could. He then went out to the guards and told them to obtain the services of physicians, knowing that Caius did not have long to live. When Agrippa learned that Claudius had been carried away by soldiers, he rushed through the crowds to find him. When Claudius told him that he was ready to let the senate make the decision concerning who should control the government, king Agrippa encouraged him not to do so, but instead to assume the government, which was his for the asking. Claudius respected king Agrippa highly, and he finally decided to seek the government because of his persuasion and also because of the boldness of the soldiers who encouraged him to accept the throne

After convincing Claudius that he should accept the government, king Agrippa retired to his residence only to learn that

Chapter 8 Events Occurring When Claudius and Nero were Emperors

he had been summoned to appear before the members of the senate. When he appeared before them, he was apprised of their opposition to Claudius as the next ruler, and their intent, if necessary, to go to war over the situation. They asked king Agrippa to give his view of this state of affairs. King Agrippa then involved himself in political double-dealing. He informed them that he was willing to lose his life for the honor of the senate, but he urged them to use caution because they did not have an army or supplies that could defeat the large and well trained army that was supporting Claudius. The senate argued that they had the money to obtain supplies, and by using slaves they could increase the number of armed men. King Agrippa replied that their own preservation was at stake because the army which would fight for Claudius is well trained for warlike activities. The army that would fight for the senate would be no better than a rude multitude of raw men who have not even been trained how to draw their swords. He told them it was his opinion that the senate should not instigate a civil war over this matter, but should send ambassadors to Claudius to persuade him not to seek the government. He volunteered to be one of those ambassadors.

The senate complied with his recommendation and sent him and others to Claudius. King Agrippa privately informed Claudius of the disorder present in the senate, but instead of trying to persuade him not to seek the government, as the senate trusted him to do, he urged Claudius to respond to the ambassadors in a commanding manner, as one invested with dignity and authority. He also suggested what Claudius might say to them. Accordingly, Claudius told the ambassadors that he understood why the senate did not want to have a ruler over them because of the harassment and barbarity they had endured at the hands of those who had formerly held the government, but they would taste an equitable government and moderate times under him. Although he would have the title of ruler, the authority would be equally common to them all, and it would be good for the senators to trust him. By his answers to their questions, he literally informed the ambassadors that he was assuming the government. He then dismissed them, and appeared with the army which had gathered. The members of the army took oaths that they would persist in their fidelity to him as emperor, upon which he gave large sums of money to the guards and captains, and promised to give the same to the rest of the army.

A hasty meeting of the senate was then called, which was poorly attended. Many of the senators had left the city because of fear of what might occur. Disarray was present among those in attendance. The soldiery who had the responsibility of guarding the senate, and who feared the prospects of a civil war, spoke for the need of a strong monarch. Several candidates were proposed as an alternative to Claudius. The debate became tense, with little headway. In frustration the soldiery drew their swords, put up their ensigns, went to Claudius, and took an oath of fidelity to him. Influential members of the army also gave their full support for Claudius. The senate then realized that its influence was powerless against the allegiance of several thousand armed men. As a consequence, it hastened to acclaim him as emperor.

His first act as emperor was to inquire of the senators what should be done about Cherea who had orchestrated the murder of Caius. They responded that even though his work was glorious, he had acted in a treacherous manner and the punishment should be death to discourage any such future actions. Thus, Cherea, Lupus and many others suspected of being involved in the conspiracy were put to death.

What Claudius Did for King Agrippa and the Jewish People

Soon after Claudius had taken over the government, he published an edict commending King Agrippa highly and confirming that he was **the ruler over the territories Caius had given him, including the tetrarchy formerly ruled by Philip, the small tetrarchy formerly ruled by Lysanias in Syria, and the tetrarchy (Galilee and Perea) formerly ruled by Antipas. Claudius also added Judea, Samaria and Idumea (formerly ruled by Archelaus) to Agrippa's kingdom.** With these additions Agrippa now ruled all the territory that had been controlled by his

Chapter 8 Events Occurring When Claudius and Nero were Emperors

grandfather [Herod the Great]. With these actions by the new emperor, Judea was no longer ruled by a Roman governor, but by a king who could trace his lineage back to Hasmoneus. King Agrippa was also given the authority to appoint and remove high priests.

King Agrippa then begged Claudius to appoint his brother Herod as the ruler of a city, and surrounding territory, known as Chalcis,[70] with title of king. This brother was married to king Agrippa's daughter Bernice, which was her second marriage. Claudius complied with this request, and as a consequence the brother of king Agrippa became king Herod of Chalcis.

Now at this time there was a continuing contention between the Jews and Greeks in Alexandria. During the reign of Caius, the Jews had been put down by the Greeks, with the full support of Caius. Following his death, the Jews took up arms to defend themselves against the Greeks. Claudius sent an order to the president of Egypt to quiet that tumult. At the request of king Agrippa and king Herod of Chalcis, he also sent an accompanying edict which read that during the reign of Caius, the Alexandrians (Greeks of Alexandria) became insolent towards the Jews because of the madness of Caius, who reduced the Jews to a low level because they would not transgress their religious laws and call him a god. Claudius decreed that the rights and privileges of the Jews, denied them by the Alexandrians with the support of Caius, should be returned to them and they should be allowed to continue with their own customs. He also charged that both parties (Jews and Greeks) should take great care that no troubles should arise after the promulgation of this edict. A similar edict was sent to "the other parts of the habitable earth," which read, "Upon the petition of king Agrippa and king Herod, who are persons very dear to me . . . I grant the same rights and privileges . . . which I have granted to those of Alexandria…to the Jews anywhere else in the Roman empire. . . It will therefore…permit the Jews, who are in all the world under us, to keep their ancient customs without being hindered . . . And I do also charge them [the Jews] to

---

70   The historic city of Chalcis was north of Galilee in Syria.

use my kindness with moderation and not to show contempt for the superstitious observances of other nations.[71]

Following the dissemination of these decrees, Claudius ordered king Agrippa to return to his kingdom. He also sent letters to the presidents and procurators of nearby provinces stating that they should treat him kindly. Agrippa traveled hastily to his kingdom and while in Jerusalem he offered all the necessary sacrifices. As a symbolic act he hung the golden chain (of the same weight as the iron chain that had bound his hands) given him by Caius in the temple over the treasury chamber. It served as a reminder that king Agrippa had once been bound in a chain for a small cause, but was now an illustrious king. Thus, they who fall may gain their illustrious dignity once again.

When Agrippa had finished all the duties of the Divine worship, he removed Theophilius, the son of Ananus, from the high priesthood, and bestowed that honor on Simon, the son of Boethus. Out of kindness, Agrippa then released the inhabitants of Jerusalem from the tax upon houses.

Agrippa was then provoked when he learned that rash young men in Doris had carried a statue of Claudius into a Jewish synagogue and erected it there, even though the edict disseminated by Claudius discouraged such activity. King Agrippa went to Petronius, who was then president of Syria, and accused the people of Doris of a seditious act. Petronius agreed totally with king Agrippa, and wrote a nasty letter to the people of Doris, accusing them of boldness or madness for their act in light of the edict written by Claudius. He ordered that the responsible men should be brought to him for punishment. He also stressed, as outlined in the edict written by Claudius, that each person should be allowed to follow one's own religious customs. Thus, Petronius took care of the matter.

---

71   These remarkable edicts show that because of his friendship with king Agrippa, Claudius gave the Jewish people their existing religious rights and freedoms throughout the Roman Empire.

Chapter 8 Events Occurring When Claudius and Nero were Emperors

King Agrippa then took the high priesthood away from Simon, son of Boethus, and gave it once again to Jonathan, the son of Ananus, stating that he was more worthy of it than Simon, son of Boethus. Jonathan, thanked him for this great honor and stated that since he had once served in the position it was proper that it should be given to someone of even greater honor, and recommended that it be given to his brother who was a man who was free of sin against God. King Agrippa was pleased with these words, and accordingly, gave the high priesthood to his brother Matthias. Soon after this appointment, Marcus succeeded Petronius as president of Syria.

At great expense, Agrippa then began repairing the walls surrounding Jerusalem, making them wider and higher, and so strong that it would take a great force to penetrate them. Alarmed at what was happening, Marcus, president of Syria, wrote to Claudius informing him that Agrippa was turning Jerusalem into an impenetrable fortress. In response, Claudius ordered Agrippa to cease building such walls. Agrippa obeyed, thinking it proper not to disobey Claudius.[72]

King Agrippa made a great effort to be a beneficial ruler, and he took great pride in acquiring and maintaining a good reputation. He was known for his compassionate and gentle temper. He was liberal in his gifts, and took great delight in giving. He was liberal to all men and humane to foreigners. He enjoyed living in Jerusalem, and he was careful to live by the Jewish laws. Each day he was diligent in carrying out the proper sacrifices. However, a certain man in Jerusalem, named Simon, who was highly knowledgeable of Jewish law, got together an assembly when Agrippa was away from Jerusalem and accused Agrippa of not living a holy life. He also claimed that Agrippa should be excluded from the temple because he

---

72   At a later time, when the Roman armies were assaulting Jerusalem, Josephus comments that the Romans would have failed in their efforts to conquer this city if these walls had been completed: ". . .for the city could no way have been taken if that wall had been finished in the manner it was begun; as its parts were connected together by stones twenty cubits long, and ten cubits broad, which could never have been either easily undermined by any iron tools, or shaken by any engines."

was not a native Jew[73] and he had been reared in Rome by gentiles. The general of the army informed king Agrippa of Simon's speech, and the king sent for Simon. He bid him to sit down by him, and then in a gentle and low voice, asked, "What is there done in this place that is contrary to the law?" Simon had nothing to say, and begged his pardon. Believing that moderation was a greater quality of a leader than passion, Agrippa gave Simon a small present and dismissed him. And such was the leadership style of king Agrippa, in contrast to that of his grandfather (king Herod).

Agrippa was a great builder. He erected a magnificent theater, amphitheater, baths, and other edifices at Berytus. He spared no costs in making these structures handsome and large. He dedicated them with shows and musicians. A major extravaganza was the use of gladiators in a fight to the finish. In an enactment of war, 700 criminals condemned to death battled 700 other criminals similarly condemned, and this manner of executing criminals was a form of recreation for the spectators at Berytus.

After completing the major projects at Berytus, king Agrippa traveled to Tiberius, a city on the Sea of Galilee. There he was held in great esteem by kings of other areas, including his brother Herod, who was king of Chalcis. He entertained these kings lavishly. While these kings were staying with him, Marcus, the president of Syria also came to visit. Out of courtesy due the Romans, king Agrippa traveled out of the city to meet him, taking with him the kings who were visiting with him. This greeting was not viewed with favor by Marcus, who was suspicious that the friendship and congeniality that existed among these kings could be a threat to Rome. Previously, Marcus had taken steps to stop Agrippa from enhancing the walls around Jerusalem. Marcus sent messengers to the kings commanding them to return without delay to their homes. This action was resented by Agrippa, and from that time on Marcus was his enemy.

---

73   Although Mariamne the Hasmonean was his grandmother, his other grandparents were Idumean (king Herod and Salome) and Arab (Costobarus).

Chapter 8 Events Occurring When Claudius and Nero were Emperors

King Agrippa then took the high priesthood away from Matthias and gave that honor to Elioneus, son of Cantheras. He then went to Caesarea for the purpose of presenting magnificent shows in honor of Caesar. On the second day of these shows he put on a garment made wholly of silver, and when he went into the theater the morning sun reflected off him in a surprising manner, and his flatterers cried out that he was a god. *The king did not rebuke them for this flattery*, but then he looked up and saw an owl sitting on a rope over his head. He viewed this owl as a bearer of ill-tidings, and he fell into a deep sorrow. A severe pain then arose in his belly and he announced to his friends: "I whom you call a god am commanded to presently depart this life; while Providence reproves the lying words you just said to me. I, who was by you called immortal, am immediately to be hurried away by death." His pain then became violent and he was carried into the palace. After five days he departed from this life at age 54, and in the seventh year of his reign, four years under Caius and three years under Claudius Caesar.[74] [75] The income he received each year during the latter years of his reign was enormous, but only about 3/4ths of that taken by king Herod. Agrippa would have earned as much except he pardoned the citizens of Jerusalem from paying taxes on their homes. He was also not as tyrannical as king Herod when it came to collecting revenues. But

---

74   From 37 AD to 41 AD, king Agrippa ruled what had been Philip's tetrarchy, and from 41 AD to 44 AD he ruled what had been king Herod's large kingdom.

75   The New Testament deals briefly with king Agrippa. In Acts, Chapter 12, it is reported that Herod the king (king Agrippa) had James, brother of John, killed with the sword. Because this act pleased the Jews, he proceeded further and placed Peter in prison. After an angel of the Lord allowed Peter to escape from prison, king Agrippa had the guards put to death. King Agrippa then departed from Judea for Caesarea. The king was highly displeased with the people of Tyre and Sidon, but they needed to have peace with him because their country was nourished by his country. To seek peace with the king, people from those cities met with him, and on a given day the king sat on his throne arrayed in royal apparel, and made an oration unto them: "And the people gave a shout, saying, it is the voice of a god, and not of a man. And immediately the angel of the Lord smote him, because he gave not God the glory; and he was eaten of worms, and gave up the ghost." This account and the one given by Josephus both give the message that king Agrippa died because he did not deny that he was a god to those who had the intention of flattering him.

even with this income, he had to borrow sums of money from others because his expenses exceeded his income, and his generosity was boundless.

What Things Were Done After the Death of King Agrippa

King Agrippa left behind a son (Agrippa II) and three daughters. Since king Agrippa had been a relatively benevolent ruler, there was great sorrow throughout most of his kingdom. Such was not the case, however, among certain inhabitants [mostly gentiles] of Caesarea and Sebaste. Upon his death they forgot his kindness to them and began berating him as if he had been a bitter enemy. Some Roman soldiers also went to his palace, hastily removed statues of his daughters, carried them to brothel-houses, and mounted them on the roofs. Various citizens celebrated his death with feasts, drinking and joyful expressions.

Claudius Caesar was extremely sad when he learned that Agrippa was dead, and he was greatly displeased when he heard that certain citizens of Caesarea and Sebaste had abused him and the honor of his daughters. **At that time Agrippa's son (Agrippa II) was at Rome being brought up with Claudius Caesar. The emperor's first inclination was to appoint Agrippa II as his father's successor and to send him home immediately. But because Agrippa II was only 17 years old, influential friends advised him that it would be a dangerous experiment to permit such a large kingdom to be placed under the rule of a young and inexperienced person. While the weight of such a large kingdom is heavy enough for a mature man, it would be too heavy for a young man of age 17 with no administrative experience. Claudius finally concurred with this advise, and sent Fadus [44 AD] to be procurator of the kingdom.**[76] Claudius

---

76   After being ruled for 3 years by a Jewish king of Hasmonean descent, **the large kingdom, once ruled by Herod the Great, was now under the rule of a Roman procurator**. King Agrippa had been a relatively benevolent ruler and the Jewish people experienced remarkable religious freedoms under him. The history of that kingdom would

also ordered Fadus to chastise the citizens of Caesarea and Sebaste and the Roman soldiers for the abuses they had committed against the deceased and for their insults against his daughters. He also ordered that the Roman soldiers who were involved in the fracas should be transferred elsewhere. These soldiers responded to this order by sending ambassadors to Claudius who were able to mollify him, causing Caesar to reverse his orders and allow the soldiers to remain in Judea. These same soldiers later were the cause of great calamities against the Jews, and helped sow the seeds of the great war that followed.

Out of respect for the memory of king Agrippa, Claudius Caesar replaced Marcus with Cassius Longinus as president of Syria. Before his death king Agrippa had written to Claudius Caesar desiring him to remove Marcus as president because he viewed him as his enemy.

Actions of Fadus and How Claudius Once Again Came to the Assistance of the Jews in Judea

Soon after Fadus arrived [44 AD] in Judea as procurator (governor), he found that quarrelsome events were occurring between the Jews of Perea and the people of Philadelphia about their borders at a village called Mia. The Jews had taken up arms and killed many of the Philadelphians. Fadus was provoked because he had been left out of this dispute and the Jews had taken actions without consulting him. So he seized the principal Jewish men and had one of them slain. He also sent for the high priest, other priests, and principal citizens of Jerusalem, and informed them that they should give him the long garment and the sacred vestments which by custom are only worn by the high priest. He stated that with the authority of the emperor he was placing these items in the fortress at Antonia under

---

likely have been much different if the lives of both Claudius and king Agrippa had been extended. The actions of Nero (the succeeding emperor) and the procurators appointed by Nero led eventually to the revolt of the Jews against Rome and the destruction of Jerusalem and the temple.

the control of the Romans. The Jews dared not contradict Fadus, but requested that they be allowed to send ambassadors to Claudius Caesar to petition him to allow the vestments to be kept by them. They also requested that they be allowed to remain in Rome until a decision was made. Fadus agreed to do so if the ambassadors would leave their sons as pledges that that they would behave in a peaceful manner. The ambassadors departed for Rome, and upon their arrival there they found that they had an influential ally in Agrippa II who was dwelling with Claudius. Agrippa II went to Claudius and urged him to grant the Jews their request concerning the holy vestments, and to send a message to Fadus accordingly. Claudius Caesar called for the ambassadors and told them that he had granted their request, and that they should give thanks to Agrippa II for this favor. He then sent a message to Fadus informing him of his decision. In this message he praised Agrippa II and king Herod of Chalcis for their loyal friendship, and stated that he esteemed them highly. He also reaffirmed that persons in Judea and elsewhere should be given the right to worship God according to the laws of their country.

King Herod of Chalcis, who was the brother of the deceased king Agrippa, then petitioned Claudius that he should be given authority over the temple in Jerusalem, control of the money of the sacred treasure, and the right to appoint high priests. Claudius Caesar responded favorably to all of these requests, and thereby took these privileges away from Fadus the procurator. King Herod of Chalcis then removed Elioneus, son of Cantheras as high priest and bestowed that dignity on Josephus, son of Camydus.

The Famine in Judea and the Assistance of Queen Helena of Adiabene

Monobarus, king of Adiabene[77] fell in love with his sister Helena and took her to be his wife. He had a son by her named Monobarus II and, in addition, he had sons by other wives. In bed

---

77   Adiabene was a small kingdom located east of the Tigris river in what is now northeastern Iraq.

Chapter 8 Events Occurring When Claudius and Nero were Emperors

one night, and while he was asleep, he placed his hand on the belly of Helena who was carrying a child. He then seemed to hear a voice telling him to remove his hand from his wife's belly and not to hurt the infant therein, which by God's providence would be safely born and have a happy end. He was so startled by what had happened that he awakened Helena and told her the story. When his son was born he named him Izates, and he openly placed all his affection on this son as he was growing up, to the exclusion of his other sons. The other sons were envious that their father would favor Izates over them, and soon learned to hate Izates. Their father was aware of their concerns and fearful that the brothers might eventually do harm to Izates, he sent him, with many presents, to Abennerig the king of Charax-Spasini, who had agreed to guarantee his preservation. Abennerig gladly received the young man, and because of the great affection he had for him, arranged to have him marry his daughter. He also bequeathed a country to him, from which he received large revenues

When king Monobazus grew old and realized that he had little time to live, he became very desirous of seeing his beloved son. He sent for him, embraced him in the most affectionate manner, and bestowed a country on him called Carae [Carron]. This country has soil with plenty of ammonium, and it also contains the remnants of the ark wherein Noah escaped the deluge. These remnants can still be shown to those who are desirous of seeing them. Izates continued to live in that country until his father died. When king Monobarus died, queen Helena asked all the principal men of the kingdom, and also those who commanded the army, to meet with her. She informed them that her husband was desirous that Izates should succeed him in the government. They voiced their joy that the king had preferred Izates over any of his brothers, because that was also their wish. After expressing themselves in this manner they announced that they wanted permission to slay all the other brothers to insure that their hatred of Izates would not prevent him from receiving the government. Queen Helena thanked them for their courtesy to Izates and to her, but requested that they defer the execution of the brothers until Izates gave his approbation. They also counseled her to assign someone, whom she trusted totally, to be governor of the kingdom until Izates arrived in the country. Queen Helena complied with their counsel and assigned Monobazus II, her eldest son, to be king. She put the diadem on his head, gave him his father's ring with its signet, and exhorted him to administer the affairs of the kingdom until his brother arrived. She then placed the other brothers and certain kinsmen in bonds. Izates came immediately upon learning that his father was dead, and succeeded his brother Monobazus II as king. Izates was then forced to make a decision about his brothers and kinsmen who were in bonds. He did not wish to have them slain or placed in prison, but because it would have been hazardous for him to set them free because of the past threats they had made against him, he sent some of them and their children to Claudius in Rome and the others to Artabanus, the king of Parthia. In these places they were treated as hostages.

When Izates lived in Charax-Spasini, a certain Jewish merchant named Ananias became acquainted with the women who belonged to him, and he taught them to worship God according to Jewish law. After he had been introduced to Izates, through the efforts of the women, Ananias also persuaded him to embrace that religion. Ananias accompanied Izates when he returned to Adiabene upon the death of his father. Upon arriving there Izates learned that another Jew had converted Helena to the Jewish religion. Both Izates and Helena were highly pleased that both of them had embraced the same religion.

After Izates assumed the government, he reached the decision, after much contemplation, that before he could be a complete Jew he must be circumcised. When he informed his mother of his decision, she attempted to dissuade him from doing so. She argued that it would be a dangerous thing for him to be circumcised because his subjects would not consent to be ruled by a Jew who would carry out rites they considered to be strange and foreign. Ananias also agreed that Izates's life would be in danger if he were circumcised, stating that it would be proper for him, under the circumstances, to worship God without being circumcised, for the worship of God is superior to circumcision, and God would forgive him as long as he followed other Jewish laws entirely. So the king complied with the persuasions of Ananias, but nevertheless had a hidden desire to become a complete Jew.

At a later time a Jew named Eleazar of Galilee arrived in Adiabene, who was esteemed to be a learned man in the learning of his country. When he observed king Izates reading the law of Moses, he lectured him on the importance of adhering to all the laws, including the law of circumcision. He stated that not to follow all the laws is injurious to God. After listening to Eleazar, king Izates knew what he had to do, so he retired to another room, called for a surgeon, and was circumcised. He then sent for his mother Helena and his tutor Ananias, and told them what he had done. They were astonished and fearful that if it became public knowledge that he had been circumcised, he would lose the government. His subjects would not tolerate being ruled by a king who was so zealous in another religion. But it was God himself who hindered what they feared from taking place, for he preserved Izates when he faced dangers, and procured his deliverance from precarious situations.

When Helena, the king's mother, saw that the affairs of Izates's kingdom were in peace and that her son was a happy man and admired by all men in his kingdom and even by some foreigners, by the means of God's providence, she decided to travel to Jerusalem to worship at the temple, and to offer her thank-offerings there. She asked her son for permission to go, which he gave willingly. He made preparations for her journey and gave her a great deal of money. He also accompanied her part of the way.

Her arrival in Jerusalem was providential, for the people

there were oppressed by a famine, with many dying for lack of food. She sent some of her servants to Alexandria with money to buy a great quantity of grain, and others to Cyprus to bring back a cargo of dried figs, and she distributed this food to those in need of it. When her son king Izates was informed of this famine, he sent great sums of money to the principal men of Jerusalem to be used to buy food for the populace. At great expense Helena then built pyramids near Jerusalem as a memorial.

Soon after king Izates came to the aid of the Jews in Judea, he came to the assistance of Artabanus, king of the Parthians, and enabled him to retain his government, for which Artabanus rewarded him with many honors. When the king's brother Monobazus II and his other kindred saw how Izates, by his piety to God, was greatly esteemed by all men, they also decided to leave the religion of their country and embrace the customs of the Jews. What they did was soon discovered by Izates's subjects who were greatly displeased by what they had learned. Influential men in the kingdom looked for an opportunity to punish their king and his kin who chose to desert the religion of their country. First they approached Abia, the king of Arabia and promised him great sums of money if he would make an expedition against Izates. Abia complied with their desires but his army was defeated by Izates's army. The influential men then wrote to the king of Parthia and requested that he kill Izates and place over them a ruler who would be a Parthian. At their request, the king of Parthia marched against Izates. With greatly superior forces they were capable of defeating Izates. In preparation for what would be the destruction of Izates and his army, the king of Parthia sent Izates a message which said that the God whom he worshipped could not deliver him out of his hands. Izates then threw himself on the ground, put ashes upon his head, fasted with his wives and children, and called upon God for help. And that same night the king of Parthia received a message that his own country had been invaded by an enemy, and his land had been made a waste. So, the king of Parthia was forced to abandon his siege against the forces of

Chapter 8 Events Occurring When Claudius and Nero were Emperors

Izates and return home immediately. And thus, Izates was saved by the providence of God.

Izates died after he had ruled his kingdom for 24 years, in the 55th year of his life. He left behind 24 sons and 24 daughters. Although one of his sons could have succeeded him, he had given the order that the government should pass to his brother Monobazus II because while he himself had been absent from the country, this brother had faithfully preserved the government for him. His mother queen Helena was greatly saddened by the death of Izates, but was comforted that her eldest son had been named king. Queen Helena died in 50 AD and king Monobazus II sent her bones as well as those of Izates to Jerusalem, with the order that they should be buried at the pyramids which their mother had erected. The site of these pyramids was north of the city, a distance of no more than three furlongs.[78]

Death of King Herod of Chalcis and the Bestowing of His Dominions on Agrippa II

Fadus was replaced [46 AD] as procurator of the kingdom by Tiberius Alexander, who was the son of Alexander, the alabarch of Alexandria, a prominent Jew, who was a principal man among all his contemporaries in Alexandria.[79] Although a Jew by birth Tiberius Alexander defected from the religion of his country. During his term as procurator, Tiberius Alexander crucified two

---

[78] The Jewish convert Monobazus II provided funds for the construction of a monument at the site known as "Tombs of the Kings" where he was buried along with his mother Helena and his brother Izates. The palace of Queen Helena was built in the southeastern part of Jerusalem. This palace was occupied by sons and kinsmen of king Izates during the destruction of Jerusalem by the Romans in 70 AD.

[79] Alexander, the father of Tiberius Alexander, was the tax administrator in Alexandria, who had great influence in Rome. His brother was Philo the famed Jewish philosopher. Alexander was the wealthiest man in Alexandria, and therefore one of the wealthiest men in the Roman empire. Because of the influence of Alexander, his son Tiberius Alexander was given the position as procurator.

sons of Judas the Galilean, who was the founder of the fourth sect of Jewish philosophy. Members of this sect opposed Roman rule, proclaiming that God alone is to be the Ruler and Lord. Judas the Galilean had caused groups of people to revolt when Cyrenius came to take an account of the estates of the Jews following the banishment of Archelaus the ethnarch to Gaul [6 AD].

During the term of Tiberius Alexander as procurator, king Herod of Chalcis removed Josephus, the son of Camydus, from the high priest position and named Ananias, the son of Nebedeus, as his successor.[80] After serving as procurator for two years, Tiberius Alexander was replaced by Cumanus [48 AD].

During the time Cumanus [48 AD to 52 AD] served as procurator, king Herod of Chalcis departed from this world. He died [49 AD] during the eighth year of the reign of Claudius Caesar. Although he had three sons and one of them could have replaced him, **Claudius Caesar chose instead to bestow the dominions of king Herod of Chalcis on Agrippa II, who now became king Agrippa II, ruler of Chalcis. Claudius Caesar also transferred to king Agrippa II the authority over the temple in Jerusalem, control of the sacred treasure, and the right to appoint high priests.**

Tumultuous Events Occurring During the Reign of Cumanus
During the administration of Cumanus an unfortunate event occurred in the city of Jerusalem. During the celebration of the Passover, at which time it was the custom to eat unleavened bread, a great multitude met in the temple and surrounding areas. Fearing that an uprising might occur, Cumanus ordered that troops should stand guard in the temple cloisters. Such precautions had been taken by previous procurators during such festivities. All went well until the fourth day when one of the soldiers let down his breeches

---

80 Ananias, the son of Nebedeus, is the high priest who condemned Paul (Acts, Chapter 24) as a pestilent fellow, a mover of sedition among all the Jews throughout the world, and a ring leader of the sect of the Nazarenes.

Chapter 8 Events Occurring When Claudius and Nero were Emperors

and exposed his private parts to the multitude. The people reacted with fury. A delegation went to Cumanus and asked whether he had ordered the soldier to behave in such a manner. Cumanus was insulted by this charge, and ordered them not to start any tumult at this festivity. He also ordered his whole army to come to Antonia, the fortress overlooking the temple. When the people saw the army in that position, they feared the worst, and began to run away. The passage ways were narrow, and believing that the army was in pursuit, trampling occurred and twenty thousand lives were lost in the stampede. So instead of being a day of festivity, it became the beginning of a period of mourning.

Another tumultuous event occurred before the mourning was over. An unruly group traveling away from Jerusalem along a public road encountered Stephanus, who was Caesar's servant. The group robbed him of all his belongings. When Cumanus heard about this thievery, he ordered his troops to plunder neighboring villages and to bring eminent persons from those villages to him in bonds. During the raids, a soldier seized the Laws of Moses which he had found in a home, and tore it apart while using reproachful language in front of the villagers. Following this insult to their religion, large numbers of citizens rushed to Caesarea where Cumanus was in residence and urged him to make amends. Fearing a major revolt, and upon the advise of friends, Cumanus ordered that the soldier who had offended the Jewish people should be beheaded. This was done to appease the Jewish people and to put a stop to a sedition that was being kindled.

That was not the end of the tumultuous events involving Cumanus. It was the custom of the people of Galilee to travel through Samaria on their way to and from Jerusalem to attend festivals. The road passed through a village known as Ginea. Samaritans from that area on one occasion attacked the traveling Galileans, killing a great many of them. When influential persons from Galilee heard of this crime, they went to Cumanus and urged him to punish those Samaritans who were guilty of the killings.

Cumanus did nothing because he had been bribed with money by the Samaritans The Galileans were irate with his failure to take action, and many of them took an oath to avenge themselves, even though they were urged by principal men among them not to do so, hoping that Cumanus would take the rightful action. The spirited Galileans could not be persuaded, so they took their weapons, and with the aid of bandits from the area, plundered many of the villages of Samaria. When Cumanus heard about their actions, he took four regiments of footmen, armed the Samaritans, and marched against the Jews, killing many of them and taking others captive. With this turn of events, there was much concern and sorrow in Jerusalem, and fearing the consequences for the whole country, principal men among them urged that the participants on both sides return to their homes. Their efforts were successful, and an uneasy peace returned to the area.

Principal persons from Samaria then went to Quadratus, president of Syria, who was then residing in Tyre. They accused the Jews of plundering their villages, thereby showing that they had no respect for the authority of Rome. The Jews replied that the Samaritans were the initiators of this tumult and fighting, and because Cumanus had been corrupted by their gifts, he had refused to bring judgment against the Samaritans. Quadratus responded that he was unable to make a decision until he had further information, and he would give sentence when he visited Samaria and Judea. It was not long before he visited Samaria, where upon hearing cause, he reached the conclusion that the Samaritans were the authors of the disturbance. However, the unbridled retaliatory actions of the Galileans and the bandits had to be avenged, so he ordered those to be crucified whom Cumanus had taken captive. He also learned that some of the Jews who had been put to death had urged a revolt against Rome. As a result he ordered that Ananias the high priest, and Ananus the commander of the temple be placed in bonds and sent to Rome to give an account to Claudius Caesar. Claudius ordered that Cumanus and principal men among the Jews and Samaritans should also go to Rome and meet with the emperor, so that he might

Chapter 8 Events Occurring When Claudius and Nero were Emperors

hear their cause and make a proper decision. With charges being made against Ananias in Rome, king Agrippa II named Jonathan to replace Ananias as high priest.

The day was established when the persons involved were to plead their case before Claudius Caesar. The emperor's freedmen and his friends were zealous in favor of the Samaritans and tried to influence him to favor them, but the Jews had a great benefactor in king Agrippa II who was then residing in Rome. He persuaded Agrippina, the emperor's wife, to convince her husband to hear both sides, and to punish those, who, by their actions, were really disloyal to the Roman government. Claudius Caesar quickly reached the decision that the Samaritans were the ring leaders of the mischievous events. He gave the order that the Samaritans who had come to him should be slain, and that Cumanus the procurator should be banished.

Additional Honors Bestowed on King Agrippa II by Claudius Caesar.

Claudius Caesar sent Felix [in 52 AD] to replace Cumanus as procurator of Judea, and when Claudius Caesar had completed 12 years of his reign as emperor, **he bestowed upon king Agrippa II [in 53 AD] the large tetrarchy formerly ruled by Philip. He also gave him Abila, which had been the tetrarchy of Lysanias. But Claudius Caesar took the small kingdom of Chalcis away from him, which king Agrippa II had ruled for four years. King Agrippa II also retained the administrative responsibility of the temple in Jerusalem with the authority to appoint persons to the high priest position.**

Soon after king Agrippa II had received the large territory to rule, he gave his sister Drusilla in marriage to Azizus, king of Emesa who had consented to be circumcised. This marriage was soon dissolved for the following reason. When Felix became procurator he saw Drusilla and fell in love with her. He sent one of his Jewish friends named Simon to her, to persuade her to forsake her present husband and marry him. Drusilla was thus prevailed upon to transgress the laws of her forefathers and to marry Felix the Roman procurator.[81]

Bernice, who was the sister of king Agrippa II, had been married to Marcus, the son of Alexander of Alexandria and brother of Tiberius Alexander who had been procurator of Judea. When Marcus died she married king Herod of Chalcis, who was her uncle. She had two sons by him. Upon his death she moved into her brother's palace. She became a constant companion of her brother king Agrippa II, accompanying him on many trips, and the rumor spread that she had criminal conversations (an incestuous relationship) with him. She persuaded Polemo, who was king of Cilcia, to be circumcised and marry her, hoping that this marriage would prove the rumor to be false. This marriage did not last long; and Bernice left him, as was said, with impure intentions, and returned to her brother's palace.

Death of Claudius Caesar

Claudius Caesar died [in 54 AD] after he had reigned for 13 years, 8 months, and 20 days. Claudius had three wives. His first wife Pelina gave birth to a daughter named Antonia. His second wife was Messalina, by whom he had Britannicus and Octavia. Out of jealousy, Claudius had Messalina slain. He then married his niece Agrippina. Agrippina's father was Germanicus, the brother of Claudius. She had a son by her first husband who was named Domitius. Following the death of her husband, and a long period as a widow, Claudius married her, adopted her son Domitius, and changed Domitius's name to Nero. He also had his daughter Octavia married to Nero. Agrippina was an ambitious person and

---

81   When Paul was in prison in Caesarea after being condemned by the former high priest, Felix the procurator and his Jewess wife Drusilla sent for Paul and heard him concerning his faith in Christ (Acts 24: 24). Felix kept him in prison for two years in order not to antagonize the Jews of Jerusalem.

Chapter 8 Events Occurring When Claudius and Nero were Emperors

was desirous that her son Nero should succeed Claudius as emperor, but feared that his son Britannicus was destined for that position. To hurry the process she took steps to have Claudius poisoned, and then arranged for the general of the army, tribunes, and freedmen with authority to take Nero to the army camp and salute him as emperor. As soon as Nero had received the government, he had his competitor Britannicus poisoned. At a later time Nero also had his own mother put to death. He also ordered the death of his wife Octavia, and many other illustrious persons, under the pretense that they plotted against him.

During the first year of his reign, Nero's entrusted Aristobulus, the son of Herod, king of Chalcis, with the government of Lesser Armenia. **Nero also bestowed on king Agrippa II, a certain part of Galilee, including Tiberius, and Tarichae, and ordered the residents to submit to his jurisdiction. He also gave him Julias, a city of Perea, and 14 villages[82] that lay about it.**

Felix soon acquired an ill-will towards Jonathan the high-priest who frequently gave him admonitions on how to govern Jewish affairs. So Felix plotted against him by persuading one of Jonathan's most faithful friends, with the name of Doras, to bring robbers into Jerusalem and kill Jonathan. Doras was promised a large sum of money for participating in this treacherous act. The robbers were a special group called Sicarii who slew men in the

---

82   During the time of king Herod and the tetrarch Herod Antipas, the territory of Perea had relatively well-defined borders, but with passing years Perea became generally known as that region east of the Jordan River extending from the east side of the Dead Sea to the southeastern side of the Sea of Galilee, and therefore including part of Decapolis which was ruled by Syria. The northern border of Decapolis in that region changed with time depending on who ruled the major cities and villages. Those decisions were made by the emperor in Rome. For example, Hippos and Gadara were ruled by king Herod during the later years of his life, but after his death these cities and surrounding areas were given to Syria. The city of Julias was built on the shore of the Sea of Galilee by Philip when that region was part of his tetrarchy. That tetrarchy was ruled by Syria upon the death of Philip, but as noted by Josephus, during the first year of Nero's reign, the city of Julias (a city of Perea) and 14 villages that lay about it, was given to king Agrippa II. Both Jewish and Roman-Grecian cities and villages developed in the northern region of Perea, with varying proportions of Jewish and gentile residents.

day time in the midst of the city. They did this chiefly at festivals by mingling with the multitude. With concealed daggers under their garments they would enter the city as if they were there for a special purpose, such as to worship God in the temple. While in a crowd of people they would single out their victim, stab him, quickly conceal their weapon, and then along with others standing by, openly express indignation at the wickedness of the crime. They killed Jonathan by using this method. The Sicarii became more numerous and more bold. At later festivals they slew many others, including their enemies and persons they intended to rob. They even had the boldness to murder men in the temple, without thinking of the impiety of which they were guilty.[83]

Following the murder of Jonathan, king Agrippa II gave the high priesthood to Ismael, who was the son of Fabi.

---

83   Following the banishment of Archelaus in 6 BC and the arrival of Roman procurators in Judea, Judas the Galilean became a spokesman against the repression of the pagan Roman rule. He became the helmsman for the political party, described by Josephus as the fourth sect of Jewish philosophy, which agreed in all things with the Pharisees but professed that God is to be their only leader. The members of this sect were willing to die for their beliefs. They were so zealous in their actions that they became known as the **zealots.** The membership consisted mostly of young men who were idealists in their philosophy, and their numbers grew when Roman procurators became more oppressive in their actions. Their opposition to Roman rule was unswerving, and they believed that God would assist them in the final confrontation with the Romans. They were quick to oppose Jews who favored peace with the Romans. Although this underground movement attracted idealists, it was also a refuge for men with unsavory reputations (described as robbers by Josephus) who used the group as an opportunity for personal or political gain. Extremists among the zealots were known as the Sicarii (from the Greek for "dagger men."). They grew in prominence in about 54 AD, by their modus operandi, as described by Josephus, of concealing daggers under their garments, and using these daggers for murdering those who opposed them, or those whom they intended to rob. These unsavory types would attack and rob Jews who were sympathetic to the Romans, or were in opposition to their cause or methods. They also attacked and robbed innocent Jews using the pretense that they were in opposition to their cause. Rationalization for their thievery was the need of resources for the good and survival of their sect. At the time of the Jewish revolt against the Romans, the zealots were a major force in Jerusalem. They led the battles against the Roman armies. However infighting and competition for power among factions of zealots were destructive and led to disastrous conditions within Jerusalem when the Jews were preparing for the attack by the Romans, and even when Roman armies were assaulting the walls of the city.

Chapter 8 Events Occurring When Claudius and Nero were Emperors

The Decision Nero Made Against the Jews in Caesarea and the Consequences of that Decision

A serious rift, with an eventual disastrous outcome, occurred between the Jews and Syrians who lived in Caesarea concerning who had greater rights of citizenship. The Jews claimed preeminence because Herod the Great was the builder of Caesarea, and he was a Jew by birth. The Syrians did not debate the role of Herod the Great, but contended that Caesarea was formerly called Strato's Tower, and at that time not a single Jew resided there. The Syrians also pointed out that because of the presence of Roman temples and images, Caesarea was clearly not a Jewish city. A contributing cause was that the wealthy inhabitants of the city tended to be Jewish, which was resented by the Syrians and other gentiles who were jealous of their achievements. The Syrians had the support of the Roman soldiers who were stationed there. From the latter days of king Agrippa these soldiers were offensive towards the Jewish inhabitants of that city. The issue became volatile with exchanges of words, physical fighting, and the throwing of rocks. When Felix saw that this argument was becoming a kind of war, he ordered the Jews to desist, which they refused to obey. So Felix turned his soldiers on the Jews, killing many of them, and putting others in bonds. He also allowed his soldiers to plunder the Jewish homes that were full of riches. Moderate Jews then pleaded with Felix to spare them from further attacks by the soldiers, which he agreed to do.

Principal Jewish inhabitants of Caesarea then went to Rome to seek an audience with Nero and to accuse Felix of murdering Jews and plundering their homes. Before they arrived, Nero had made the decision to replace Felix as procurator by Porcius Festus, who was then on route to Judea. **An important event then occurred.** Two principal Syrians in Caesarea were able to bribe Burrhus, who was Nero's influential tutor and secretary for his Greek epistles, to convince Nero to side with the Syrians of Caesarea. **An epistle was written by Nero that denied the Jewish citizens the equality of privileges that they had hitherto enjoyed in that city. The meaning of this epistle was of great concern to Jews throughout** the Roman empire, and especially to those Jews living in Caesarea.[84]

Many problems faced Festus the new procurator.[85] Members of the fourth sect became more politically active, and by doing so, gained many followers. These zealots openly expressed resentment of the presence of the Romans and promoted revolt as the only means of obtaining freedom. The Sicarii, who were the radicals among the zealots, also increased in numbers and became more active. In addition to mingling with the crowds at festivals and stabbing and robbing persons, they also proceeded to burn and plunder villages. Festus sent forces, both horsemen and footmen, to destroy members of the Sicarii and to quell the seditions. Another group of persons preying on the multitude were the impostors who poised as prophets who proclaimed to their followers that they would deliver freedom

---

84　　This epistle was a major turning point in the relationship between Judea and Rome. Whereas the Jews had experienced remarkable freedom of religion under Claudius Caesar, his successor Nero was now proclaiming that the Jews of Caesarea (and in essence elsewhere) could be denied basic freedoms. The racist tone of this doctrine written by the Roman emperor gave license to Gessius Florus, who succeeded Albinus as procurator, to commit atrocities against the Jews for his own material benefit. This behavior was the primary cause of the revolt of the Jews against the Romans.

85　　Festus arrived in Caesarea as procurator and three days later he traveled to Jerusalem (Acts, Chapter 25, 26). The high priest urged Festus to return Paul to Jerusalem so he could be judged, knowing that persons would lay in wait for Paul and kill him. Upon his return to Caesarea, Festus asked Paul if he would return to Jerusalem to be judged, but Paul, knowing the consequences, requested to be judged instead by Caesar in Rome. After conferring with his council, Festus told Paul that since he had appealed unto Caesar, "unto Caesar shall thou go." Several days later king Agrippa II and his sister Bernice arrived in Caesarea to salute Festus. Festus commented to them that Felix (the former Procurator) had left a certain man (Paul) in bonds in Caesarea (for two years). After hearing the circumstances of the case king Agrippa requested that he be allowed to hear what Paul had to say. The next day Agrippa, Bernice, the chief captains, and principal men of the city entered the place of the hearing, and at Festus's command, Paul was brought into the room. After hearing Paul bear his testimony, king Agrippa announced that Paul had almost persuaded him to be a Christian. At the conclusion of the meeting, the governor, king Agrippa, and Bernice talked among themselves and concluded that Paul had done nothing worthy of death or bonds. King Agrippa then said to Festus that Paul might have been set free if he had not appealed to be heard by Caesar.

Chapter 8 Events Occurring When Claudius and Nero were Emperors

from their miseries, and from the Romans, if they would just follow them.

About this same time king Agrippa II built himself a very large dining room in the royal palace at Jerusalem formerly occupied by the Hasmonean leaders. This palace was at a high elevation and from the dining room he had a unique view of the city. Its location also allowed him to see what was happening within the walls of the temple while he was eating. The chief men of Jerusalem were displeased with this dining room, because it was the law that what was done in the temple, and what was offered as sacrifices, could not be viewed by others. Therefore they erected a large wall upon the uppermost building that obstructed the view from the palace dining room. It also disrupted the view of the Roman guards who stood guard at another location at the time of festivals. Both king Agrippa II and Festus the procurator were displeased with the presence of the wall, but especially Festus, who ordered the Jews to remove it. The Jews petitioned him to allow them to take the case to Nero in Rome, by arguing that they could not endure to live if any part of their temple were destroyed. Festus agreed that they could seek an audience with Nero, and allowed ten of them to make the journey, in addition to Ismael the high priest and Helcias, the keeper of the sacred treasure. When Nero heard what they had to say, he forgave them for building the wall and allowed it to stand. He had been influenced by his wife Poppea, who was a religious person and who had requested that he honor the request of the Jewish ambassadors. She then urged that the ten ambassadors should be allowed to return to the home land, but Ismael and Helcias should be retained as hostages.

As soon as king Agrippa II heard that Ismael was being held in Rome, he appointed Joseph, who was called Cabi, as high priest. He was the son of Simon who had formerly been high priest.

Josephus

The Death of James, Brother of Jesus

Upon the sudden death of Festus [in 60 AD], Nero sent Albinus to Judea as procurator. Before Albinus arrived in Judea, king Agrippa II deprived Joseph of the high priesthood, and bestowed that dignity on Ananus, who was the son of Ananus. [This elder Ananus, who was the son of Seth, had served formerly as high priest. Five of his sons and a son-in-law had also served as high priest.] The younger Ananus was a member of the Sadducees sect, and members of this sect were very rigid in judging offenders. Ananus, upon being named high priest, took the opportunity to exercise his authority, and one of his first acts was to call an assembly of the sanhedrin of judges, and bring before them James, the brother of Jesus, who was called Christ, and some others.

Book XX Chapter IX, Antiquities of the Jews

"So he assembled the sanhedrin of Judges, and brought before them the brother of Jesus, who was called Christ, and some others [or, some of his companions]; and when he had formed an accusation against them as breakers of the law; he delivered them to be stoned."

Those who were the most equitable of the citizens, disliked what he had done, and they sent a message to king Agrippa II, urging him to inform Ananus that he should not act in such a manner, for what he had done could not be justified. Some of the citizens also went to meet Albinus who was traveling to Judea from Alexandria. They informed him that it was not lawful for Ananus to assemble the sanhedrim without his consent. Upon learning that Ananus had condemned James (brother of Jesus who was called Christ) and others[86], Albinus wrote to Ananus in anger, and threatened to punish

---

86   Several references are given in the New Testament of the brothers and sisters of Jesus. The brothers (James, Joses, Judas, and Simon) are named in Mark 6:3 and Matthew 13:55-56. Tradition states that his brothers did not believe in him (John 7:35), but that changed when Jesus appeared to James following his resurrection (1 Corinthians 15:7). With full faith in the divinity of his brother, James then became a major leader in the early

Chapter 8 Events Occurring When Claudius and Nero were Emperors

him for what he had done. King Agrippa II reacted by taking the

Christian church in Jerusalem, and was known as James the Just and James the Righteous. This situation is not fully delineated in the writings included in the New Testament. It has been proposed by many different New Testament scholars that beginning in the Second Century there was a concerted effort to downplay the role of James, the brother of Jesus Christ, in the history of Christianity. The reason was to turn attention away from the possibility that Jesus had younger siblings born to Mary. Based on the supernatural birth of Jesus presented in Luke and Matthew, *Mary's perpetual virginity* became a theological affirmation of Christianity during the Second Century. Thus, Mary could not have had any additional children, even though Jesus is clearly said to be her "firstborn son" in Matthew 1:25 and Luke 2:7, which implies she later gave birth to other sons. In essence, the one-child family consisted of Joseph, Mary, and Jesus, and it was often inferred that any stated brothers and sisters of Jesus were actually cousins or "half-siblings" born to Joseph by an earlier wife. There is no mention in any of the gospels and letters in the New Testament, or in any other early Christian writing, that Joseph was a widower when betrothed to Mary. When the family of Jesus is mentioned in John (2:1-11, 12; 7:3-51 19:25-27) or Mark (3:31-35; 6:3-4) the brothers and sisters of Jesus are presented as if they are full biological siblings. Paul (Gal 1:18-19; 2:9) refers to James as the brother of the Lord. Gnostic gospels such as the Gospel of Thomas and Gospel of Hebrews also refer to James as the brother of Jesus. The same situation is true of Josephus and early Christian writings referred to by Eusebius in his *Ecclesiastical History* written after AD 325. These many references, without any qualification, were problems for the proponents of perpetual virginity, and one apparent solution beginning during the Second Century was to eliminate discussions of James when possible from the early writings, or by not designating who he really was and thereby allowing him to be confused with James the son of Zebedee and brother of John, James the son of Alphaeus, or some other James. When James is first introduced in Acts 12:17 as a major leader of the Jerusalem Christian church, there is no mention that he was the brother of Jesus or how he arrived at the position he was occupying. It is told in Acts 12 that Herod (King Agrippa 1) in order to vex the church had James the brother of John killed with the sword, and because he saw that it pleased the Jews, he proceeded to apprehend Peter (during the Passover) and place him in prison. The night before King Agrippa 1 was to deliver him to the people, an angel appeared to Peter and set him free. Peter fled to the house of Mary the mother of John, whose surname was Mark, where many were gathering and praying. They were astonished to see him. Acts 12:17 states that he told them how had he had gotten out of prison, and before he departed to another place he asked them to tell these things *to "James and to the brethren."* James, the brother of Jesus, cannot be confused here with James, the brother of John, because the latter James had previously been killed by King Agrippa I. The prominence of James as one of the leaders of the Jerusalem Christian church is contained in the writings of Paul. Gal 1:18-19 reads, *"Then after three years I went up to Jerusalem to see Peter, and abode with him fifteen days. But other of the apostles saw I none, save James the Lord's brother."* Fourteen years later he returned once again to Jerusalem (Gal 2:9) and met with "three pillars" of the church, James, Cephas (i.e., Peter), and John. The prominence of James is also indicated in Acts 15:13, Acts: 15:19 and Acts 21:18. In all situations the name of James is presented first when mentioned with other leaders of the Christian movement, such as Peter and John, suggesting that James was the person of authority. Supporting this

high priesthood away from Ananus (who held the position for only

view is the role James played in resolving whether circumcision was a requirement of gentiles who were followers of Jesus. This controversial situation is introduced in Acts 15:1 where it is stated that certain men from Jerusalem had gone to Antioch and taught the doctrine that *"Except ye be circumcised, after the manner of Moses, ye cannot be saved."* Greatly concerned about this situation Paul and others traveled to Jerusalem to learn from the apostles and elders of the church whether this doctrine represented their view (Acts 15:2). At the council meeting where both views were presented, it was James who made the decision (Acts 15:19). He decreed that gentiles who have turned to God did not need to be circumcised as long as they abstained from eating food offered to idols, from fornication, from eating animals that have been strangled, and from eating blood (i.e. under cooked meat). Because this decree came from the brother of Jesus, who was the person of authority in Jerusalem, it is likely that the future of Christianity among gentiles would have been altered if James had made a different decision. Although some of the accounts lack historical credibility, the authority of James is also reported in the early Christian literature. Clement (quoted by Eusebius) wrote "Peter, James and John, after the Ascension of the Savior, as if preferred by the Savior, did not struggle for glory, but chose James the Just as the Bishop of Jerusalem." However, another quotation from Eusebius indicates that James had the leadership role from the time of the resurrection. It is also implied in Eusebius that James was chosen as the leader because he was the brother of Jesus. Eusebius gives the names of the fifteen persons who served in the prestigious position as Bishop of the Jerusalem Church, with the first being James the brother of Jesus Christ. The second was Symeon (son of Clopas) who was the cousin of James because Clopas was the brother of Joseph. The others were Justus, Zacchaeus, Tobias, Benjamin, John, Matthias, Philip, Seneca, Justus, Leir, Epres, Joseph, and Judas. Hegesippus (quoted by Eusebius) gives an account of the death of James, who was taken into custody and demanded to deny his faith in Christ in the presence of the people. When he refused to do so, he was thrown down from the pinnacle of the Temple, stoned, and finally killed by a fuller's club (62 AD). Following this event plots were made against the other Apostles, and they had to flee from Jerusalem to save their lives. According to Eusebius, the people of Jerusalem, who believed in Christ, were commanded by an oracle to depart from Jerusalem and go to the city of Pella in Perea beyond the Jordan River. A footnote in Eusebius states that Pella was located in northern Perea, within the territory of king Agrippa II, and the people in the vicinity of Pella were for the greater part Gentiles. Pella may have been one of the 14 villages given to king Agrippa II during the first year of the reign of Nero (See Footnote #13 in this Chapter). The departure to Pella occurred just before Jerusalem and surrounding areas were destroyed by the Romans. Eusebius wrote that after the destruction of Jerusalem by the Romans, the Apostles and disciples of the Lord who were still alive, along with available family members of the Lord, returned to Jerusalem, took counsel together, and unanimously decided that Symeon son of Clopas was worthy of serving as the second Bishop of Jerusalem. The succeeding bishops of Jerusalem, whose terms were short-lived, served up to the time of the rule of the Roman Emperor Hadrian (117-138 AD). The Jews were then driven out of Jerusalem by Hadrian. That was the end of the historic Christian church in Jerusalem, headed in the beginning by James the brother of Jesus. The mission of James (as was the mission of Jesus) was to the Jewish people who followed the Mosaic law (including circumcision), and he expected Jesus to return momentarily as the Messiah to

Chapter 8 Events Occurring When Claudius and Nero were Emperors

three months), and gave it to Jesus, son of Damneus.

Problems then started to occur in the temple. The elder Ananus [who had formerly been high priest and whose five sons and son-in-law had been given this honor] continued to increase in power each day.[87] He was a hoarder of money, and he cultivated the friendship of the Roman governor Albinus and the high priest Jesus by giving them presents. He also had servants who were wicked. They went to the thrashing-floors and took away by violence the tithes that belonged to the priests, and they did not refrain from beating those who would not give the tithes to them. Following the pattern set by the elder Ananus, certain other high priests acted in a similar manner, as did their servants, without anyone being able to prevent them from doing so. Some of the priests who were old, and who were supported totally by these tithes, died for want of food. This impudent behavior and corruption by persons of authority in the temple cast a dark shadow on the holiness of the temple, causing much discontent and loss of faith in the priesthood leadership by members of the multitude.

As soon as Albinus arrived in Jerusalem, he made every effort to bring peace to the country by destroying many of the Sicarii. But the Sicarii continued to be seditious. They went into the city by night and captured the scribe belonging to the governor of the temple. This governor was Eleazar the son of the elder Ananus. The Sicarii bound the scribe and carried him out of the city. They then sent a ransom note to Ananus stating that they would release him if

---

Jerusalem where he would bring about everlasting social and economic reforms. But the growth of Christianity occurred elsewhere among the gentiles, and with time the importance of James in early Christianity was minimized or ignored.

87 This section describes the corruptness of the elder Ananus, the son of Seth, who was an influential person in the Temple. His son-in-law Caiaphas was high priest when Jesus of Nazareth was condemned, and his son Ananus had James, the brother of Jesus Christ, stoned to death. Although there was only one high priest (who was the presiding officer), persons who had held that position formerly were also dignified by *being* called high priest. They often remained active in temple activities, and because of their seniority and influence, some had great power, such as Ananus, the son of Seth.

Albinus would release 10 prisoners who belonged to their group. Ananus made this request to Albinus, who obliged and released the 10 prisoners. This success caused the robbers to become more bold, and they proceeded to kidnap servants belonging to Ananus, stating again that they would not be released until they recovered some of their own Sicarii. The bold actions of the Sicarii and other robbers, who were increasing in numbers, became a great concern for the whole country.

Albinus was soon despised as a governor by the populace of Judea because he executed his office as governor in a heinous manner. He had his hand in any sort of wickedness that could be imagined. He burdened the entire nation with excessive taxes and also stole and plundered everyone's substance. When Albinus heard that Gessius Florus was coming to succeed him as procurator, he became desirous to do something that he thought would endear him to the citizens of Jerusalem. He killed prisoners who he thought were worthy of death, but all other prisoners were dismissed after money had been taken from them. The consequences were that the prisons were now empty, but the country gained many more robbers.

About this time king Agrippa II built Caesarea Philippi larger than it was before and renamed it Neronias, in honor of Nero.[88] King Agrippa II also built at great expense a theater at Berytus, where shows were presented each year. He also adorned that city with statues, making it a show place. His subjects were disturbed by the high cost and the continuing use of their funds, obtained by taxation, for enhancing that city. As a consequence he acquired many enemies. He then caused controversy by replacing Jesus the son of Damneus with Jesus the son of Gamaliel as high priest. This appointment was not favored by certain principal men of the temple, and a rift occurred among them. They resorted to speaking in a reproaching manner to each other, and even throwing stones at each other. The elder Ananus, because of his wealth, was able to bring

---

88 Upon the death of Nero, the name of this city reverted back to Caesarea Philippi because of the extreme misery that Nero caused the Jews.

Chapter 8 Events Occurring When Claudius and Nero were Emperors

receptive men to his point of view and resolve the concern of this appointment. Nevertheless, king Agrippa II soon deprived Jesus the son of Gamaliel of the high priesthood, and gave it to Matthias the son of Theophilus, under whom the Jew's war with the Romans was initiated

The High Priest Position in Judea

According to history, Aaron, the brother of Moses, officiated as high priest. After his death, he was succeeded by his sons, and in later generations, it became the custom that no one could assume the high priest position unless he was a descendant of Aaron. At the beginning of the Hasmonean era, Judas Maccabeus was named to be high priest and ruler. This position then remained in the Hasmonean family line until Antigonus was defeated and king Herod appointed Ananelus to be high priest.

In the early years the newly appointed high priest retained the position until his death, but beginning with Herod the Great, the person holding the position could be replaced at any time. Beginning with Ananelus, 28 persons held this position until Jerusalem and the temple were destroyed by the Romans in 70 AD. Twenty seven of the 28 High Priests were appointed by a King or Ethnarch, (appointed by Rome) or by a representative of Rome (governor, senator, or president of Syria). Many were not qualified for the premiere position as High Priest, who was expected to perform sacred ceremonies in the Temple and be the religious leader of the people. These 27 High Priests served at the will of the appointer and hence their allegiance was to that person and not to the Jewish people or to the ideals of the position. Because of the political nature of these appointments the tenure of a High Priest was often tarnished by corruption. The assignment of Phannias the son of Samuel (#28) to the position was done in a bogus manner (See Chapter 10).

Josephus

High Priest	Appointed by:
1. Ananelus	King Herod
2. Aristobulus	King Herod
3. Jesus, the son of Phabet (Fabus)	King Herod
4. Simon, the son of Boethus	King Herod
5. Matthias, the son of Theophilus	King Herod
6. Joazar, the son of Boethus	King Herod
7. Eleazar, the son of Boethus	Archelaus the Ethnarch
8. Jesus, the son of Sie	Archelaus the Ethnarch
9. Ananus, the son of Seth	Cyrenius the Senator
10. Ismael, the son of Fabus	Gratus the Procurator
11. Eleazar, the son of Ananus	Gratus the Procurator
12. Simon, the son of Camithus	Gratus the Procurator
13. Caiaphus, son-in-law to Ananus	Valerius the Procurator
14. Jonathan, the son of Ananus	Vitellius, president of Syria

Chapter 8 Events Occurring When Claudius and Nero were Emperors

15. Theophilus, the son of Ananus	Vitellius, president of Syria
16. Simon, the son of Boethus	King Agrippa
17. Matthias, the son of Ananus	King Agrippa
18. Elioneus, son of Cantheras	King Agrippa
19. Josephus, the son of Camydus	King Herod of Chalcis
20. Ananias, the son of Nebedeus	King Herod of Chalcis
21. Jonathan	King Agrippa II
22. Ismael, the son of Fabi	King Agrippa II
23. Joseph Cabi, the son of Simon	King Agrippa II
24. Ananus, the son of Ananus	King Agrippa II
25. Jesus, the son of Damneus	King Agrippa II
26. Jesus, the son of Gamaliel	King Agrippa II
27. Matthias, the son of Theophilus	King Agrippa II
28. Phannias the son of Samuel	Zealots

Josephus

Chapter 9

THE BEGINNING OF THE JEWISH REVOLT AGAINST ROME

Gessius Florus, who succeeded Albinus [in 64 AD] as procurator, filled Judea with an abundance of miseries. Florus brought with him to Judea his wife Cleopatra, who was a close friend of Nero's wife Poppea. It was this friendship that allowed Florus to obtain the position as governor. Florus was so mischievous and so violent in the use of his authority, that the Jews actually remembered Albinus as being their benefactor. Florus, in a pompous manner, made no effort to conceal his wickedness. Nor could anyone outdo him in disguising the truth. He thought it was such a petty offense to obtain money from individuals, that he plundered entire cities. It was almost as if he had the license to personally obtain the riches of the nation. He also became a partner with the robbers that imposed themselves on the country, by sharing in the results of their plundering, and making no effort to punish them for their crimes. There were no bounds to the miseries of the Jews who had to bear the devastations caused by Florus and the robbers. Those Jews who were able to do so began moving away from Judea, believing that they could dwell more easily elsewhere than in their own country. And it was this Florus who ultimately caused the Jewish people in Judea to take up arms against the Romans, believing that it is better to be destroyed at once, than little by little.

Because of the fear of Florus, no one dared send ambassadors to Cestius (Roman president of Syria) for the purpose of bringing charges against Florus. However, when Cestius arrived in Jerusalem to attend the feast of the unleavened bread, no fewer than three million people besought him to commiserate the calamities of the country and to blame Florus for their miseries. Florus was present when these charges were leveled at him. He stood by the side of Cestius and laughed at their words. Cestius quieted the multitude and assured them that in the future Florus would treat them in a gentler manner. Cestius then returned to Antioch, with Florus accompanying him as far as Caesarea. On this trip Florus deluded Cestius, for although he suggested otherwise, he intended to continue showing his anger toward the Jews. And fearing that influential persons such as king Agrippa II or Cestius might send negative reports about him to Rome, he encouraged the Jews in a deceptive manner to revolt against Roman rule, believing that open warfare would draw attention away from the extent of his crimes against the Jewish people.

A major conflagration leading to the revolt of the Jews against the Romans took place in Caesarea [66 AD] in the 12th year of the reign of Nero, and in the 17th year of the reign of king Agrippa II. The Syrians of Caesarea had previously obtained a decree from Nero giving them authority over the Jews in determining governmental judicial matters. This decree, which denied the Jews of that city their civil rights, made living difficult for the Jews who resided there. A conflict with serious consequences occurred when the Jews attempted to purchase land adjacent to their synagogue. The owner was a Caesarean Greek. He refused their financial offer which was many times higher than the value of the property. Then in a defiant manner he began to construct buildings (work shops) on the property that would allow only a narrow passageway to the synagogue. Young and bold Jews wishing to take matters into their own hands went to the workmen and forbade them to continue their work. Prominent Jews also went to Florus and gave him money which he accepted with the promise that he would stop the construction of the workshops. Upon obtaining the money Florus departed for Sebaste, allowing the controversy to take its full course. A young Grecian then got an earthen vessel, set it with the bottom

Chapter 9 The Beginning of the Jewish Revolt Against Rome

upward at the entrance to the synagogue, and sacrificed birds on it. Such a sacrifice is to cleanse a leper and doing it at the entrance of the synagogue implied that the Jews were a leprous people and the synagogue was polluted. The Jewish people were furious. The older and moderate Jews wished to bring this matter before the governor, but many of the young Jews, because of the fervor of their youth, wanted to fight. Certain Syrians were also ready to fight the Jews because they were the ones who had sent the man to sacrifice the birds on the earthen vessel in front of the synagogue. Fighting commenced, and many Jews escaped to Narbata (7.5 miles away) taking with them their books of law. Twelve principal men among them then went to Sebaste to complain to Florus, and to remind him that he had been given money by them to stop the construction of the workshops on the property. He responded by accusing them of carrying their books of law out of Caesarea without authority. He then put them into prison.

Florus enflamed the situation further by sending persons to Jerusalem with the order to take 17 talents from the sacred treasure, with the explanation that Nero wanted the money. In retaliation, and in an effort to mock Florus and to cast reproaches on him, young zealots carried a basket around Jerusalem begging in a mocking manner for contributions of money for Florus as if he were destitute of any possessions and in a miserable condition. Florus was enraged by this mockery, and instead of going from Sebaste to Caesarea and quenching the flames of war that were starting there, he gathered an army and marched towards Jerusalem. It was his plan to use the Roman forces to terrorize the Jews in Jerusalem and subject them to his total authority. When the Jews learned of this event, they planned to mock him further by meeting him with acclamations and receiving him submissively. Knowing their intention, Florus ordered that his horsemen disperse them before they could salute him or manifest any submissive behavior. Following this encounter the Jews retired to their homes and spent the night in fear and confusion.

Florus then took up residency in the palace, and the next day called the high priest, men of power, and those of greatest eminence in the city to sit before him. He commanded them to deliver to him those who had reproached him, stating that they would be subjects of his vengeance if they did not produce the criminals. They begged him to forgive those persons who acted improperly because of their youth, immaturity, and foolishness. They also commented that it was impossible to distinguish those who offended from the rest. To provide for the peace of the nation and to preserve the city for the Romans, they urged him to forgive the few that were guilty. Florus was highly provoked at this response and ordered his soldiers to plunder the Upper Market Place in the city, and to slay anyone they met. With this license for material gain, the soldiers plundered as told and in addition forced themselves into many houses, killing the inhabitants. They also captured persons known or suspected to have mocked Florus in a submissive manner. These persons were then brought before Florus, who had them whipped and then crucified. The number of persons killed that day, including wives and children (and even infants), was about 3,600. What made this calamity even more unusual was that Florus did something that no other Roman governor had done before. He had Jews whipped and crucified even if they had the dignity of being Roman citizens. According to Roman laws, this should not have occurred.[89]

About this time king Agrippa II was traveling to Alexandria, to congratulate Tiberius Alexander on being named governor of Egypt by Nero.[90] While he was on that journey his sister Bernice, who was his constant companion, came to Jerusalem to perform a vow of 30 days of fasting and to make preparations for a sacrifice. Upon witnessing the plundering and vicious killings, she begged Florus

---

[89] Paul had been protected by centurions because although a Jew, he was a Roman citizen. Acts, Chapter 23: 27.

[90] Tiberius Alexander, the son of the wealthy Alexander of Alexandria and the nephew of Philo, the Jewish philosopher, had previously been governor of Judea from 46 to 48 AD.

Chapter 9 The Beginning of the Jewish Revolt Against Rome

to spare the Jews. He would not comply with her requests, and she had to flee to the palace where she was protected by guards from the madness of the soldiers. No regard was given her by Florus, even though she was the sister of king Agrippa II, the daughter of king Agrippa, and the wife of a former king (King Herod of Chalcis).

The high priests were so frightened by the events that had occurred, that they urged the multitude to be submissive. Florus was troubled that the disturbances might be over, and he tried to kindle the flames of war once again. He sent for the high priests and told them that they should urge a multitude of persons to go out and meet the soldiers who were coming from Caesarea. Previously he had informed the soldiers not to return the salutations of the Jews who would meet them, and if the Jews replied in any discourteous manner, they should use their weapons against them. When the high priests assembled the multitude in the temple and instructed them to go out and meet the Romans, the young zealots objected, and only agreed to do so out of consideration for those who had already been killed. As instructed, a large group went out to meet the soldiers, and at the proper time saluted them in a courteous manner. When the soldiers did not return the salute, some of the younger Jews made uncomplimentary remarks against them which was the signal that the soldiers should attack them. The soldiers struck the multitude with clubs, and as the Jews tried to flee away, the horsemen trampled them, killing many of them. Others were killed by the stampede that occurred. There was a terrible crowding at the gates of the city, and the soldiers beat anyone in their path, without showing any mercy. The soldiers then tried to seize the temple and obtain the treasures found there, but the Jews began throwing darts from the tops of their houses, and forced the Romans to retreat. Fearing that the soldiers might obtain access to the temple through Antonia, the Jews climbed upon the cloisters that joined the temple with Antonia, and forced them away. Realizing that his attempt to obtain the treasures of the temple had failed, Florus called off the siege. He then met with the high priests and members of the sanhedrin, and told them that he was returning to Caesarea, but would leave a garrison to maintain peace.

Upon returning to Caesarea, Florus wrote to Cestius, president of Syria, and accused the Jews of revolting against the Roman government and blaming them for the disturbances that had occurred. In rebuttal, influential leaders in Jerusalem and also Bernice, the sister of king Agrippa II, wrote to Cestius complaining about the illegal actions of Florus. Upon reading both accounts, Cestius conferred with his captains for advice. Some of them thought it best to send an army to Jerusalem to learn the true state of affairs. If the Jews were truly revolting, the army should punish the Jews, but if the Jews were still loyal to Rome, the army should settle their affairs peacefully. Cestius decided to send one of his intimate friends to Jerusalem, whose name was Neopolitanus, with the expectation that he would give him an honest account of what was happening.

At this time king Agrippa II was returning from Alexandria. Neopolitanus met him in Jamnia and informed him of the purpose of his mission. It was also in Jamnia that the high priests and members of the sanhedrin also met with king Agrippa II, where they congratulated him on his safe return from Alexandria. After paying him respects, they informed him of the tyranny and cruelty of Florus. The group then traveled to Jerusalem. They were met 7.5 miles out of Jerusalem by people who came to greet them, including the wives of those who had been killed by Florus's soldiers. They lamented about the miseries Florus had caused them. When they entered the city they showed king Agrippa II and Neopolitanus the market place that had been made desolate and the homes that had been plundered. Neopolitanus was encouraged to walk around the city with only one servant to learn by himself whether there had been a revolt against Rome or only a revolt against the barbarity of Florus. He followed this suggestion and assessed the situation by conversing with many different persons. After doing so he called the multitude together in the temple and commended them for their fidelity to Rome, and

Chapter 9 The Beginning of the Jewish Revolt Against Rome

urged them to keep the peace. He then traveled to Caesarea, on the first leg of his journey to give his report to Cestius.

The multitude then urged king Agrippa II to send ambassadors to Nero in Rome to complain against Florus. King Agrippa II knew that it was too dangerous at that time to accuse Florus in front of Nero, but he also knew that the serious concerns of the people should not be ignored. It was apparent to him that many, and especially the younger ones, [i.e. the zealots] were eager for immediate war. So he called the multitude together in a large gallery, placed his sister Bernice in a position so they could all see her, and spoke to them. In a long and emotional speech king Agrippa II counseled the multitude to consider the consequences of going to war against the Romans, realizing that certain groups among them [i.e, members of the fourth sect] were disposed to initiate the revolt because of their belief that only God should be our ruler. He was concerned about the youth who had not experienced the miseries of war, in addition to those who had an unreasonable expectation of gaining freedom. He said that although certain procurators had been severe in their actions, not all of them in the past had been injurious, and neither had Nero, whom you would be going to war against. *Those in authority that live in the west cannot see those that live in the east; nor is it easy for them there even to hear what is done in the east.* This statement was to implore the Jews to have patience and to understand that influential authorities in Rome often do not know what certain procurators are doing in Judea, and when they learn that unjust acts have been done, they will make the needed changes. He reminded them that the present procurator will not serve forever, but will eventually be replaced by another, and with that replacement tolerable conditions may occur once again. He told them to reflect on the vastness of the Roman empire and the power of the Roman armies that control the world. He then asked them questions: What sort of an army do you rely on? Where are the arms you depend on? Where is your fleet to conquer the Roman seas? You would have no hope of defeating the Romans in battle, who are invincible in all parts of the world. The outcome of war would be the total destruction of your country, Jerusalem and the temple. Therefore have pity on your children and wives, and upon Jerusalem and its sacred walls. Spare the temple--preserve the holy house with its holy furniture. The danger involves not just the Jews in Judea, but Jews everywhere, because once war is begun, Jews will be slaughtered in every city in which they live throughout the Roman Empire. For those who put their trust in God, he said that Divine assistance was already on the side of the Romans, because it is impossible that so vast an empire could be obtained without God's providence. He urged them to withstand the present storms, and if they do, they will eventually have the peace that they desire.

When he had finished his impassioned speech, he and his sister Bernice wept, and their tears had an influence on many of the people. However the zealots cried out that they would not fight the Romans, but they would fight Florus. Agrippa replied that what they had already done was similar to making war against the Romans, such as failing to pay their annual tribute (forty talents) to Caesar, and tearing down the cloisters between the temple and Antonia. He hoped they would make amends. This advice was followed by some who went to the temple and began to rebuild the cloisters. Others also went out to the villages and collected the forty talents, which was the sum that was deficient. King Agrippa II also attempted to persuade the people to obey Florus until Caesar sent a replacement. The zealots were provoked at this advice, rebuked him, and forced him out of the city. Some of the zealots even had the impudence to throw stones at him. Dismayed at their actions, king Agrippa II traveled to his own country.

The Sicarii, who were the most anxious of the zealots to go to war against the Romans, then made an assault on Masada. The leader of this group was Eleazar the son of Jairus, who was a descendant of Judas the Gaililean , founder of the fourth sect of Jewish philosophy. The Sicarri seized Masada by treachery, killed the Romans that were

Chapter 9 The Beginning of the Jewish Revolt Against Rome

there, and then secured it with their own comrades.[91]

At that time Eleazar, a very bold youth and son of Ananus the former high priest, was governor of the temple. He used his influence to persuade the officers of the temple not to receive any gift or sacrifice from a foreigner. This edict was leveled at the Romans. The implications of this edict were profound, because by adhering to it any gift or sacrifice even offered by Caesar would be rejected. Many of the former high priests and principal men of the temple urged them to change this policy, and especially before word of it got to Rome. They emphasized that all of their forefathers, out of courtesy, had received sacrifices from Rome and foreign nations. In spite of their pleas, the officers of the temple would not relent. And this was the true beginning of the war with the Romans, because by this edict any sacrifice offered by the Emperor of Rome would be rejected.

The Beginning of Civil War in Jerusalem

The split between the zealots (those favoring war against the Romans) and the moderates (those favoring peace) then led to a civil war within Jerusalem and elsewhere in Judea. The zealots gained control of the temple and the lower city. Fearing the worst, the moderates sent ambassadors to Florus and to king Agrippa II urging them to come with an army, subdue the zealots, and return peace to the city and temple. This message was good news for Florus, who wished to kindle a war. Thus, he did not respond to the request of the ambassadors. King Agrippa II, who realized the gravity of the situation, and the possible outcome if peace was not restored, sent 3,000 horsemen to put down the sedition that was occurring.

---

91   Somehow the Sicarii were able to seize Masada by treachery. Because of its location and design, this famous fortress was impregnable to an assault by an army of footmen and horsemen. Thus, the Romans who held Masada could easily have defended it against any attack by the Sicarii. The Sicarii remained at Masada, where they were protected, during the major war against the Romans in defense of Jerusalem.   Other groups of Sicarii fled to Alexandria and adjoining regions before the Roman armies began their siege on Jerusalem (See Chapter 12).

When these soldiers sent by king Agrippa II arrived in Jerusalem, they assisted the moderates (high priests, principle men among of Jerusalem and others of the multitude who desired peace) and went to battle against the zealots. In addition to fighting hand to hand, they made use of stones, slings, and darts. The king's soldiers were superior in skill, but the zealots were superior in boldness. The moderates and the king's soldiers were able to seize the upper city, and from there they made attacks on the temple, while the zealots, headed by Eleazar, the son of Simon, made forays against the upper city. They fought each other for seven days with slaughters occurring on both sides, but neither side was able to make inroads into the territory defended by the other.

The advantage shifted in favor of the zealots when they obtained the aid of many Sicarii, who mingled with the multitude and used their hidden daggers at opportune times. The king's soldiers were overpowered and driven out of the upper city. The zealots then set fire to the home of Ananias the high priest [high priest prior to Jonathan] and to the palace of king Agrippa II and Bernice [Hasmonean palace]. They also set fire to the archives containing all contracts belonging to creditors, and thereby removed any proof that debts were owed. They attacked the men of influence among the moderates, claiming them to be their enemies and forcing them to hide themselves in vaults under ground. The king's soldiers and many others fled to the royal palace [Herod's palace] and shut the gates. The zealots then made an assault on Antonia, captured it, and slew the garrison stationed there. Following that success they attacked the royal palace, but resistance was strong there, and they were forced to terminate their assault.

In the mean time Manahem, the son of Judas the Galilean left Jerusalem with a group of supporters and went to Masada which was controlled by the Sicarii. The leader of the Sicarii at Masada was Eleazar, the son of Jairus, who was a descendant of Judas the Galilean, and therefore a kin of Manahem. Judas the Galilean was the

Chapter 9 The Beginning of the Jewish Revolt Against Rome

founder of the fourth sect of Jewish philosophy which proclaimed that God alone is our ruler and taxation by the Roman is a form of slavery. At Masada, Manahem opened Herod's armory and obtained arms for his supporters and others who joined him. With this well armed group he returned to Jerusalem in a kingly manner and became the leader of the siege against the royal palace. They attempted to undermine the walls surrounding the palace, hoping to make them fall. Fearing the consequences, those within the palace sent a message to Manahem and other leaders of the sedition that they wished to capitulate and negotiate their freedom. This was granted for the king's soldiers and others from their country, but for no one else. With the departure of the king's soldiers from the city, Roman forces that had been camped within the palace fled to the safety of the royal towers (Hippicus, Phasaelus, and Mariamne), but many were caught and slain before they reached the towers. Manahem and his party then plundered what they left behind and set fire to their former camp.

The next day Ananias, the former high priest and his brother Hezekiah were captured hiding in an aqueduct, and were slain by Manahem. His party then placed guards at the royal towers to insure that none of the Romans could escape. His success in the siege of the royal palace and the death of Ananias so puffed up Manahem that he imagined that he was now the uncontested leader of the zealots in Jerusalem. Eleazar, the son of Simon, viewed him with contempt and proclaimed that it was his party (zealots) that had first revolted against the Romans and if they were obliged to chose a leader they would not give that privilege to Manahem.

In a pompous manner and adorned in royal garments, Manahem went to worship in the temple. He had with him his followers who wore their armor. As an expression of disgust at this show of royalty and arrogance, Eleazar and his party, and other members of the multitude, attacked Manahem and his followers. Manahem and his followers put up resistance until they realized that they were out-numbered, and then they tried to flee away. Those that were caught were slain. Some were able to escape to Masada, and included among them was Eleazar, the son of Jairus.[92] As for Manahem, he escaped to a place called Ophla, where he and the captains under him were soon captured and slain.

Divisions then occurred within the zealots, with many being incensed at the barbarity of some of their own against their own Jewish people. Certain factions hoped that the death of Manahem would bring an end to the more seditious practices. At this time the Roman general, who was trapped with his men in the towers of the royal palace, sent a message to Eleazar, the son of Simon, and petitioned that he and his men be given safe passage out of the city. If granted, they would surrender their shields, swords, and all their belongings. Some of the zealots readily agreed with this petition and sent messengers to them agreeing that their lives would be spared. But when the Romans placed their shields and swords on the ground, and began to march away, they were barbarously murdered by some of Eleazar's men. Only the general was spared. He begged for mercy and promised that he would become a Jew and be circumcised. The consequences were immense. The moderates were saddened by the wickedness of some of the zealots. They knew that revenge could be expected from the Romans when they learned of this atrocity. It was especially ominous that these murders occurred on the Sabbath, when the Jews should have a respite from their works according to Jewish laws.

The Calamities and Slaughters that Befell the Jews in Caesarea and Elsewhere

By coincidence the very same day that the Roman soldiers were murdered in Jerusalem, over 20,000 Jews living in Caesarea

---

[92] Eleazar the son of Jairus was the leader of the Sicarii who had seized Masada from the Romans by treachery. He was with his kin Manahem in this skirmish, but was able to escape and return to Masada. Eleazar the son of Jairus played a major role at Masada when it was taken by the Romans in 73 AD.

Chapter 9 The Beginning of the Jewish Revolt Against Rome

were slaughtered by the gentiles (Syrians, Roman soldiers, and others) living in that city. As a consequence Caesarea was emptied of all Jewish inhabitants. This slaughter, which was well planned by Florus, took place in one hour's time. Many Jews who tried to escape were captured and killed or placed in bonds in galleys. This carnage was the final outcome of the conflict between the Jews and gentiles of that city, and was justified by Florus and others by the edict written by Nero denying basic rights to the Jews of that city.

What happened in Caesarea united the Jews of the whole nation who sought immediate revenge. They divided themselves into large armed groups and attacked the Syrian villages and neighboring cities: Philadelphia, Sebonitis, Gerasa, Pella, Scythopolis, Gadara, Hippos, and Gaulonitis. Many of these cities were burned and laid to waste. Then they attacked Ptolemais, Gaba, Sebaste, Caesarea, and Gaza. An immense slaughter was made of the men who were caught in these cities and villages. The Syrians, who had a long hatred of the Jews, attacked back and the total number of Jews killed was about equal to the number of Syrians who were killed in these battles. It was common to see cities filled with dead bodies lying unburied. Many of bodies were old men, women, children, and infants. Even though king Agrippa II was in good graces with Rome, there were plots by the Syrians against the Jews living in his kingdom.

The zealots were often the leaders in these battles. They captured the citadel called Cypros, which was above Jericho, and killed the Roman soldiers who were there. At this same time the Jews at Macherus persuaded the Romans to leave. These Romans, who feared for their lives, left this fortress and turned it over to the Jews.

Seditions against the Jews then broke out in Alexandria. In order to pacify the Grecians of the city, Tiberius Alexander, who was governor of Egypt, sent two Roman legions and 5,000 other soldiers from Libya to attack the Jews. The soldiers were permitted to plunder, kill, and set fire to homes. No mercy was shown to infants or the aged. Finally the governor commiserated with the condition of the Jews and the amount of blood that had been shed, and gave orders for the Romans to retire. They obeyed, but the Grecians had such a great hatred for the Jews that it was difficult to restrain them from committing further atrocities when presented with the opportunity.

The March on Judea by Cestius, the President of Syria

With Jewish groups attacking Syrian cities and villages, and Syrians responding with their own vicious attacks, Cestius, president of Syria, knew that he could no longer remain inactive. So he left Antioch with a large army and marched toward Galilee. King Agrippa II also supplied footmen and horsemen and served as a guide and director as the army marched across his country. Cestius's goal was to put an end to the fighting by the Jews. Resistance was heavy as his army marched across Galilee and Samaria and to the outskirts of Jerusalem. When the Jews saw the army approaching Jerusalem, they took up their arms, gained courage, and fell upon the Romans, causing much damage.[93] The losses were heavy on both sides, and at one point, because of their fervor, the battle almost turned in favor of the Jews. The Jews controlled the mountainous areas around Jerusalem, the elevated parts of the city and had all entrances to the city well-fortified. Nevertheless, the Romans still had the superior forces and the potential for causing heavy destruction to the city.

At this time king Agrippa II decided to attempt to convince the

---

93   Josephus mentions the name of a zealot who participates in a battle in a mountainous region about 6 miles north of Jerusalem. This zealot later becomes a major leader among the Jews in the battle against the Romans in the defense of Jerusalem. His name was Simon of Gerasa, and also known as Simon the son of Giora. As the Roman army headed by Cestius ascended up Bethoron, the rear of the army was attacked unexpectedly by zealots who were followers of Simon. The resulting disarray among the Romans allowed the zealots to capture beasts that carried weapons of war. These beasts and what they carried were then taken to Jerusalem.

Chapter 9 The Beginning of the Jewish Revolt Against Rome

Jews to stop fighting. He sent two ambassadors to talk to the Jews, and to tell them that if they would put down their arms the Romans would forgive them for what they had done. To the alarm of the people, some of the zealots, fearing that the entire multitude might go over to king Agrippa II and Cestius, attacked the ambassadors. One ambassador was killed, but the other, although wounded, was able to escape. The people were angry at the zealots for this act, and had the responsible persons beaten with stones and clubs, and driven from the city.

Noting the division that had occurred in Jerusalem, Cestius moved closer and made his camp about a mile from the city. There he tarried for 3 days, hoping that the Jews might yield. On the fourth day he moved towards the city and pitched his tent near the walls of the royal palace in the upper city. At that time, many of the principal men of the city invited Cestius and his army to enter the city. They were about to open the gates for him and his army, but Cestius was angry at the Jews and did not believe that they were in earnest, so he delayed. The zealots, when they learned of this treachery, threw the responsible persons over the wall, pelting them with stones. The next day Cestius ordered his army to begin the siege against the walls near the temple, but they were repulsed by the Jews. At this time many of the zealots, fearing that the entire city would soon be taken, ran out of the city. The moderates were then willing to open the gates and admit Cestius as their benefactor. If Cestius had continued the siege a little longer, the war would have ended, but for some unknown reason, other than his belief that he might not be able to take the city, he recalled his troops and began to march away from the city. He did not know that many of the influential Jewish people in the city would have welcomed an end to the bloody siege, and especially because of the promise made by king Agrippa II that the Romans would forgive them for past offenses.

When the zealots and other defenders of the city perceived that the Romans were marching away from Jerusalem, they regained their courage and followed the retreating army. Although greatly outnumbered, they began attacking the rear of the departing troops causing many Roman casualties. *Cestius then made a grave tactical error.* He had a vastly superior army, and if he had stopped the march and turned his army against the Jews, he would have caused them to flee. Not knowing how many Jews he was facing, and imagining that the number in pursuit was immense, he kept marching. Consequently, those at the rear were vulnerable. The next day, there was a repeat of the attacks on the troops bringing up the rear, resulting again in many Roman casualties. At opportune places the Jews also attacked from the sides, but the Romans made no effort to drive them away because of the fear of breaking their ranks. In one narrow passage where the Romans were penned in, the Jews pelted them with darts from above, killing a large number of them, including key commanders. Soon the Romans were in disarray. After three days of this type of warfare, Cestius became greatly distressed. Fearing that he was facing a vast number of enemies, he gave the order to cast away what might hinder their march. They killed the mules and other animals except those that carried their darts and machines. To get further away from the Jews, Cestius began marching at night and discarding key instruments of war including their engines of war used for throwing stones. The Jews pursued them as far as Antipatris, and then seeing that they could not overtake them, they turned back, collected the valuable articles discarded by the Romans, and returned in a joyous manner to Jerusalem, celebrating their victory. The Jews lost only a few warriors, but they had slain 5,038 Roman footmen and 388 Roman horsemen. The Jews had also collected valuable instruments of war. It was a decisive victory for the Jews, and the zealots took credit for the victory.

This calamity befalling Cestius occurred in the 12th year of the reign of Nero [66 AD]. After Cestius returned to Antioch, he sent emissaries to Nero to inform him of the situation and to blame Florus for kindling the war. He hoped to invoke Nero's indignation against Florus, and thereby to alleviate his own danger because of his ineptitude as a military leader.

Previous to this time, about 10,000 Jews living in Damascus had gathered together (cooped up) in one area because the people were suspicious of them. When the people learned of the destruction of the Roman army led by Cestius, they went to the area and slaughtered the Jews by cutting their throats. All of the Jews were unarmed, and unprotected, and were killed within a period one hour.

Preparation for War in Jerusalem
Following this victory the zealots in Jerusalem were euphoric, believing that since they had met the enemy and were victorious, they would also be the winners of future battles. However, the realists in Jerusalem, knowing the power of the forces that Rome would now throw at them, feared the worst. Consequently many of the most eminent Jews departed from the city believing that it would soon be attacked by the Romans.

The leadership of Jerusalem then gathered a large crowd in the temple and made preparations for the war that would surely come. At this stage the moderates and zealots were united in the common cause to defend the city. One of the first steps was to appoint generals to command forces in Judea and surrounding areas. Ananus the son of Ananus, the former high priest, and Joseph the son of Gorion, were chosen as governors of all affairs within Jerusalem, and with a particular charge to repair the walls of the city. The leadership did not ordain Eleazar the son of Simon to that office even though he had in his possession the weapons of war that had been taken from Cestius, and he and his zealots controlled the temple with all its public treasures. They considered him to have a tyrannical temper. They also had a great concern about his followers because they often behaved like guards in his presence, and listened only to him. But he could not be ignored because he possessed resources which would be needed in the defense of the city. Therefore the leaders in Jerusalem were forced to submit to his authority on many issues. **Among other appointments, Josephus was made governor and general of Galilee**[94].

The Appointment of Vespasian to Command the Army to Attack Judea

When Nero was informed of Cestius's defeat in Judea, he became very concerned and angry, stating that what happened was due to the negligence of the commander (Cestius) rather than any valor of the enemy. He deliberated about whom he should select to punish the Jews for their rebellion, and found no one but Vespasian equal to the task, even though he was no longer a young man. From his youth Vespasian had excelled in warlike exploits under Claudius Caesar, subduing the west (Germany) and conquering Britain. Vespasian was known to have good leadership skills, and Nero believed that Vespasian's age gave him the experience needed for the task. Vespasian also had sons to serve with him. So Nero commissioned Vespasian to take command of the army to attack Galilee and then Judea. One of Vespasian's first assignments was to send his son Titus to Alexandria to obtain the Roman legions that were stationed there. Vespasian then traveled to Syria and gathered together the Roman armies stationed in that province. Considerable additional forces were contributed by the kings in that neighborhood. The gathering place was Antioch, known as the third greatest city in the Roman Empire, behind Rome and Alexandria). King Agrippa II met him there with his forces, and they marched to Ptolemais.

Titus sailed to Alexandria, gathered his army together and

---

94 In *The Life of Flavius Josephus and The Wars of the Jews,* Josephus describes in detail his experiences as governor of Galilee and the problems he faced as the military leader as he prepared for the war against the Romans. That account is not presented here. He did not personally support the war because of the invincibility of the Romans, but as general of an army he prepared for the battles that were certain to come. His views were similar to those expressed in the impassioned speech king Agrippa II gave to the people of Jerusalem after arriving there from his trip to Alexandria where he had met with Tiberius Alexander.

Chapter 9 The Beginning of the Jewish Revolt Against Rome

marched hastily up the coast line to Ptolemais, where he met with his father. There a massive army was put together for an assault on cities in Galilee and surrounding areas, and then eventually on cities in Judea, including Jerusalem. The army consisted of Romans and their instruments of war plus footmen and horsemen contributed by King Agrippa II and various Arabian kings. All together the army consisted of over 60,000 men not counting servants.

The army then marched in the direction of Galilee, with the deployment living up to the fame of Roman armies. In the front were the troops provided by the kings, which acted as scouts. Next came heavily armed Roman troops, followed by engineers and a cavalry detachment. Vespasian rode at the front of the foot soldiers, a special group of cavalrymen, and lancers. They were followed by the legionary cavalry (120 horsemen per legion), war machines pulled by mules, and officers escorted by special soldiers. Then came the ensigns encompassing the eagle which is at the head of every Roman legion. These sacred ensigns were followed by trumpeters. Then came the main army, marching in columns of six and commanded by centurions. They were followed by the military servants, beasts of burden carrying or pulling military equipment, mercenaries, and a rear guard of foot soldiers and horsemen. It was an impressive sight, meant to strike fear in the hearts of the enemy.

On the borders of Galilee, Vespasian made camp, where he had to restrain his soldiers who were eager for battle. One reason for camping there was to show the size of his army to the enemy in Galilee and thereby give them a chance to repent and change their minds about confronting the Romans in combat. And indeed, the sight of the might of the Roman army caused many to flee. This was most discouraging to Josephus who saw his army depleted because of the large number of deserters. He knew that he did not have an army sufficient to engage the enemy. As general of the forces in Galilee, he was not hopeful of any success, and made the decision to go to Tiberius, where he sent a letter by messengers to the principal men in Jerusalem informing them of the state of affairs in Galilee, and what now faced the Jewish nation because of the presence of Vespasian's mighty army. Josephus was of the opinion that the Romans would forgive them if peace were sought, but he would rather die than dishonor his country or the supreme command of the army that had been given him. His letter said that if they thought it best to come to terms with the Romans, they must inform him immediately, but if they were still resolved to fight the Romans, they must send him an army sufficient to do so.

Vespasian's army then marched to the city of Gadara, southeast of the Sea of Galilee. He subdued all resistance at the first assault, and found it destitute of grown men fit for war. His army slew the youth and all others in the city, showing hatred for the Jewish people because of what had happened to Cestius and his army. Vespasian then burned the city and all villages surrounding it. The inhabitants of all of these villages were either slain or placed into captivity.

Vespasian was then intent on capturing Jotapata[95], located about 8 miles northeast of Nazareth in Galilee, because he had obtained intelligence that the greatest part of the Jewish forces in Galilee was stationed there. If that city and all the forces contained within it were destroyed, his forces would have little resistance until they reached Judea. He had also learned that Josephus had arrived in Jotapata from Tiberius, and his presence there had raised the drooping spirits of the Jews. Vespasian wished to capture Josephus alive, and to bring this about, he had his forces circle the city, sealing off all the obvious escape routes. The sight of the vast Roman outside their city caused a great deal of consternation to the residents, but even though their situation was desperate, they were motivated to fight boldly. At the first assault by the Romans, Josephus and many followers leaped out, fell upon the Romans, and

---

95   The modern community near the site of Jotapata is known as Yodfat. The site of the fortress is now a national monument, commemorating the importance of the events that occurred there.

drove them away from the walls. The next day the Romans made another attack on the walls, fighting more vigorously because of the shame of their defeat the previous day. These attacks continued for many days, with neither side showing any advantage. Jotapata was located on the side of a mountain with cliffs which gave it a natural protection from enemies. In addition it was protected by high walls. In preparation for the eventual attack, Josephus had increased the height of the walls and made them even more impenetrable. Finally, in desperation, Vespasian made the decision to stop the assault which was not succeeding, and to starve the residents of the city. He believed that when they were fatigued and demoralized by lack of food and water, they would be easy to conquer in battle. The strategy was well thought out because although there was plenty of food in the city, there was a shortage of water. It was summer and not the rainy season, and there was no fountain within the walls of the city. The situation became desperate for the inhabitants and Josephus began to ration the water. Because of the extreme water shortage, Vespasian believed that it was just a matter of time before the Jews would be unfit to defend themselves. However, to convince the Romans that the lack of water was not a problem, Josephus ordered that clothes should be soaked in water and hung over the walls, allowing the water to run down the wall in clear view of the Romans. The purpose was to make the Romans believe that they had ample water, and therefore it would be wise to resume their attacks on the city. They had made the decision that they would rather die in battle, than die because of the lack of water. The stratagem worked, because when Vespasian learned that the Jews were making sport of their water, he made the decision to continue the assault on the walls.

Although the Romans made every effort to insure that no resident of Jotapata was able to leave the city, the mountainous terrain and cliffs made one region difficult to ascend, and for that reason it was not well guarded by the Romans at nighttime. Josephus was able to send messengers out of the city in that region at nighttime by having them wear sheepskins on their backs. They appeared to be dogs when creeping close to the ground. By using this method Josephus was able to send letters to whom he pleased. When the assault began again Josephus knew that the city could not hold out long, and he made plans for him and certain other influential persons to flee the city at night using the mountainous region as the escape route. When the multitude learned of his plans, they came to him and begged him not to leave them, stating that he was needed to help bring deliverance from the Romans, and without him they were doomed. Instead of telling them that he was going to provide for his own safety, he informed them that he was going for their sakes, for if he were able to escape the siege he would mobilize the Galileans in another part of the country to draw the Romans away from Jotapata. He also said that Vespasian wished to capture him, and when it was learned by Vespasian that he was no longer in the city, his interests would shift elsewhere. This argument did not convince the residents. Old men, women, children, and infants came in mourning to him, fell down before him and lamented what would happen to them if he left them. They were adamant in their belief that he was needed to defend them against the Romans.

So he resolved to stay. He announced to the residents: "Now is the time to begin to fight in earnest." He energized the residents, and they fought valiantly. They moved the Romans away from the walls, charged out of the city and even attacked some of their camps. Successes of this type, based partly on acts of heroism, went on for many days, to the consternation of the Romans. During one of these battles Vespasian was wounded in the foot by an arrow. His troops were alarmed when they saw that their general was bleeding, but the wound was not serious, and he ordered the troops to continue the siege. Vespasian then unleashed a new weapon of war, the battering ram, and the wall of Jotapata was not able to withstand its constant blows. The fighting became intense, and the forces within the city, although fighting heroically under the creative leadership of Josephus, began to dwindle. On the 47th day of the siege, a

Chapter 9 The Beginning of the Jewish Revolt Against Rome

deserter informed Vespasian of the weakened conditions within the city, and told him that the city was vulnerable during the last watch of the night. Vespasian did not trust the deserter, but made the decision that nothing would be lost by following his suggestion. A massive assault took place during the time suggested by the deserter, and it was successful. The Romans were able to enter the city, and the attacks by the Romans were vicious. The Jewish men they encountered were killed outright by the Romans or were pushed down the steep precipices, with the fall killing them. Women and infants were taken into captivity. There was mass suicide by many of the Jews, choosing that honorable death over death at the hands of the Romans. Forty thousand Jews were killed during the siege of the city. Once the city was taken, Vespasian gave the order that the city should be entirely demolished, and all fortifications burned down. The battle ended at Jotapata in the thirteenth year of the reign of Nero [67 AD].

The Capture of Josephus

The day Jotapata fell to the Romans, Josephus was no where to be seen. The Romans searched for him because Vespasian was desirous to have him taken captive if he were still alive, believing that if he were taken, the greatest part of the war in Galilee would be over. They searched for him in concealed recesses of the city, and also among the dead, but could not find him. Where was he? When the Romans surged into the city he leaped into a pit which was adjoined to a large den, which could not be seen from above. In the den were 40 persons of eminence who had concealed themselves with enough provisions to satisfy them for several days. During that day Josephus hid himself from the enemy in this den, but when night came he left the den and looked for ways to escape from the city. His search was in vain. All exits from the city were well guarded. He concealed himself for two days in the den, but on the third day a woman was captured who had been concealed with them in the den, and she informed the Romans where he was hiding. Vespasian sent two tribunes to the entrance of the den to encourage Josephus to come out, promising him that his life would be preserved if he surrendered to the Romans. Josephus was reluctant to come out fearing that he would be punished and then killed. Vespasian sent a third tribune Nicanor who had been Josephus's acquaintance in past years. He encouraged Josephus to surrender, stating that Vespasian would not punish him and was determined to preserve a man with his reputation and courage. He remarked that if the Romans wanted to do harm to him, all they had to do was set fire to the den, which Vespasian had already prevented the soldiers from doing.

After rationalizing that God had foretold him in dreams about the calamities of the Jews and events that concerned the Roman emperors, and that God wanted him to foretell what is to come to pass, Josephus made the decision to accept Nicanor's invitation. Placing himself in God's hands he said, "And I protest openly that I do not go over to the Romans as a deserter of the Jews, but as a minister from Thee." When the Jews in the den with him understood that he had accepted the invitation to surrender they reacted vehemently, accusing him of being a traitor. They surrounded him and threatened him with their swords, shouting that they would kill him if he thought of yielding himself to the Romans.

After philosophical appeals failed to convince his fellow captives that he should leave the den, he decided to trust himself to the will of God. He proposed to them that since they were all resolved to die, he would join them, but they should die in a manner determined by a lottery system. That would be preferable, he said, than mass suicide, because at the last second some might refuse to do it, or might inflict a wound that is not fatal. It would be better if each had his throat slit by someone else in view of all the others. He proposed that by randomly selecting lots, the one with the first lot would be killed by the one with the second lot. The one with the second lot would then be killed by the one with the third lot, and this procedure would continue until only one person was left, who would then kill himself. This procedure was accepted by all in the

Chapter 9 The Beginning of the Jewish Revolt Against Rome

den, because each believed that their general would die with them. So lots were drawn and the one with the first lot laid his neck bare for the one with the second lot, and the killings continued, with each disclosing his number at the proper time.

Whether it was a matter of chance or an act of providence, Josephus and one other person were left to the last. Because Josephus did not wish to die or kill a fellow countryman, he persuaded the other remaining person to trust in his fidelity and choose to live. Thus, Josephus survived the war with the Romans and the war with his friends in the den, and was led by Nicanor to Vespasian.[96]

As he was led away from the den, the Roman soldiers ran to see him, and some clamored for his death. When he met with Vespasian and his son Titus, a strong bond was formed immediately between Josephus and Titus, for they were about the same age (30 years) and only a short time before they had been fighting each other. Both Vespasian and Titus had great respect for the military and leadership skills of Josephus. Even though the soldiery and commanders wished to put this enemy to death, Vespasian gave strict orders that he should be kept alive and sent to Nero in Rome. When Josephus heard Vespasian give this order he said that he had something that he should relate to him and requested that he be able to say this to him in private. Vespasian then ordered that all should withdraw except Titus and two of their friends. Josephus then announced that he came as a messenger of good tidings, for he had been given a revelation by God. He said there was no reason why he should be sent to Nero *because in the near future Vespasian would be Caesar and emperor, and he would be succeeded by his son Titus*. Therefore, he should be bound and kept as a captive for Vespasian. He then venerated Vespasian with the expression, "*For thou O Caesar, are not only lord*

---

96   Josephus justifies his drawing of the highest number on good fortune or an act of providence. Some cynical writers have suggested however, that because Josephus devised the lottery system he was able, by using deception, to obtain the number that allowed him to survive.

over me, but over the land and the sea, and all mankind." Vespasian was astounded by these words and did not believe him, assuming that it was some kind of trick to seek mercy. However, both he and Titus were flattered by Josephus's words, and hoped that what he had said was true. After pondering what Josephus had prophesied, and making further inquiries, Vespasian learned that Josephus was a man who spoke the truth. He also learned from other captives that Josephus had predicted to the people of Jotapata that the city would be taken on the 47th day, and that he would caught alive by the Romans. Vespasian began to believe that Josephus, who was from a family of priests, had a gift of prophesy, and therefore he was an unusual captive who should be given special consideration and privileges. As a consequence, even though Josephus was kept bound in chains, Vespasian bestowed upon him suits of clothes and other precious gifts.

There was gloom in Jerusalem when the fate of Jotapata became known, but the news was slow in coming because there were no survivors who could bring the news to Jerusalem. Rumors were rampant, and it was first reported that Josephus had been slain by the Romans when the city was taken. There was great sadness throughout Jerusalem because of the loss of this Galilean general, and the public mourning lasted for many days. Then the truth became known that Josephus was not dead, had been captured alive by the Romans, and was being treated by the Roman commanders in a special manner. At this news the mourning in Jerusalem turned into general anger, and Josephus was accused by many of being a traitor and a coward.

After the victory at Jotapata, Vespasian and part of his army went to Caesarea where they rested. The other members of his army were sent to Scythopolis because Caesarea was not large enough to absorb the whole army. Josephus was brought to Caesarea by Vespasian, where he remained for two years as a captive bound in chains. There he was treated well as a prisoner, and Vespasian even

Chapter 9 The Beginning of the Jewish Revolt Against Rome

commanded him to marry a Jewish prisoner, who was a virgin.

The War Continues in Galilee

After resting in Caesarea, Vespasian accepted an invitation from king Agrippa II for him and part of his army to visit Caesarea Philippi. There the troops were refreshed for 20 days and Vespasian was feasted and entertained extravagantly.[97] King Agrippa II had a motive for treating Vespasian so well. He needed military assistance because two major cities in his kingdom had large anti-Roman factions, and he had lost control of these cities. These cities were Tiberius and Tarichae on the shore of Lake Genesareth [Sea of Galilee]. Vespasian agreed that it was important to stop the revolts in these cities. He sent his son Titus back to Caesarea to bring additional footmen and horsemen. Titus brought these troops to Scythopolis where he met his father. An army was then put together for the march on the two cities. A camp was made near Tiberius. The presence of Vespasian's army caused the anti-Roman faction in the city to flee to Tarichae, and the pro-Agrippa faction in the city came to Vespasian asking for peace and his compassion. Thus, king Agrippa II once again had control of the city.

Titus then led the fight against Tarichae, and it was he who first led the charge into the city. A major battle took place on boats and rafts on the lake. The Romans had a decisive victory. At the end of the sea-fight the shore of the lake was laden with dead bodies which putrefied and corrupted the air. The number of Jews slain, including those that were killed in the city, was 6,500.

Vespasian then committed a cruel and barbaric act. At the conclusion of the battle at Tarichae, he had prisoners who had been long-time inhabitants of the city in addition to foreigners who had been living there. He blamed the foreigners for the war, but was undecided what to do with the long-time inhabitants. He considered

---

97   During this visit to Caesarea, Titus would have met Bernice, the sister of king Agrippa II, who later became his mistress in Rome.

saving them, but many of his commanders argued that if they were set free they might eventually fight against Rome. Vespasian followed the advice of his commanders. The prisoners, believing that their lives would be spared, were marched from Tarichae to Tiberius, with Roman soldiers guarding the road so none could escape. In Tiberius they were ushered into a large stadium. Vespasian entered the stadium and ordered that all old men, and others that were useless, should be killed. The number slaughtered was one thousand and two hundred. He then chose six thousand of the strongest young men, and sent them to Nero to dig a canal across the Isthmus of Corinth. The rest (30,450) were sold into slavery. He gave king Agrippa II those prisoners that belonged to his kingdom, giving him the privilege of making the decision as to their fate. King Agrippa II sold these prisoners as slaves.

Vespasian then turned his attention to three other fortified cities in the northern part of the country, which were revolting against the Romans: Mount Tabor, Gamala and Gischala. Mt. Tabor was taken quickly, but Gamala, located across the Jordan, presented problems to the Romans because of its location on a mountainous peak and its high walls. The Romans assembled at the base of the city and prepared to assault the city. Before doing so, king Agrippa II approached the wall and urged the inhabitants to surrender as a means of preventing bloodshed and the destruction of the city. He was rebuffed and hit on the right elbow by a stone thrown by one of the slingers. The Romans then attacked the city using their instruments of war. Because of the fortifications of the city, the siege was not easy. Finally, one of the large towers was undermined, and it collapsed, allowing the Romans to enter the city. The Romans were enraged at the long time it took to enter the city and as a consequence the massacre of the inhabitants was almost total.

The last city in Galilee with a major faction hostile to the Romans was Gischala. The leader was John (of Gischala) who was a sworn enemy and antagonist of Josephus when Josephus was

Chapter 9 The Beginning of the Jewish Revolt Against Rome

governor and general of Galilee.[98] Gischala was a small city in northern Galilee. It was not well fortified, and Vespasian knew that it could be taken easily. He assigned the task to Titus, who took with him one thousand horseman. As Titus approached Gischala and viewed the city and surrounding area, he knew that he could take it on the first assault. He also knew that the multitude would be destroyed without mercy by his soldiers. Since he was already satiated with the shedding of blood, he hoped that the city would surrender so the innocent citizens could be spared. He made such a proposal to the inhabitants, and received a response from John, who said that the Sabbath was upon them, and on such days it was unlawful to fight or work, or even to consider a proposal of peace. He hoped that Titus would allow them to honor that day properly. Out of compassion, and hoping the surrender would take place after the Sabbath, Titus suspended all activities for the day and pulled guards away from the city. But it was a subterfuge, because when John observed that the Romans guards had withdrawn, he and his followers and whole families left the city at night under the cover of darkness and headed for Jerusalem. The next day as Titus approached the wall the gates opened and he was greeted with joy by those who had remained in the city. When he was informed that John and many others had fled the city on the Sabbath, he sent part of his horsemen in pursuit. John had too much of a head start, and they could not catch him, but they over took many of the others. His horsemen slew six thousand of the women and children, and returned to the city with three thousand others, whom Titus made slaves. The inhabitants who had remained in Gischala were allowed to live, and he placed a garrison in the city to keep it secure.

All of Galilee was now taken, but at great cost to the Romans. Assessing what had happened in Galilee, and especially at Jotapata, Vespasian knew that the assault on Jerusalem would be difficult, and careful planning was needed.

---

98   Josephus gives detailed accounts in *The Life of Flavius Josephus* and the *War of the Jews* of the devious behavior of John (of Gischala) and the animosity that existed between them .

Josephus

Chapter 10

THE SEDITIONS WITHIN JERUSALEM

When John of Gischala entered Jerusalem after escaping from Gischala on the Sabbath, the inhabitants of Jerusalem were in an uproar. They gathered about him to learn what miseries the Romans had inflicted on the Jewish people in Galilee.[99] John did not mention that he had fled Gischala by subterfuge and left many of the inhabitants of that city to the mercy of the Romans. He said instead that he had chosen to fight the Romans in Jerusalem rather than in a weak city such as Gischala. He emphasized that the Jewish people should save all their weapons and zeal for their defense of their major metropolis. He urged them to go to war and announced that they should have high hopes of defeating the Romans who were in a weakened condition following all their battles in Galilee. He extolled his own power as a military leader, and declared that the Romans were unskillful and *even if they had wings they could never fly over the walls of Jerusalem.* He also declared that the Romans had encountered great difficulty in taking the villages of Galilee and that their feared engines of war had actually broken down against the walls of the Galilean cities. These harangues of John inflamed even more the young men of Jerusalem who were eager for war, and especially those who still celebrated the military success over the retreating Roman army led by Cestius.

John's influence intensified the conflict between the zealots

---

[99] It is noted in Chapter 9 that when Josephus was governor and general of Galilee he encountered John of Gischala who become his enemy. Josephus described him as a treacherous person whose character was that of a very cunning and very knavish person. He also described him as a ready liar, who was very sharp in gaining credit for his fictions, and who thought it a point of virtue to delude people, even those who were dearest to him.

who wanted war and the more prudent ones who feared the consequences of war and therefore wanted peace with the Romans. In the beginning the zealots were idealists and advocates of the fourth philosophy promoted by Judas the Galilean in 6 AD, who taught that God is their only ruler. But some men joined the ranks of the zealots only because they had lost family members and belongings to the Romans. Because of their bitterness, they were eager to fight the Romans. The number of the zealots was also swelled by immigrants into the city who were robbers. These persons with unsavory backgrounds joined the ranks of the zealots because they found camaraderie and protection among the zealots. The confrontation became bitter between the two factions. Families were split over this issue, and even those who were dearest to each other found themselves on opposite sides of this quarrelsome matter. And those that were desirous for war, because of their youth and vigor, would not listen to the older and more prudent men.

At this time anarchy reigned in Jerusalem. There was no central government, and men got together in bodies to rob the people of their own city and country. With no authority to pursue them, they committed barbarities, with no fear of punishment. And to make matters worse, each day there was a huge influx of persons arriving from far and nearby areas who were fleeing the Romans. These persons had lost their belongings and had arrived in the city with no food and only the clothes on their back. It was the ancient custom of Jerusalem to receive all such persons without distinction and to treat them with kindness, for in the past such visitors had usually come to attend the temple. Many fleeing the Romans came with good intentions and were treated kindly. They had come to Jerusalem believing that it was a refuge against the Romans because it contained the temple and also because of the high walls around the city. However, many of the robbers who had come took advantage of the lawless condition in Jerusalem. They joined with others in the city with similar intentions and proceeded to rob, plunder, and murder.

Chapter 10 The Seditions Within Jerusalem

The zealots who still occupied the temple were led by Eleazar the son of Simon. They prepared for war against the Romans and opposed bitterly anyone who disagreed with them or their tactics. They especially opposed the elderly priests [including former high priests] who favored peace because of the fear that the Romans would destroy Jerusalem and their holy temple. The zealots, with a high degree of insolence, then gave themselves the authority to name the high priest,[100] which they said should be by lot. They falsely justified this method by saying that it was done that way in ancient times, but in reality, it was a contrivance by them to seize the government by profiting from the one placed in the position. They specified that the new high priest should be from one of the pontifical tribes (called Eniachim), and the procedure of casting lots should decide which member should be high priest. By this method Phannias, the son of Samuel, was chosen. He was not worthy of the high priesthood, and in fact, he did not know what the high priesthood was, or what the holder of this priesthood did. The zealots brought this rustic and simple person into the temple from his own country, without his own consent, placed the sacred garments upon him, and gave him instructions as to what he should do, as if they were directing a play on the stage. They viewed this event as a sport, and found much humor in what they had done. This wickedness brought tears to the eyes of the other priests who viewed this event as a mockery of a sacred tradition.

The multitude who valued the dignity of the temple and the authority of the high priest position were prompted to rise against the zealots for their actions. Urged on by Ananus the son of Ananus and Jesus the son of Gamaliel, the former high priests in high esteem began circulating in crowds, urging the people to unite and to purge the temple of the bloody polluters. At a large assembly, Ananus

---

100   No mention is made of the whereabouts of the high priest Matthias, the son of Theophilus, who was the high priest named by king Agrippa II. Apparently he was deceased at that time in history.

stood in their midst and with a flood of tears in his eyes as he looked up at the temple, he said that it would have been better for him to die than to see the house of God full of so many abominations, and the sacred places trodden upon by the feet of blood-shedding villains. In a long speech he exhorted the people to unite and go against the zealots, and at its conclusion he organized his followers to do battle.[101]

The civil war now became intensified, with the followers of Ananus being more numerous than the zealots, even though the zealots had better weapons and were more experienced in the use of them. A great slaughter occurred, with a large number being killed or wounded on both sides. The tide turned in favor of the followers of Ananus. With greater numbers and fighting courageously because they believed that God was on their side, they were able to contain the zealots within the inner chamber of the temple. Ananus did not think it proper to make any attack against the holy gates, or to have the multitude invade the sanctified region of the temple, so he selected 6,000 armed men by lot to stand guard. These guards were rotated with time.

The civil war raging in Jerusalem became known to Vespasian from persons who had who had fled from that city because of the existing turmoil. Vespasian's commanders advised him that now would be the time to march on the city because of the disarray that

---

101   Ananus the son of Ananus, was the high priest who was responsible for the stoning of James, the brother of Jesus Christ. He served as high priest for only three months. At the time of the Roman revolt he was considered by the multitude to be the best of the Jews and the most revered among the former high priests. Following the defeat of Cestius, he was named as one of the governors of Jerusalem to help prepare for the anticipated onslaught by the Romans. In this position he was responsible for all affairs within the city, with a particular charge to repair the walls of the city. He was a prudent man who feared the consequences of a war with the Romans, and preferred a solution to this dilemma other than fighting the Romans. But he joined the anti-Roman movement at the time Cestius was assaulting Jerusalem, emphasizing that if war was necessary, he would rather die at the hands of the Romans in a noble war in defense of Jerusalem and the holy temple, than to end up as a Roman slave. He soon found himself in a conflict with the zealots led by Eleazar son of Simon.

Chapter 10 The Seditions Within Jerusalem

was present there. Being a wise person Vespasian thought otherwise, stating that an attack by the Romans at this time might unite the divisive groups. It would be better he said to let them continue fighting among themselves, because further killings and desertions would make them even weaker.

A decisive event then occurred because of the devious actions of John of Gischala. This man went to great extremes to cultivate a friendship with Ananus, by claiming falsely to be one of his devoted followers and an enemy of the zealots because of what they had done to the temple. Once this friendship was established, he accompanied Ananus when he consulted with eminent persons throughout Jerusalem and attended meetings with his advisers. Then in secret, John divulged what he had learned to the zealots, enabling them to know in advance what to expect from Ananus. Realizing that the zealots were able to anticipate their military moves, John was suspected by some of Ananus's advisers of betraying them. When this suspicion surfaced, John gave an impassioned oath of loyalty to Ananus stating that he supported his views, would not betray any secrets, and would defend him and any of his followers who might be attacked by their enemies. Ananus became convinced of his loyalty and his close advisers finally began to trust him. They took him into their confidence and even sent him into the temple as their ambassador to the zealots with proposals of accommodation. At one time John stood in the midst of the zealots and informed them that their lives were in great danger because Ananus had convinced his followers that a message should be sent to Vespasian asking him to come and take the city. He also proclaimed that the followers of Ananus were making plans to invade the temple and attack them even though Ananus had announced his opposition to any shedding of blood in the sanctity of the temple. John told the zealots that he did not see how they could survive the attacks by the followers of Ananus and the Romans who were going to be invited into city. One solution was to ask for foreign assistance, and in a covert manner he intimated that the Idumeans should be invited to rescue them before the Romans arrived. Although the Idumeans had maintained their ethnic differences, they were strong in the Jewish faith and viewed that the temple in Jerusalem was also their temple.

The zealots were greatly disturbed by John's message, and after much consideration Eleazar the son of Simon and the leader of the zealots, decided to ask the Idumeans to come to their assistance. A letter was written and carried under cover by messengers to their leaders stating that Ananus had imposed his will on the people, and was betraying Jerusalem to the Romans. The letter also stated that those loyalists who were committed to protecting Jerusalem from the Romans were confined to the temple. It also said that unless the Idumeans came immediately to their assistance, they would soon be under the power of Ananus, and the city would soon be in the hands of the Romans. The leaders of the Idumeans were surprised by the content of the letter. Fearful of losing Jerusalem and the holy temple to the Romans, they responded quickly and put together an army of twenty thousand men, and marched on Jerusalem.

Ananus did not know that the letter had been delivered to the Idumeans, but he soon learned that they were approaching the city wall and the reason for their coming. He gave orders for the gates to be locked, and the walls to be guarded. Then Jesus, the son of Gamaliel, who was a former high priest, stood on the tower and spoke to the Idumeans, telling them that they had been asked to come to the assistance of the vilest of men, who are barbarians and who at this time were drinking themselves drunk in the sanctuary. He also stated that these vile persons had told you a falsehood when they informed you that we intend to betray the city to the Romans. What they told you is not true. The Romans have subdued Galilee and are now proud and insolent, and any effort to please them at this time, when they are so close to us, would bring reproach on us worse than death. As for myself, I would have preferred peace with them, but now that we have made war with them, and fought against them, there is no turning back, and I prefer death with reputation before

Chapter 10 The Seditions Within Jerusalem

being enslaved by them. You have been betrayed by these defilers of the temple. If you want to enter the city in peace and not in war, we will show you the houses that have been depopulated by their rapacious actions. We will also show you those wives and family members who wear black because of the slaughter of their relatives by them. Jesus, the son of Gamaliel, then urged them to put down their weapons or go away, but the Idumeans paid no attention to what they said, and were in a rage because they were refused entry into the city. A spokesman of the Idumeans then shouted that the real patrons of liberty are under custody in the temple, and those who will not allow us to enter the gates of our common city are prepared to admit the Romans. These traitors are also disposed to crown the gates with garlands at the coming of the Romans. At these remarks Jesus sorrowfully went away.

That night a terrible storm hit the area, and believing that because of its ferocity nothing of consequence would happen, Ananus allowed the guards at the temple to go to sleep. However, the zealots took advantage of this situation, and using saws belonging to the temple, they crept to the gate of the city near where the Idumeans were camping, and cut the bars of the gate to pieces, allowing the gate to open. The noise of the saws was not heard because of the fierceness of the storm. The Idumeans entered the city, went immediately to the sanctuary of the temple and freed the zealots who were waiting for them. The Idumeans and the zealots then attacked the sleeping guards. Because of the element of surprise, the guards were no match, and they were slaughtered. The Idumeans and zealots then turned their attention on their adversaries in the outer temple, and the battle continued through the night. At dawn the outer temple overflowed with blood and eight thousand and five hundred bodies were there. The Idumeans and zealots were not satisfied with these slaughters, and the next day they went into the city, plundered homes, and killed everyone they met. A special goal was to find Ananus and Jesus, the former high priests. As soon as they captured them, they slew them, stood on their bodies, made jest concerning them, and then cast their bodies aside denying them a proper burial.

The slaughter of the populace continued until the Idumeans became weary of all the killing. Many also repented of what they had done, with the realization that they had been deceived by the zealots because there was no evidence that the Romans had been invited to take the city. Finally, ashamed at what they had done, the Idumeans left the city and returned home. This was a great surprise to both the zealots and their adversaries. Before leaving, the Idumeans freed two thousand prisoners, who immediately left the city and joined the forces of Simon of Gerasa, and also known as Simon the son of Giora.[102] These forces were in a nearby mountainous region.

With the departure of the Idumeans, the zealots continued their slaughter of persons in the city, seeking out persons of eminence. One person they sought was Matthias, who was a close friend of Ananus and Jesus, the former high priests who were killed. In addition to his close relationship with these leaders, **Matthias was also the father of the "traitor" Josephus** who was captured alive by the Romans in Jotapata and who was now in custody in Caesarea. As soon as he was captured, Matthias was placed in prison by the zealots.

The goal of John of Gischala was to become the military and political leader of the Jews in Jerusalem in the war against the Romans. He had effectively gotten rid of Ananus and his followers, and by gathering together the most wicked of the zealots, he formed a separate party that tried to set policy and gain influence. He did this by persuasion and by tyranny, hoping to replace Eleazar son

---

102   Simon of Gerasa, also known as Simon the son of Giora, was introduced in Chapter 9 when he and his followers attacked the rear of the Roman army, headed by Cestius, as it ascended Bethoron in a mountainous region on the outskirts of Jerusalem. They were able to capture beasts carrying weapons of war, which they then took to Jerusalem. This Simon eventually became a powerful zealot who had a major impact within Jerusalem during the siege by the Roman army.

of Simon as leader of the zealots. Many of the zealots opposed him because of the fear of a monarchy with him as the ruler. Some joined him because of their personal fear of him. Many also joined him because they admired him, and his strongest supporters were the Galileans who were residing in the city. The two competing leaders of the zealots (i.e., Eleazar and John), competed with each other, but would unite in actions against the populace, and especially against anyone who favored peace with the Romans, or was suspected of having that frame of mind. Many residents departed from the city because the preferred taking their chances with the Romans rather than with the two competing zealot factions led by Eleazar son of Simon and John of Gischala.

There was also terror in other regions. South of Jerusalem in Idumea near the Dead Sea was the fortress Masada located on top of a mesa and protected by steep cliffs. The *Sicarii*, under the leadership of Eleazar the son of Jairus, had taken control of it, and were now using it as a hideout and a base from which they raided nearby regions. They became especially bold when civil war was occurring in Jerusalem. One night they raided cities and villages and killed all persons (including women and children) who could not run away, and seized provisions from the homes, which they carried back to Masada. This continued until the whole region was made a waste land. By these means they obtained supplies for their fortress which would allow them to withstand a long siege from any enemy. Similar activities of robbers and seditious persons occurred throughout Judea, turning regions that were once peaceful into regions of fear and discord. Thus, the anarchy present in Jerusalem was also present throughout Judea and surrounding areas.

The Decision by Vespasian to Conquer Regions Surrounding Jerusalem

Before assaulting Jerusalem, Vespasian made the decision to conquer nearby cities containing seditious Jewish forces, believing that defeating these cities would allow him to devote full attention to attacking the walls of Jerusalem. He went with his army to Perea,[103] located east of the Jordan River, and subdued the major cities in that area. As his army approached Gadara, the Jews who controlled that city fled away to a village called Bethennabris. Vespasian directed his tribune Placidus to subdue them and any other seditious Jews in that region. Vespasian then returned to Caesarea with the rest of his army, and Placidus attacked key cities and villages east of the Jordan River as far south as the Dead Sea (Lake Asphaltitis), leaving the fortress Macherus, on the east side of the Dead Sea, as the only city in Perea not conquered by the Romans.[104]

While in Caesarea, Vespasian heard the news that there was a commotion in Gaul because the principal men in that country had revolted against Nero. This report was ominous because it was further evidence that civil unrest was continuing to occur in various regions of the empire, causing danger to the present government. Vespasian received the message that it would be beneficial to Rome if matters in Judea were settled as soon as possible. Winter was his hindrance, but when spring came he led his army from Caesarea to Antipatris, where he took control of the affairs of that city. He then laid waste and burned the neighboring villages. He moved on to Lydda, Jamnia, and Emmaus, seizing these cities. After taking all the strongholds in that area near Idumea, he veered north and then east until he came to Jericho and the lush Jordan valley, where he found that most of the inhabitants had fled. He traveled south to the west side of the Dead Sea, where he was intrigued with the notion that the salty water of this sea lake prevents persons from

---

103   Gadara was part of king Herod's kingdom, but upon the death of Herod this city was added to Decapolis, which was administered by Syria. With this change it slowly became a Roman-Grecian city but still contained a sizeable group of seditious Jews who opposed the Romans. At that time in history Perea was generally known as that region east of the Jordan River (see Footnote 13 in Chapter 8). Josephus described Gadara as being the metropolis of Perea.

104   Placidus knew that he did not have the size of army and weapons of war that were needed to conquer the formidable fortress at Macherus.

sinking. In order to verify the correctness of this information, he commanded that certain persons who could not swim should have their hands tied behind them, and thrown into a deep part of the lake. He observed that all were able to stay afloat.

The Reprieve Given Jerusalem Because of the Death of Nero

Vespasian now had control of the key areas surrounding Jerusalem. Three fortresses (Herodium, Masada, and Macherus) had not been destroyed, and he had not invaded the region of Idumea directly south of Jerusalem. It was his assessment, however, that the forces in these areas would be of no threat to his army when he attacked Jerusalem.

Vespasian returned to Caesarea to make final plans for the assault on Jerusalem. Upon arriving there he was informed that Nero was dead. After abusing his power in government for many years, Nero killed himself [68 AD] in the suburbs of Rome. He had served as emperor for thirteen years and eight days.[105]

---

105   Nero, who was the son of Agrippina the Younger, succeeded Claudius as emperor. He was born in 37 AD and died in 68 AD. After poisoning her second husband, Agrippina the Younger became the wife of her uncle, who was emperor Claudius, and persuaded him to favor Nero over his own son Britannicus as his successor. She also convinced Claudius that he should allow his daughter Octavia to be married to her son Nero. Previously she had helped bring about the murder of Messalina, who was her predecessor as the wife of Claudius. In her efforts to have her son named emperor, she poisoned her husband Claudius in 54 AD, and then immediately had the Praetorian Guard, through the influence of the prefect Burrus, declare Nero as emperor. This declaration forced the senate to accept him as emperor even though Nero was only 16 years old. Agrippina hoped to control the government, but Burrus and Nero's former tutor Seneca, had other plans, and until 62 AD they were the effective rulers of the Roman empire. They encouraged Nero to be independent of his mother, and in 56 AD Agrippina was forced into retirement. Nero had his mother murdered in 59 AD because of her erratic behavior. He also had his wife Octavia murdered in 62 AD so he could marry Poppaea, who had been his mistress. In the beginning, through the influence of Burrus and Seneca, Nero acquired a good reputation as emperor by bringing about many positive changes in government, but then he underwent a bizarre change in behavior. While Burrus and Seneca were running the government, Nero chose to immerse himself in art, poetry, and music, and in 59 AD began giving public acting performances. His public performances on the stage in many different roles were an embarrassment to the Romans, which they believed were unfitting for an emperor. He also became infamous for his extravagances. After Burrus died in 62 AD, Seneca retired from

Vespasian learned that Galba was made emperor and had returned to Rome from Spain to assume the position. It was now proper that the assault on Jerusalem be delayed until Vespasian had learned Galba's desires concerning the war against the Jews in Judea. The Jewish war had been ordered by Nero, and the new emperor might have other priorities. So Vespasian sent his son to Titus to salute the new emperor and to obtain directions. King Agrippa II accompanied Titus on this trip to pay homage to the new emperor. It was winter time, and they sailed along the northern coast line making frequent stops. In Greece they learned that Galba had been slain after serving as emperor for only seven months and seven days, and that he had been replaced by Otho. King Agrippa II decided to continue his journey to Rome to salute the new emperor, but Titus sailed back from Greece to Syria, and went in haste to his father in Cesarea. They were both in suspense about the future of their government and made the decision not to make any further expeditions against the Jews until conditions were stable and orders had been received.

Concerning Simon of Gerasa

A very influential person then arrived on the scene in Jerusalem. Simon of Gerasa, also known as Simon, son of Giora, was born in Gerasa located in northern Judea. He was a man of great physical strength and courage, and was one of the zealots who

---

political life believing that he was no longer able to have an influence on Nero. Nero gave certain freedmen much authority in running the government while he spent his time on artistic endeavors. Following the fire that ravaged Rome in 64 AD, Nero began a massive rebuilding program. It was commonly believed that Nero had the fire started so he could rebuild Rome following his own tastes, but Nero blamed it on the Christians who lived there. It was this fire that initiated the persecution of the Christians. Because of his lack of attention to governmental affairs, revolts were occurring in various areas in the empire. His massive expenditures in rebuilding Rome following the fire and his megalomaniac behavior caused many influential persons in Rome to oppose him. In 65 AD there was a plot to overthrow him by various senators and influential military officers, but he was protected by supporters who warned him of the plots against him. The revolt against him spread, and when the Praetorian guard and his palace guard abandoned him, Nero fled the city. He then committed suicide [68 AD]. His failure to be an effective ruler sparked a series of civil wars within the empire, such as the one that occurred in Judea.

Chapter 10 The Seditions Within Jerusalem

defended Jerusalem from the attacks by Cestius and his army. A rebel by nature, he was the leader of a group that controlled the Acrabattene toparchy in Judea[106] until driven out by Ananus the former high priest. He then went to Masada to join the Sicarii who had seized that fortress, but they were suspicious of him and only allowed him and the women who accompanied him to dwell in the lower section of this fortress. They trusted him enough, however, that they allowed him to join them when they ravaged the villages and areas near Masada. When he encouraged them to expand their territory and raid other areas, they resisted, preferring to remain close to their fortress which they viewed as their hiding place. When Simon of Gerasa learned that Ananus was dead, he left Masada and went into a mountainous region. Because of his charismatic personality, he was able to attract a large body of men (mostly slaves and robbers), who, with him as their leader, began to overrun the villages located in the area. When his army grew in strength, he moved out of the mountainous area and raided many different cities as far south as Idumea. His followers, who revered him as king, grew in great numbers. Two thousand men who joined his army were the prisoners released by the Idumeans in Jerusalem. It was his grandiose ambition to have a large enough army, with the necessary weapons of war and resources, to defend the entire region, including Jerusalem, against the pending assault from the Romans. He began making plans for this defense, which included gaining control of Jerusalem.

Learning of his growing army, the zealots in Jerusalem now feared that Simon of Gerasa would soon attack Jerusalem, so they made the decision to leave the city and confront him. A battle ensued and Simon drove them back into the city. Believing that he was not quite ready to tackle the walls of the city, he withdrew and with twenty thousand men marched into Idumea for the purpose of obtaining needed resources. A fierce battle with the Idumeans took

---

106 The Acrabattene toparchy was in a mountainous region north of Jerusalem near the border of Samaria.

place on the border between Idumea and Judea, with neither side gaining a victory. Each side withdrew, but Simon soon returned with the determination to take the country by force. Before any additional battle took place, one of the Idumean commanders made the decision to betray his country for his own personal benefit. He went to Simon and convinced him that he could persuade his country to surrender if Simon would reward him properly. After being feasted by Simon and promises were made, the commander returned to Idumea and convinced the other commanders and the multitude not to resist Simon's army. As a consequence, Simon was able to march into Idumea without any opposition. He made an attack on Hebron[107] and, obtained many needed resources. From there Simon moved across Idumea, where he and his army ravaged villages and cities, and made a waste of the whole country.

The zealots in Jerusalem were now greatly alarmed by the threat of Simon. Because of his massive army, they dared not fight him openly in a fair battle, so they set an ambush and seized his wife and a considerable number of her attendants. They took them back to the city, rejoicing that his wife could be used for ransom. They assumed that he would lay down his arms out of concern for the safety of his beloved wife, but instead of negotiating for her release, he approached the gates of the city, and in a rage took vengeance on anyone who tried to leave the city through the gates to gather sticks or herbs. He tormented some and killed others. To the astonishment of the multitude, he cut the hands off many and sent them back into the city with the warning that he had sworn by the God of the universe that unless his wife is returned, he would break down the walls of the city and inflict a similar punishment upon all the citizens. This would be done without sparing age or distinguishing between the innocent and those who authored the capturing of his wife. These threats so frightened the multitude and the zealots that they sent his

---

107   Hebron is the ancient city where Abraham, the progenitor of the Jews, lived after he had migrated from Mesopotamia.

Chapter 10 The Seditions Within Jerusalem

wife back to him. This made him milder and he retreated from the gates of the city.

News from Rome

Although Otho was made emperor after Galba had been assassinated, he was challenged by Vitellius who had been chosen to be emperor by the Roman legions in Germany. These legions then proceeded to move towards Rome. A battle ensued between the forces of Otho and the stronger forces supporting Vitellius, and Otho's army was defeated. Otho then committed suicide after serving as emperor for only three months and two days. Otho's army then joined Vitellius's army, and the combined army returned to Rome, hailing Vitellius as the new emperor.[108]

Conditions in Jerusalem Because of the Mischievous and Seditious Behavior of John of Gischala

In the meantime John of Gischala rose to great power in Jerusalem, gaining many followers of Eleazar, son of Simon who was the initial leader of the zealots. Eleazar and his zealots were entrenched in the inner court of the temple, where they had huge amounts of provisions intended for priests. By their presence they controlled the activities of that sacred part of the temple. John

---

108   Three emperors who succeeded Nero and served briefly were Galba, Otho, and Vitellius. Galba was a man of wealth who had enjoyed the favor of the emperors Augustus and Tiberius. He served as a senator as a young man. In 68 AD he was appointed governor of Spain, but believing that Nero was planning his assassination, he started a rebellion against Nero with the support of many others throughout the Roman empire. When Nero fled Rome and committed suicide, Galba was acclaimed as emperor by the Senate. Upon his arrival in Rome he executed many highly placed Romans and refused to pay the members of the Praetorian Guard for the reward they said they deserved for having deserted Nero. Otho had been governor of Lusitania for ten years, and ruled with integrity. He had joined in the rebellion against Nero led by Galba, and he assumed that he would be designated as Galba's successor, but when this did not happen, Otho prepared to seize power with the aid of the Praetorian Guard. Galba was killed by the Praetorian Guard and Otho was proclaimed as emperor. However, before Galba was slain, the legions in Germany acclaimed Vitellius as emperor. Otho sent forces against Vitellius, but the forces of Vitellius were stronger. Otho was defeated and he committed suicide. With the support of his army, Vitellius then marched to Rome as the new emperor.

received the strongest support from his fellow Galileans, and because of that support he allowed them to do whatever they pleased such as prowling through the city, robbing the houses of the rich, murdering men at will, and sexually abusing women. It was all sport to them. However, the extent of their wicked behavior soon caused a revolt by the multitude. They rebelled against John and his followers and drove them into the outer confines of the temple. John threatened a massive retaliation. The leaders of the multitude considered how they were going to deal with the situation. They were not as worried about any battle with the followers of John, as they were about the madness of John who threatened to have his followers set fire to the entire city. In desperation they decided to invite Simon of Gerasa and his army into the city to overthrow John and his followers. They sent Matthias, son of Boethus, an influential priest, to Simon with the request for his assistance. In an arrogant manner Simon granted them his protection. He and his army then marched into the city with the intention of getting rid of John and his followers. Simon was acclaimed joyfully by the multitude as their savior and preserver, but he quickly took care to impose his own authority even upon those invited him into the city. And this is how Simon of Gerasa and his army obtained entry into Jerusalem.

Simon then made an assault on John and his followers, with the assistance of able men belonging to the multitude. But having the advantage of position, John and his followers fought back effectively and inflicted great damage on Simon's troops. John and his followers occupied strategic positions high in elevation on the cloisters of the temple and on four towers they had constructed there. Looking down on their adversaries, their darts and stones often hit their targets. With increasing losses, Simon attacked with less fury and especially because the majority of his men grew weary of the battle. Yet he did not quit because he had the advantage of a much larger army, and his enemy was contained within the outer confines of temple with no means of escape. The battle continued with neither side gaining an advantage. Caught in this battle, but not

Chapter 10 The Seditions Within Jerusalem

participating in it, were Eleazar son of Simon and his zealots who were entrenched in the inner court of the temple.

How Vespasian was Proclaimed Emperor by the Soldiers in Judea and Egypt

Learning what Simon of Gerasa had done in Idumea and elsewhere, and the support he had been able to enlist, Vespasian left Caesarea with his army and marched into Judea to overthrow any area with forces loyal to Simon that could threaten the Romans. He went up into the mountainous region and took the Acrabattene toparchy formerly controlled by Simon of Gerasa. He then took Bethel and Ephraim, two small cities, and nearby areas. He marched towards Jerusalem, taking many prisoners. He then dispatched Cerealis, one of his commanders, with footmen and horsemen to Idumea to put down any areas of resistance. Cerealis made waste to upper Idumea. He then went on to Hebron, where he broke through the walls around the city, killed the multitude and troops left there by Simon, and then destroyed the city with fire. Now all regions near Jerusalem, except Herodium, Macherus, and Masada, were under the control of the Romans. Vespasian could now turn his full attention to the pending assault on Jerusalem, which was his main objective.

Vespasian then returned to Caesarea and learned that Vitellius had arrived in Rome with his army and assumed the position as emperor. His army occupied the city, making Rome a huge army camp. The presence of the victorious army was a threat to the populace, because the soldiers seemed covetous and ready to plunder and slaughter any who stood in their way. This news and other news from Rome produced indignation in Vespasian who had no respect for Vitellius. It was believed by Vespasian that the Roman Empire now had a new emperor who was as morally corrupt and sordid as Nero. Vespasian worried about the future of his nation, and he was distressed because the distance and the winter season prevented him from avenging what had happened. Furthermore, he decided not to enter into any new battles in Judea because his own country was in such dire straits with Vitellius as emperor.

His commanders and soldiers then took a united action. They met and voiced their opinion that Vespasian was much more qualified to be emperor than Vitellius. He had earned that honor by his many years of service for his country. Why should the Roman troops serving in Germany believe that they can select the new emperor? Their wars had not been as laborious as the wars experienced by Vespasian's army in Galilee and Judea, and thus Vespasian's army was more entitled to select the new emperor. Besides, the senate and the people would not accept such a lascivious emperor as Vitellius. Vespasian is a chaste man of great honor who would be acclaimed throughout the empire. And, importantly, he has an heir in his son Titus. All of Vespasian's armies would give their allegiance to him, and similar support would come from the other eastern armies. In addition, Vespasian's brother Sabinus and his other son Domitian, both influential men in Rome, would be of assistance in helping him obtain the government. They made the decision that they should not delay in acclaiming Vespasian as emperor.

A delegation of commanders, soldiers, and other prominent supporters, then went to Vespasian and expressed their opinion that the government was in great danger, and Vespasian must save it. They declared him to be emperor. But being a private and reticent man, and not desiring to campaign for the position, or take steps to obtain it, he informed them that he had given the matter considerable thought, and would choose not to be emperor. In response, the soldiers drew their swords and threatened to kill him if he refused to accept their acclamation. After expressing reluctance a little longer, he finally announced that he would abide by their wishes. His commanders, including Mucianus, who was president of Syria, cried out that they would go to battle against anyone who opposed him for the position.

Chapter 10 The Seditions Within Jerusalem

With the important support of Mucianus, Vespasian then wrote to Tiberius Alexander, governor of Egypt. Vespasian informed Tiberius Alexander what his army had thrust upon him, and since he now had the burden of accepting the government, he desired to have him as a supporter and confederate. Upon receiving this letter, Tiberius Alexander immediately obliged his legions and multitude to take an oath of fidelity to Vespasian. The full support of Tiberius Alexander and the armies of that country were essential because Egypt was the main supplier of grain to Rome. Vespasian knew that Vitellius would not last long as emperor if grain and other needed substances were not being shipped to Rome from Egypt. With the full support of the armies in the eastern countries, from Syria to Egypt, and especially those in the strategic country of Egypt, Vespasian assumed, in essence, that he was now the emperor. News of what had transpired traveled abroad rapidly. Festivals were held in eastern cities acclaiming Vespasian as emperor, and armies in various parts of the empire, who were distraught at the actions of Vitellius, were happy to take an oath of fidelity to Vespasian.

Release of Josephus from Bondage

Vespasian then moved from Caesarea to Berytus, where many ambassadors came to him from Syria, and other eastern provinces, bringing him congratulations from the people. Mucianus, president of Syria also came, and told him that the people from all cities in Syria had taken the oath of fidelity to him.

Vespasian then proclaimed that Divine Providence had given him the government. He recalled that Josephus had prophesied that he would be emperor, and he became concerned that this prophet was still in bonds. So he called in Mucianus, and other commanders, and after informing them how valiant Josephus had been in the battle at Jotapata, he related the details of the predictions that Josephus had made immediately after he had been captured. He informed them that although he suspected these predictions to be fiction in the beginning, as a ruse by Josephus because of his predicament, he later came to believe that Josephus was divinely inspired. Recent events gave further testimony of that belief. He then announced, "It is a shameful thing that this man, who had foretold my coming to the empire beforehand, and who had been the minister of a Divine message to me, should still be retained in the condition of a captive or prisoner." So he called for Josephus and commanded that he should be given his liberty. Titus, who was present, suggested that it would not be fitting merely to remove the bonds from him, for the scandal of being a prisoner must also be removed. This man should never have been placed in chains, and it would be proper to remove them by cutting them to pieces, as is done for those cases when a man was placed in bonds unjustly. Vespasian agreed to this advice, so a man came in, and in front of Vespasian, Titus, Mucianus, and the other commanders, removed the chains by cutting them to pieces. By this ceremony Josephus received a testimony of his integrity and was thereby esteemed as a man of credit now and in the future.

The Death of Vitellius

Even though his support was crumbling, Vitellius nevertheless was emperor with a power base in Rome. To settle this matter Vespasian traveled to Antioch, considered various plans, and then decided to send Mucianus with a considerable army of footmen and horsemen to Italy to fight Vitellius. Because it was winter time Mucianus preferred to travel by land rather than by sea. Vespasian also sent Primus, president of Mysia [province in a region that is now western Turkey] with an army to Italy. Because it had less distance to travel, Primus's army was the first to reach Italy. To contest Primus, Vitellius commissioned Cecinna to march quickly out of Rome with a large army. Vitellius had confidence in Cecinna because he had beaten Otho, but when Cecinna viewed the largeness of the army headed by Primus, he decided to betray Vitellius and have his army join Primus's army. He was able to convince his tribunes and centurions under his command that changing allegiance was proper because the future of the Roman Empire was in the hands of the revered Vespasian and not Vitellius. However, that same night the soldiers who feared the consequences of such action in case Vitellius did persevere, decided to rebel. They drew their swords, captured Cecinna, and intended to kill him, but were persuaded not to do so by the tribunes. Instead, they put him in bonds as a traitor, and were about to send him to Vitellius when Primus ordered his army to attack. The battle ended quickly, with the destruction of what remained of Vitellius's army. Cecinna was released and was sent to Vespasian to tell him the good news. Vespasian received him well and gave him unexpected honors.

Primus then marched towards Rome. At the news that this army was approaching Rome, Sabinus, who was Vespasian's brother, decided that now was time to take action in Rome for Vespasian. He assembled a cohort of soldiers and at night time seized the capital. Vitellius was furious with the soldiers who had revolted with Sabinus, and ordered his army stationed in Rome to put down Sabinus and those with him. These soldiers from Germany were too numerous for the forces headed by Sabinus, and during the struggle, Sabinus was captured and taken to Vitellius, who had him slain. Domitian, who was Vespasian's son, with the aid of providence, was able to escape along with many other principal Romans. Within a day Primus marched into Rome and confronted Vitellius's army, which was quickly defeated. And then Vitellius came out of the palace, satiated with drink and an extravagant and luxurious meal. He was captured, dragged through the multitude, from whom he suffered much abuse, and then beheaded in the midst of Rome after having served as emperor for eight months and five days.

The next day Mucianus came into the city with his army and ordered Primus and his army to quit killing, for they were still searching houses for members of Vitellius's army and members of the populace known to be loyal to Vitellius. Mucianus then introduced Domitian to the multitude and recommended that he represent his father until Vespasian appeared in Rome. The people made acclamations of joy for Vespasian as emperor, and celebrated with festivities the death of Vitellius.

The Trip Made by Vespasian to Alexandria, and then to Rome to Receive the Government. The March on Jerusalem by Titus

In the meantime Vespasian traveled to Alexandria where he received the good news from Rome. Ambassadors came from afar to Alexandria to honor him. Alexandria was so besieged by ambassadors and well-wishers that the city could not accommodate all of them.

Traveling with Vespasian to Alexandria, among others, were Titus and Josephus. Although Josephus had been married in Caesarea, the marriage ended in divorce soon after he was released from his bonds because the Law of Moses states that it is unlawful for a priest to marry a captive woman. Vespasian had commanded Josephus to marry the captive virgin girl, and Josephus, who was of priestly origin, did so in order not to offend his benefactor. But upon becoming a free man, Josephus put this wife away, and soon after arriving in Alexandria, he married again.

After his affairs were in order in Alexandria, Vespasian made arrangements to leave for Rome, but before doing so he made plans to send his son Titus with a large army to destroy Jerusalem. He also asked Tiberius Alexander to accompany Titus, believing that this governor of Egypt was worthy to be general of an army. He would also be a valuable counselor to Titus because of his age, wisdom, and administrative skills. Another benefit was his knowledge of the terrain around Jerusalem because he had been procurator of Judea in 46-48 AD. He also gave Tiberius Alexander this honor because he had been influential in helping him obtain the government.

So Titus led his large army on the long journey from Alexandria to Caesarea, which was the staging area for the siege on Jerusalem. Accompanying Titus was Josephus, who would be a bystander as plans were made to destroy his native city that contained members of his family and many close friends.

Chapter 11

THE DESTRUCTION OF JERUSALEM BY THE ROMANS

Before Vespasian departed from Alexandria for Rome and before Titus led his army from Alexandria to Judea, the news reached Alexandria that the civil war in Jerusalem had now broken into three warring factions. Each of the adversaries (Eleazar, John, and Simon) desired political power, and this desire was so overwhelming that they fought each other rather than uniting and preparing for the siege that was coming. Eleazar and his followers controlled the inner court of the temple, and they had an advantage of having the large amount of supplies meant for the priests that they had commandeered. Another advantage was their location in the inner court of the temple which allowed them added protection. A marked disadvantage was their small number, being outnumbered by the followers of John, who, in turn were outnumbered by the followers of Simon of Gerasa. John and his followers controlled the outer perimeter of the temple, including the cloisters and towers. With Simon of Gerasa controlling the outer regions of the city, John now found himself facing enemies on two fronts. He was often forced to line his men back to back to throw darts against his opponents who were attacking from different directions. The city was so engaged by this civil war, causing so much distress, that many of the aged men and women wished the Romans would come quickly and end the miseries caused by these combatants. This civil war also led to the death of many skilled warriors who were needed to fight the Romans.

The Tragic Event That Shaped the Outcome of the Coming Siege by the Romans

To prepare for the coming siege, steps had been taken to store enough grain and other provisions to feed the defenders and populace of Jerusalem for many years. These huge amounts of provisions were kept and guarded in storehouses designed for that purpose. The army of Simon, which controlled the parts of the city where these buildings were located, began using these provisions for their subsidence. Although John and his followers were restricted to the outer perimeter of the temple, they were often able to leave this area at night undercover when there was a lull in the fighting, usually because Simon and his followers were tired and drunk. Believing that access to the provisions gave Simon a tactical advantage, the followers of John and his followers went one night to the buildings containing these valuable food substances and burned them to the ground. Simon retaliated in a like manner by destroying provisions available to John which had been stored in preparation for the siege. The madness of these individuals served the Romans well by ultimately causing a devastating famine in Jerusalem.

The March on Jerusalem by Titus

From Caesarea, Titus began his march to Jerusalem. He had with him the three legions used by his father for the siege of Galilee. In addition there was the legion from Syria that had been embarrassed by the Jews when Cestius was the commander. This legion was eager to avenge themselves against the Jews in Jerusalem. A large army from Egypt, in addition to auxiliaries sent by various kings of Syria and Arabia, contributed to the forces led by Titus.

The civil war within the city took a bizarre turn as the Roman army approached the walls of Jerusalem. At this time it was the feast of the unleavened bread, and in order to accommodate the people, Eleazar and his party opened the gates leading to the inner court of the temple and admitted those who wished to enter and worship God. John took advantage of this situation by sending a

Chapter 11 The Destruction of Jerusalem by the Romans

major proportion of his followers into the temple with weapons hidden under their garments. When they were admitted into the inner court they threw their garments aside revealing their armor and weapons. The result was chaos with innocent people being beaten and killed. Eleazar's zealots, knowing they had no chance of defending themselves because of the bedlam, tried to escape into the subterranean caverns of the temple. Many were caught and killed, *and among the casualties was Eleazar.*

Some of Eleazar's followers, forgiven for their former transgresses, were allowed to come out of the caverns and join John's followers. By this means John of Gischala and his followers obtained control of the inner court of the temple and all the warlike machines, armaments, and provisions contained there. And thus, the civil war that had consisted of three warring parties was now reduced to two, consisting of zealots headed by John of Gischala and zealots headed by Simon of Gerasa. John, who had now seized the temple, had 6,000 armed men, in addition to the 2,400 zealots formerly under Eleazar who had come over to him. Simon had 10,000 men in addition to 5,000 Idumeans who paid homage to him. These two factions continued to fight against each other and also to prey upon the people. This madness prevailed within the city even though Roman armies were camped outside the walls of the city and were preparing to make attacks on the city.

Jerusalem was protected by ravines and three walls, with each wall having massive towers. The ravines, the design of the walls, and the position of the towers made the city impregnable to an invading army consisting of footmen and horsemen, but the walls were vulnerable to the powerful battering rams of the Romans. Because of the height of the walls, embankments were needed to bring the battering rams adjacent to the walls. In order to obtain materials to build the embankments, Titus gave orders to cut down all trees near the city. The Romans then began to build embankments in key positions along the third wall. In an effort to protect this wall,

251

Simon ordered his followers to cast stones and arrows at the Romans making the embankments. Even though John himself stayed in the temple, many of his men participated in this sally against the Romans. To combat the Jews who were successfully protecting the third wall, Titus gave orders for the erection of towers near each embankment. These towers were troublesome for the Jews because they were protected by plates of iron. Soldiers on top of them were able to drive the Jews away from the wall by the use of darts, arrows, stones and light engines of war. Consequently, the construction of the embankments continued with a minimum of impedance. The Jews became discouraged, and soon the third wall was breached. The Romans who got over the wall opened the gates, which allowed the Romans to secure the area within the wall. This event occurred on the fifteenth day of the siege. The third wall and the parts of the city within that wall, known as the new city (or new quarter) were then mostly destroyed by the Romans.

Titus then prepared to attack the second wall which adjoined the tower of Antonia and the northern cloister of the temple. Because of the vigor of their attack the Romans were able to breach this wall five days after they had breached the third wall. This gap in the wall allowed 1,000 Roman soldiers to enter that part of the city. Hoping that the Jews would realize that their situation was now hopeless and thereby surrender, Titus gave the order that his troops should not widen the gap in the wall caused by the battering rams. Furthermore, they should not destroy that part of the city or kill any of the inhabitants. He wished to preserve the temple and the remaining part of the city. By his actions he anticipated that the Jews would realize that he did not want to cause any further bloodshed. Many members of the populace were now willing to concede victory to the Romans. However, the followers of Simon and John argued that the lull in the siege by the Romans was a sign of their weakness and evidence that they were unable to take the rest of the city. They threatened death to anyone who talked of surrender, and they cut the throats of those who talked of peace.

Chapter 11 The Destruction of Jerusalem by the Romans

The zealots attacked the Romans who had come through the gap in the wall, and having the advantage of the larger number of fighting men and knowledge of the lanes and layout of this part of the city, they were able to drive the Roman troops out of the city. The zealots were elated with this victory, and some actually believed that the Romans would not dare enter the city a second time. But, to the contrary, Titus ordered a full attack on the second wall, and after four days the Romans demolished it completely. Titus then placed troops in strategic positions and considered how he might best assault the first wall.

Titus Sends Josephus to Urge His Own Countrymen to Seek Peace

A decision was then made by Titus to relax the siege temporarily in order to afford Simon and John time to contemplate their situation. Titus learned that extreme famine was eminent within the city, and expected that the zealots would realize that the alternative to peace was death by famine or at the hands of the Romans. He also took this opportunity to show the Jews the might of the Roman army. It was time to distribute subsistence money to his soldiers, so he gave orders to the commanders to put the soldiers in battle array and parade with all their trappings to receive their pay. With the horsemen leading their horses, and the sun reflecting off the breast plates of the soldiers, the sight was devastating to the Jews who lined the walls and witnessed the event that lasted for four days. On the fifth day, when no sign of peace came from the Jews, Titus divided his legions and began raising embankments at Antonio and elsewhere with the intention of taking the temple. He then sent Josephus to speak to the Jews hoping that they would yield to the persuasion of one of their own countrymen.

Josephus went around the wall to find a place where he was out of the range of darts but could still be heard. In a long speech he besought them to spare the city, the temple, and themselves.

He told them that the Roman army was invincible, but Titus was now offering them a chance for their safety. If they refused his offer, Titus would take the city by force and might not spare any of them. And even though their fortifications might forestall their demise, the famine in the city would favor the Romans. While Josephus was making these exhortations to the Jews, many of them reproached him and threw stones at him. Josephus then shouted at them, calling them insensible creatures, more stupid than the stones they had thrown. He admonished them to look at their precarious position with discerning eyes and to have pity upon their families, their children, and wives, and parents, who will eventually be consumed by famine or by war. He reminded them that this danger also extended to his mother, *his wife*[109], and other members of his family. He added, however, that if they believed that it was on account of his family that he urged them to seek peace, then they should kill them and also take his own blood, for he was ready to die if it would procure the preservation of the city, the holy temple and the remaining inhabitants of the city. As Josephus was speaking, a large segment of the populace had an inclination to desert to the Romans, and many who were able to escape the vengeance of the zealots left the city for what they hoped would be safety among the Roman troops. Some of them, if they were able to do so, sold what they owned for small amounts, swallowed pieces of gold, and after going to the Romans recovered the gold from their stools, which gave them the wherewithal to provide for themselves. As promised by Josephus, Titus let them go away into the desert as free persons. Simon and John tried to prevent these desertions, and especially by men who had gold or access to gold. If there was the least shadow of suspicion that a man intended to desert, his throat was cut immediately. The zealots then began preying on wealthy persons and put many to death under the pretense that they were

---

109   In this speech Josephus states that he has a wife living in Jerusalem, indicating that he was married before he was commanded by Vespasian to marry the captive Jewish girl in Caesarea. As noted above, Josephus dissolved that marriage upon being released from bondage by Vespasian, and acquired another wife.

going to desert. As a consequence, many men were killed merely because the zealots wanted what they had. A dilemma was then faced by wealthy persons. They would be killed by the zealots if caught while trying to desert, or they might be killed by the zealots if they remained in the city.

This madness of the zealots increased in intensity as the famine in the city reached a critical stage. The zealots preyed on wealthy persons, or even persons with moderate means, for food in addition to gold and other valuable resources. They broke into private homes looking for food. If food was found they took it, but if food was not found, they often used terrible methods of torture to make persons confess where they had stored their food. Starvation also drove people who had previously been model citizens to commit crimes to obtain food for themselves and their family, with food even being taken from the mouths of babies.

> *"Neither did any other city ever suffer such miseries, or did any age ever breed a generation more fruitful in wickedness than this, from the beginning of the world."*

The Crucifixion of Jews before the Walls of Jerusalem

To prevent food from being brought into the city, Titus sent a party of horsemen to intercept those who had left the city and gone out into the valleys in search of edible plants for their starving families. If they were fortunate to find food, they had the problem of getting back into the city without being captured by the Romans. If they were able to get back into the city, they had the problem of hiding the food from the zealots or someone else. Some leaving the city had the intention of deserting to the Romans, and hoped that they might be allowed to continue into the desert as free persons. But the situation was now different and the Roman horsemen took into custody all those they were able to catch, including the food gatherers and the deserters. The number captured each day was about 500, and on some days the number was even larger. The Romans first whipped and tormented them, and then, upon the orders of Titus, crucified them in plain view of the Jews who mounted the wall. Although Titus pitied them, he justified this cruel act as a means of enticing the Jews to seek peace out of fear that they themselves might also be tortured in the same manner. Because there was soon a shortage of crosses for the number of captured Jews, the Romans resorted to cutting off the hands of the persons they captured, and sending them back into the city with the message to John and Simon that death or a similar fate will occur to anyone who opposes them. The zealots lectured to the people that this barbarism of the Romans is an example of what happens to persons who surrender to them. These acts of the Romans kept some persons from deserting who had a mind to do so, but it did not prevent others from fleeing the city. Those that left had reached the decision that it would be better to face death at the hands of the Romans than to die from starvation in the city or at the hands of the zealots.

The Destruction of the Embankments Against the First Wall by the Zealots

The Romans now proceeded to raise four different embankments against the first wall. They worked continuously for seventeen days to complete the task, and when finished they proceeded to move their battering rams up the embankments. One embankment was against the tower of Antonia. Prior to its construction, John and his followers had been able *from within* to undermine the space where it was going to be built with a pit covered with cross beams of wood.[110] Not knowing that this had occurred, the Romans constructed the embankment, partially made of wood from trees that had been cut

---

110   Josephus does not give details concerning how John was able to build and disguise this pit outside the wall. He merely writes that "John had from within undermined the space." The wording implies that knowing where the embankment would be built, the followers of John dug *from within* a tunnel under the wall, and then in the darkness of night they dug a large pit outside the wall which they covered with cross beams of wood, disguised with a layer of earthen materials.

Chapter 11 The Destruction of Jerusalem by the Romans

down on the outskirts of Jerusalem, on a foundation supported by cross beams over the top of the pit. When the construction of the embankment was finished by the Romans, the Jews set fire to the cross beams using materials daubed with pitch and bitumen. At first a thick smoke rose from the area, then as the fire spread, the cross beams gave way and the embankment crashed into the pit with an enormous noise. Deeply concerned by the shrewdness of the Jews, the Romans watched in awe as the flames grew in intensity. They made no effort to extinguish the fire because the burning embankment, which had been swallowed up by the pit, was now useless to them.

Two days later Simon and his party attacked the other embankments as the battering rams on them were shaking the walls. Again the Romans were taken by surprise. Courageous men snatched torches and rushed quickly through the midst of the Romans towards the battering rams and set them on fire. When the Romans finally realized what was happening, they threw darts at them and assaulted them with swords. But the Jews persisted until the engines were on fire. Large numbers of Romans came running from their camps and tried to put out the fires, but the Jews, with the advantage of height at the top of the wall, hindered their efforts by throwing darts at them. Other Jews came out from behind the walls and fought with the Romans with their swords without any regard for their personal safety. The Romans tried to pull the engines away from the fire, but the Jews caught hold of the battering rams and held them fast even though the iron was hot, and this caused the fire to spread from the engines to the embankments. Soon the embankments were engulfed in flames. Realizing that they could not save their engines and embankments, the Romans retired to their camps. What had taken over seventeen days to build was demolished in one hour's time, and what had happened, convinced some Romans that they could never take the city with their usual engines of war.

The Wall Built by Titus that Encompassed Jerusalem

Following the loss of their embankments, Titus consulted with his commanders about what was to be done. Some recommended storming the city with the entire army, believing that such an attack could not be withstood by the Jews. Some favored building additional embankments, while others favored doing nothing more than blockading the city completely, believing that preventing the Jews from obtaining supplies would hasten the famine and their quick surrender. After listening to these recommendations, Titus expressed concern that because the wall and the fortifications gave the Jews an advantage, storming the city would result in a large number of Roman deaths. It was not practical to build additional embankments at the present time because of the absence of available materials. All trees in the area had already been cut down and used in the construction of the former embankments. Furthermore, his army was not large enough to form an effective blockade. Spreading the army around the city would thin its ranks and make the troops in any area vulnerable to concentrated attacks by the Jews. It was his opinion that the right strategy was to build a wall that would contain the Jews within the city and prevent them from obtaining any supplies from outside the city. An effective wall would cause increased famine within the city, and when the Jews were in a weakened condition because of the famine, and unable to protect their walls, embankments would be built from trees in outlying regions. The construction of the wall would also keep his army from being idle, a situation that Titus wanted to avoid. He also believed that the construction of the wall would hasten victory, which was greatly desired, because the reputation of a Roman commander can be tarnished if a long time is required to achieve success in the battlefield.

His arguments prevailed and Titus gave the order that the various legions of the army should be assigned to areas around the city and be given the responsibility of building sections of the wall. The legions worked energetically in competition with each other,

Chapter 11 The Destruction of Jerusalem by the Romans

to complete their assignments. What would have usually taken months to build was finished in a few days. The wall was 5 miles in length, and enclosed the city. Garrisons were then placed at various positions around this wall, and the areas between garrisons were patrolled to make sure that the wall was an effective blockade of the city.[111]

The Jews now had less hope of escaping from the city, and the famine continued to increase in intensity, resulting in the deaths of entire families. Lanes of the city were laden with persons who had died. When burial was not possible, the bodies were thrown over the walls into the valleys below. When Titus made his rounds and viewed these valleys and experienced the thick putrefaction coming from them, he gave a groan, and spreading his hands towards heaven, called God to witness that this was not his doing.

The Romans had ample food brought in from Syria, and they would stand near the wall and show the Jews what great quantities of provisions they possessed, hoping that this would bring the Jews to their senses and open the gates of the city. The zealots would not yield, and Titus made the decision to build the embankments once again. Materials for these embankments came from trees cut down in areas far from Jerusalem.

Further Crimes of Simon of Gerasa

Matthias, son of Boethus, was an influential priest who was greatly esteemed by the people. He was also the person who invited Simon and his army into Jerusalem. At this time Simon took vengeance on Matthias, using the excuse that Matthias was on

---

111 Josephus gives no details on the height of the wall or what materials were used to build it. In order for the wall to be finished in a few days the materials had to be readily available. One source of stones would have been the second and third walls that the Romans had already demolished. Wood and stones from the vast number of homes that the Romans had destroyed would have also been available. Because it was built hurriedly and from different materials, perhaps it might have been better described by Josephus as a barricade rather than a wall.

the side of the Romans. First, he killed three of Matthias's sons in his presence, and then he killed Matthias. He also killed another eminent priest, the scribe of the sanhedrin, and fifteen other men of eminence. He also slew those who lamented the deaths of these persons. Simon also kept Josephus's father in prison and made a public proclamation that no citizen whatsoever should speak with him or go near him. He also killed a group of mutinous men, led by an officer in charge of one of the towers who expressed concern with Simon's barbaric actions and the hopelessness of the situation. This officer convinced his cohorts they should assist the Romans in taking the city, but when the officer called to the Romans from the tower with the proposal, Simon had his men kill him and the other mutinous men in view of the Romans. Their bodies were then mangled and thrown down from the wall of the city.

Josephus Presumably Killed by a Stone and Comments by his Mother

One day when Josephus was walking near the wall of the city, he was hit in the head by a stone that was thrown at him by one of the zealots. He fell to the ground, and the Jews made a sally in an attempt to capture him. They would have succeeded if Titus had not sent men to protect him. The Romans carried him away, and Josephus knew little of what had transpired because of his unconscious state. The zealots rejoiced because they believed that they had slain the man whom they were the most desirous of killing. The announcement of his death was made in the city, and many of the multitude were saddened at the news, because they viewed him as a person who could protect them if they decided to desert to the Romans. When Josephus's mother heard in prison that her son was dead, she said that it was always her opinion, since the siege of Jotapata, that he would be slain and she would never enjoy him alive again. She also made great lamentation privately that she would not be able to bury that extraordinary son of hers, whom she expected to bury her. Josephus soon recovered from his head wound, went out to the wall, and shouted that it would not be long before they (the zealots) would be punished for the wound they had given him. He also once again encouraged the people to surrender and to receive the security of the Romans. Upon hearing Josephus's words, some of the Jews leaped down from the wall. Others rushed out of the city as if to intercept them, and then they deserted. As Josephus had said, they were received kindly by the Romans, who offered them food, but for some of these persons the consequences were disastrous. They were in a critical stage of starvation, and upon gorging themselves, their bodies rebelled. Being unaccustomed to food, they suffered gruesome deaths. Those deserters who survived were those who were able to contain their appetites and only consume traces of food at the outset.

However, some the Jewish deserters who believed in the words of Josephus, unfortunately, found themselves in the camps of the Syrians and Arabians, who comprised the auxiliary troops of the army under Titus Knowing that some of these deserters swallowed gold coins before leaving the city, the Syrians and Arabians dissected their bellies and searched for gold pieces among the excrement. When Titus was informed of this barbaric practice, he gave the order that it must stop. He also said that he would kill all offenders. He did not do so however, because the number of offenders was great, and Titus also learned to his chagrin that even some Roman soldiers were guilty of this offense. In one night's time about two thousand deserters were dissected. Even after the order had been given by Titus that this infamous practice must cease, some Syrians and Arabians still did it privately, after looking around to see that no Roman was spying on them. Their hatred of the Jews and their love of money were more overpowering than the fear of their own death if they were caught. This slaughter of Jews continued even though gold was found in only a small percentage of those who were dissected. Thus, Jewish deserters who believed they would find refuge in the camps of the Roman army, as assured by Josephus, did not find it in the camps of the Syrians and Arabians, and even in some of the camps of the Romans.

Josephus

Continuing Effects of the Famine in Jerusalem

The miseries of the famine grew worse each day. The number that perished by famine was prodigious, and the misery of the people was unspeakable. One zealot, who was entrusted to guard one of the gates, deserted to the Romans and told Titus that no fewer than 115,888 bodies had been carried out through that gate and cast away. Various eminent men deserted to Titus and informed him that no fewer than 600,000 persons had died of starvation. When the bodies were not carried out through the gates or cast over the walls, they were laid in heaps in large houses with shut doors, or they were laid in heaps in the lanes of the city. The multitude of carcasses that lay in heaps, one upon another was a horrible sight, and produced an unbearable stench.

The hunger was so intolerable that the people would eat things that even animals would not touch. People were driven to search common sewers and old dunghills of cattle and to eat the dung they found there. Girdles, shoes, and leather were chewed, and pieces of old hay became food for some. And one woman did an unthinkable thing. She snatched up her infant son who was sucking at her breast, and said, "O thou miserable infant! For whom shall I preserve thee in this war, this famine, and this sedition? . . . This famine will destroy us. . . Come on, be thou my food. . ." She then slew her child and roasted him. She ate one half of him, and concealed the other half. Zealots who were passing by smelled the scent of food. They entered her home and threatened to slit her throat if she did not show them what food she had cooked. She replied by saying that she had saved a good portion for them, and produced what was left of her son. The men left trembling, and soon the whole city was lamenting the insanity of this poor woman who had committed this horrid act.

The Breach of the First Wall by the Romans

Titus, who was distressed by what he was hearing about the conditions within the city, ordered that the embankments against the

Chapter 11 The Destruction of Jerusalem by the Romans

walls should be constructed with haste. The Romans concentrated their efforts at the wall adjoining the tower of Antonia which protected one corner of the temple. This tower was controlled by John and his party of zealots. To build the embankments, all trees were cut down within 15 miles of the city, causing those places that were formerly dense with trees to become a desert. The new embankments were a worry to the Jews and the Romans. The Jews feared that if they could not destroy them by fire the city would be taken. The Romans knew that if the embankments were burned, they could not build new ones in the near future because of the scarcity of trees. For this reason the new embankments were guarded carefully by the Romans. The Romans were also perplexed because the zealots were fighting with courage and alacrity, which was an unexpected situation. They expected that the famine would be taking its toll on the defenders of the city as well as the multitude. However, John and his party who controlled the temple still had provisions to sustain them. He used the food substances that had been stored in the temple for priests. He also emptied the vessels of the sacred wine and oil which the priests had kept to be poured on burnt offerings and distributed it to his followers, stating that it was proper to use divine things while they were fighting for the Divinity.

Even though the embankments against the wall adjoining Antonia were heavily guarded by the Romans, the followers of John went out with torches to do damage to them. But they were not united in action, went out in a slow and timid manner, and hesitated when they saw the large number of Romans guarding the embankments. When the Romans began throwing darts and stones at them, causing many casualties, they retreated back into the city. Following this retreat the Romans brought their battering rams against the wall, even though stones were thrown at them from above. Because of the massive structure of the wall it did not yield to the blows given it by the battering ram. Several of the Romans then covered themselves with armor to protect themselves from the stones coming from above, and by using their hands and iron tools, they were able to undermine the wall by removing four of its large stones. That night the wall in that region where John and his followers had previously dug the pit from within was so shaken by the battering rams that it finally fell.

The Jews were disheartened by this turn of events, but took courage because the tower of Antonia was still standing. The Romans were elated by the collapse of the wall, but then were discouraged when they discovered that John and his followers had built another wall behind the one they had just brought down. Titus cheered them on by promising that victory was in sight and that the newly-built wall would be easy to ascend and destroy. Forays were then made up the wall by using ropes and ladders. Following vicious battles with the guards, the Romans obtained control of the wall and then the tower of Antonia. The Romans then turned their attention to the temple, but the zeal of the Jews was too much for the limited number of Romans engaged in that battle. The Romans were driven away from the temple and back to the tower of Antonia.

Titus then gave orders to his soldiers that they were to dig up the foundations of the tower of Antonia, and make a passage large enough for his army to enter that part of the city. He then commanded Josephus to speak once again to the zealots, and especially to John, urging them to surrender in order to save their temple and city, or at least to fight in an area that would not defile the temple. Josephus beseeched them earnestly and emotionally to come to their senses and to spare their holy temple and city from further destruction. At his words there was great silence and sadness among his people, but John responded by casting many reproaches on Josephus and stating that Jerusalem was God's city and could not be taken. Following the words of Josephus, some of the more eminent persons in the city, including priests and sons of these priests fled away to the Romans. Titus gave security to these persons and sent them away to Gophna where they would be safe. He also told them that when the war was over, he would restore their possessions to them. When they

Chapter 11 The Destruction of Jerusalem by the Romans

disappeared from the camps of the Romans, the zealots announced that these deserters had been killed by the Romans, and a similar fate would happen to any other deserters. To stop this rumor, Titus recalled the deserters from Gophna, and had them walk around the wall with Josephus in plain sight of the Jews who lined the top of the walls. When they were observed by the people, many others fled to the Romans. The men recalled from Gophna also stood before the wall, and with tears in their eyes urged the zealots to save the city and the temple by allowing the Romans to enter the city. The zealots cast bitter reproaches upon these deserters. Titus was deeply affected with this state of affairs, reproached John and his party, and warned them of the consequences of their actions.

In the meantime, the Romans destroyed much of the foundation of the tower of Antonia and made a broad passage way to the temple. The legions then entered and began to raise embankments against the walls of the temple. Engines of war began battering the western edifice of the inner temple, but when six days passed and no impressions were made because of the massive stones used by Herod in the construction of the temple, Titus then ordered that the gates should be set on fire.

Prominent guards numbered among the followers of Simon then deserted to the Romans, hoping that they would be received safely. Titus objected to giving these zealots any consideration, suspecting that their desertion might be some sort of trick. He argued that these warriors only sought sanctuary because their cause was lost. But since he had promised security to deserters, he relented, but did not give them the same privileges that he had given the others.

The fire on the gates took hold and caused the silver over the gates to melt. Soon the cloisters above the gates were also in flame. The fire prevailed for two days, but the fire did not spread to all the cloisters. The soldiers were forced to burn one section at a time. On the next day Titus commanded part of his army to quench the fires and to make a road allowing his legions to march into that part of the city. Then he called a meeting of his commanders, including Tiberius Alexander, and asked for advice on what should happen to the temple. Some recommended that it should be destroyed, arguing that the Jews would continue to rebel as long as it stood. Others recommended that it should not be destroyed if the Jews would agree to vacate it and not store any arms in it. If they refused, then it should be considered to be a citadel rather than a holy house, and should be demolished by fire. Titus then gave his opinion that it would be mischievous to burn such a magnificent structure and it should be saved as an ornament for the Roman government. Tiberius Alexander and two other principal commanders agreed with Titus, and the assembly was dismissed. Action was then taken to quench all fires in the vicinity of the temple and to prevent any other fires from starting there.

Titus retired to the tower of Antonia and resolved to storm the temple early in the morning with his entire army, but events then got out of hand. After Titus retired, the zealots attacked the Romans who were trying to quench the fire that was burning the inner court of the temple. The Romans put the Jews to flight, and then one of the Roman soldiers, being driven by some kind of divine fury, took burning materials, and being lifted up by another soldier, set fire to a golden window through which there were passage ways to rooms in the temple. The flames spread upward and into these rooms, and soon it was evident that the temple was doomed. Other soldiers rushed to the scene and being caught up in the frenzy of the situation, they helped spread the fire. Since Titus was unable to control the fury of the soldiers, the fire proceeded on and on, and soon the holy house was engulfed in flames. While the temple was burning, plundering was carried out by the Romans. They also killed ten thousand persons they had caught, without any consideration of age or position. Numbered among these persons who were killed were many followers of John, but John himself and many zealots were able to escape into the upper city. About six thousand of the persons killed were men, women, and children who were in the temple because a false prophet had made a public proclamation that God wanted his people to go to the temple where they would receive miraculous signs of their deliverance.

Upon the flight of the zealots out of the temple and into the upper city, the Romans set fire to places around the temple, including the cloisters and the gates. And there was great wailing by the populace as they viewed the flames reaching to the sky from their holy house. This destruction of the temple by fire occurred in the second year of the reign of Vespasian [70 AD].

The Romans then brought their ensigns to the temple, set them against the eastern gate, and offered sacrifices to them. At the same time they made acclamations of joy and proclaimed Titus as imperator. These acts were the greatest of insults to the Jews who witnessed their holy house being dishonored in this manner.

When the zealots were encompassed on all sides and there was no way of escape, they petitioned for an audience with Titus. Hoping that complete surrender would come from this meeting, Titus agreed to meet with them. He positioned himself and part of his army on one side of a bridge that connected the upper city with the temple. On the other side were John, Simon, and the zealots who hoped to be pardoned. Titus ordered his soldiers to control their rage and not to attack their adversaries with darts. He then appointed an interpreter, which was the sign that he was the conqueror. After listening to their supplication he lectured them about their insolence, stating that on different occasions he had given them opportunities to save themselves, their families, their temple, and their city. Yet, in each case they showed contempt for his proposals. He told them, however, that if they would now throw down their arms and deliver themselves to him, he would grant them their lives, but he as their conqueror would decide the fates of certain individuals. The zealots replied that they could not accept his offer because they had sworn never to give up their arms and surrender. What they desired was to be able to depart in safety into the desert with their wives and children. Titus was indignant with this response stating that since they would soon be his captives, they should not be dictating terms to him. He then proclaimed to them that they should be prepared to defend themselves against his army.

At the conclusion of the meeting with Titus at the bridge, the zealots rushed to the royal palace (Herod's palace) in the upper city. They drove away the Romans who were there, killed all the people who had sought safety within the palace, which numbered about 8,400, and plundered them of what they had. The zealots also dispersed themselves throughout the upper city, where they plundered and killed without mercy anyone they suspected of having food.

Titus gave orders to continue burning and plundering the city. The next day the Romans drove all the zealots out of the lower city and began to destroy it by fire, including the palace of Helena. At that time the sons and brethren of Izates, the former king of Adiabene, were living in the palace, together with other eminent men from Adiabene. They petitioned Titus for their freedom. He admonished them in an angry manner for remaining in the city throughout the war, and decided to keep all of them in custody. He placed the king's sons and kinsmen in bonds and sent them to Rome where they served as hostages as insurance that Adiabene would remain loyal to Rome.

When Titus perceived that the upper city could not be taken without raising embankments against it and destroying the walls, he assigned several units of his army to the task. He designated that a major embankment would be against the wall of the royal palace (Herod's palace). It took 18 days to build the embankments and bring engines of war against the walls of the palace. Even though some of the zealots sought refuge in subterranean vaults

Chapter 11 The Destruction of Jerusalem by the Romans

or elsewhere in the city, a great many of them tried to prevent the Romans from battering the walls. However, the Romans had greater numbers and the zealots, weakened by numbers, famine, and low morale, were ineffective. Soon the walls were breached and the zealots who opposed the Romans then began to flee in terror. Some sought refuge in subterranean caverns. Others fled from the city and tried to force their way past the wall built around the city by the Romans, and find safety in the desert. The Romans guarding these walls repulsed them and they had to retreat back into the city. A slaughter then began. The Romans went into the lanes of the upper city, and with their swords drawn, slew the zealots they encountered. They often set fire to houses without determining if inhabitants were present. When they entered homes for the purpose of plundering, they frequently found entire families who had died from the famine. In some cases upper rooms were filled with corpses, testifying to the tragedy of the famine. At the sight of this horror, and because of the stench, the Romans went out of these houses without touching anything.

Because the Romans were tired of killing, and a great multitude still remained alive, Titus gave orders that they should kill only those that possessed arms and opposed them. All others should be taken as captives. But the Romans did kill the aged and the infirmed. Those not slain were driven into the temple where one of Titus's freedmen determined the fate of each according to his merits. All captives who were impeached by others to be seditious and robbers were killed. Among the young men, the tallest and most beautiful were chosen for the *triumph in Rome*. Those remaining who were under 17 years old were sold as slaves. Many captives above 17 years were chosen to work in Egyptian mines. A great number of the captives were sentenced to be killed in theaters either by the sword or wild beasts in various provinces. The number of captives was so great it was difficult for the Romans to find food for them, and about 11,000 died for want of food while decisions were being made concerning them. Some refused to eat even when food was offered to them, preferring to die of starvation rather than to be a slave, or to die later in a theater at the hands of the Romans.

The Capture of John of Gischala

The Romans then made a search of the underground caverns where they found about two thousand persons who had died from the famine, by their own hands, or by the hands of others. They also found John of Gischala and members of his party hiding in these caverns. John wanted food and he also begged the Romans for his personal security. *John was taken captive, but instead of being slain, he was condemned by Titus to perpetual imprisonment.*

The Destruction of Jerusalem Except for Three Towers and the Capture of Simon of Gerasa

When the army had no more persons to kill, Titus gave the order that they should demolish the entire city and temple, but should leave the wall that enclosed the city on the west side. Titus also ordered that because of their superior structure and eminence, the three towers (Phasaelus, Hippicus, and Mariamne) comprising the royal palace built by Herod should also be left intact. When Titus visited the upper city he admired the design of the royal palace and the strength of these towers. He marveled at the size of the stones, the exactness of their joints, and the breadth of the walls. He proclaimed that these towers should be preserved as a monument of his good fortune. They should also be spared to give protection for the troops that would be stationed there. The rest of the city was so thoroughly destroyed, that persons who later visited the area could not believe that it had ever been inhabited.

With the completion of the war, Titus rewarded his commanders and troops in a tribunal that lasted three days. He then sent sections of his army to various destinations, leaving the tenth legion to guard Jerusalem. He then traveled to Caesarea with his army, spoils of the war, and the captives. From Caesarea Titus went to Caesarea

Chapter 11 The Destruction of Jerusalem by the Romans

Philippi where he staged many shows.[112] A great many captives were destroyed in these shows by being thrown to wild beasts, or being forced to kill each other in games, with one group fighting another group as if they were enemies.

Titus was informed at Caesarea Philippi that Simon of Gerasa (son of Gioras) had been captured in Jerusalem. When the Roman army broke into the upper city, Simon and some of his faithful friends went into a subterranean cavern that was not discovered by the Romans. Numbered among his friends were stone cutters who had tools of their trade. The group had also been able to obtain a great quantity of provisions that would sustain them for a long period of time. Their objective was to dig a tunnel from this cavern to a safe location beyond the wall where they might escape. They proceeded at a good pace until they hit solid earth, and then their progress was greatly slowed. Because of the time required to complete the tunnel, it became apparent that the provisions they had with them, no matter how carefully they were rationed, would not last. Simon then thought that he might astonish the Romans and therefore elude them by putting on a white frock and a purple robe and appearing suddenly out of the ground, as an apparition, in the place where the temple had stood. And indeed, the Romans who first saw him were astonished, but he was soon identified and placed in bonds. The subterranean area from which Simon had risen was then searched by the Romans, and the other members of his party were taken captive. *When Titus was informed of Simon's capture, he ordered that Simon should be taken in bonds to Caesarea, and eventually to Rome where he would be a key person in the celebration of the triumph.*

---

112   It has been conjectured that the incentive for Titus to stage these shows in Caesarea Philippi was the opportunity to be with Beatrice, the sister of king Agrippa II, whom he had met on an earlier visit to this city and who later became his mistress in Rome.

Josephus

Chapter 12

THE TRIUMPH IN ROME AND THE DESTRUCTION OF REMAINING JEWISH STONGHOLDS

After returning to Caesarea from Caesarea Philippi, Titus celebrated the birthday of his brother Domitian in a splendid manner and staged shows and games that inflicted a great deal of punishment on the Jews who were his captives. The number of captives, who were slain by beasts, by fighting each other, or by burning, exceeded 2,500. Titus then went to Berytus, a city of Phoenicia, where he celebrated his father's birthday by holding magnificent shows during which another multitude of Jewish captives were killed. After spending time in Berytus, Titus visited various cities in Syria where he also put on similar shows resulting in the slaughter of captive Jews. From there he went to cities on the Euphrates where he received messengers from the king of Parthia, who sent him a crown of gold in honor of his victory at Jerusalem. With the winter season now almost ending, Titus made plans for his return to Rome via Egypt. One stop was in Antioch where he learned that the gentiles residing there wanted him to eject all the Jews from their city, or at least deny them any privileges. He met with the senate and multitude in a theater, and after listening to their pleas, he responded that he could not honor their request because the country of the Jews had been destroyed and they had no place to go. He also refused to take away their privileges, but permitted the Jews of Antioch to continue to enjoy the same privileges which they had before. His proclamation was a surprise and a great disappointment to the gentiles of Antioch.

From Antioch, Titus traveled to Jerusalem, where he compared the present desolation and melancholy with the glory of the past. He

Josephus

viewed the ruins with great pity and cursed the zealots, who because of their revolt against Rome were the authors of the destruction of that magnificent city.

Titus then traveled hurriedly with his army across the desert to Egypt, and finally arrived in Alexandria, where he made plans to travel to Rome by sea. In Alexandria were John of Gischala and Simon of Gerasa, the leaders of the captives, and 700 captives who had been selected because they were tall and handsome of body. Titus ordered that they should be taken to Rome where they would play roles in the *triumph*.

Josephus was in Alexander with Titus, and when Titus was making plans for his trip to Rome he invited Josephus and his wife, whom Josephus had married in Alexandria, to sail with him. The bond of friendship was strong between these two men, and Titus was always quick to be of assistance to him. During the siege of Jerusalem, Josephus's life was threatened frequently by both the Jews and Romans. The Jews were anxious to get him in their power and punish him, and the Romans, whenever they were beaten in a battle, wanted to put the blame on Josephus, accusing him of conspiracy with the Jews. In every situation, however, Titus always came to the defense of Josephus and refused to listen to any vehement charges against him from his soldiers. When the city of Jerusalem was destroyed, Titus invited Josephus to take whatever he wanted from the ruins. Josephus responded by requesting that members of his family be given their liberty, and that he also be given the "holy books." Titus released from bondage the brother[113] of Josephus and also gave liberty to 50 of his friends. Josephus went to the place where a large number of captive women and children were being held. Among them were many friends and acquaintances, and he was able to obtain the freedom of 190 of them. Josephus was then sent with a Roman general to a village to determine if it were suitable for

---

113   Since only a brother was released from bondage, it is assumed that all other close relatives, including his parents and wife, were deceased.

Chapter 12 The Triumph in Rome

a camp. Upon his return he observed many captives being crucified, and recognized three of them as being former acquaintances. With tears in his eyes he went to Titus and asked that they be released. Titus commanded that they be taken down immediately from their crosses and be given assistance in order that they might recover. Unfortunately, two of them died while in the care of physicians, but the third recovered. Titus also conjectured that lands owned by Josephus in Judea would not bring any profit because a garrison had been placed there to guard the country. To make amends he gave him lands elsewhere. Titus did all this for Josephus because of the great respect he had for him. One of the great honors was for Titus to invite Josephus and his wife to accompany him on his voyage by sea to Rome.

In Rome Titus was met in a glorious ceremony by his father Vespasian, his brother Domitian, and all of Rome. The multitude expressed great joy at the sight of the emperor and his two sons. The decision was then made to hold a single triumph, celebrating the victories of both Vespasian and Titus, even though the senate had previously voted that each should have a separate triumph. On the appointed day no one remained in their homes, for all departed to obtain positions that would allow them an advantage in viewing the pageantry. The initial parade consisted of soldiers and commanders, followed by Vespasian and Titus, crowned with laurel and clothed in ancient purple habits. They proceeded to Octavian's Walks, where they were received by the senators and other principal persons. There, Vespasian and Titus sat on ivory chairs and received acclamations from the soldiers. Vespasian and Titus gave prayers, and after a short speech by Vespasian to the people, the soldiers were sent away to a dinner given by the emperor. Food was served and sacrifices were offered to the gods. A magnificent parade was then held. Workmen with great skill had created floats three and four stories high, adorned in gold and silver. These floats were designed to proclaim the power and riches of the Roman Empire. Images of gods were carried along, as well as many different species of animals. Even the captives appearing in this pageantry were adorned. Along came floats showing the captured cities with each having a caricature of the conquered general appearing on the top of the float showing how he had been taken.[114] Treasures taken from the temple in Jerusalem and elsewhere were put on display. The climax was the appearance of Vespasian and Titus in chariots, with Domitian riding along side them on a stately horse.

The parade proceeded to the temple of Jupiter Capitolinus. There they stood still, for it was an ancient Roman custom for every one to remain silent until someone brought the news that the general of the enemy had been slain. *This general was Simon of Gerasa (son of Gioras)*, who had been selected for this important symbolic ceremony.[115] Simon had been in the parade with the other captives. With a rope around his neck he was tormented by those who dragged him along. He was taken to a designated place in the Forum where it was Roman law that captured generals condemned to die should be slain. There Simon was ceremoniously beheaded. When it was announced that he had been slain, all the people shouted for joy in unison, and prayers and sacrifices were offered. Banquets were then held throughout the city, which brought an end to the festival celebrating the victories of the Roman armies over the enemy.

Concerning Herodium, Macherus, and Masada, Three Jewish Strongholds that Remained Following the Destruction of Jerusalem

Even though the triumph had been held in Rome celebrating the defeat of the Jews, three Jewish strongholds had yet to be conquered by the Romans. These citadels were Herodium, Macherus, and Masada. The Roman general Bassus was sent to Judea to resolve

---

114   Because of his friendship with Vespasian, it is highly unlikely that a caricature of Josephus would have been present on the float celebrating Vespasian's victory at Jotapata in Galilee.

115   John of Gischala had previously been sentenced to life imprisonment for his role in the revolt.

Chapter 12 The Triumph in Rome

this problem. He assumed command of the forces stationed in Judea and first marched on the fortress at Herodium only about 7 miles south of Jerusalem, where Herod had been buried. The Jews who defended the citadel on top of the cone-shaped hill were quickly subdued by the Roman army led by Bassus.

The next citadel to be attacked was Macherus located on the eastern shore of the Dead Sea. Bassus was told that it was necessary to demolish this citadel, because otherwise it might be used as a refuge by those who wish to continue their battles against Rome. When Alexander Janneus was king of the Jews, he built a citadel there because of the natural terrain of the area. The citadel was located on top of majestic peak nearly 4,000 feet above the level of the Dead Sea, and was protected on three sides by deep ravines. It was later demolished by the Roman forces led by Gabinius in his war against Aristobulus. When Herod became king, he reached the conclusion that because of ongoing political problems with Arabia, the formidable fortress at Macherus should be rebuilt. Petra, a prominent Arabian city, is located not too far away from Macherus. Herod selected a site on one of the northern slopes and built a city there, known as the lower city, and protected it with high walls and towers. From that city he built a pathway to the top of the mountain, where he rebuilt the citadel enclosed by high walls with towers erected at the corners. King Herod built a magnificent palace[116] within the walls, containing large and beautiful edifices. He also built many facilities for receiving and storing water, so that defenders of the citadel would have plenty of water to meet their needs during a long siege.[117] He also stored darts and other machines of war within the walls that would contribute to the security of the defenders during a long siege.

---

116   With the death of king Herod, Macherus was located within the tetrarchy ruled by Herod Antipas, and it was at Macherus that John the Baptist was imprisoned and slain

117   Recent excavations have revealed that the lower city and upper city (citadel) were connected by an aqueduct that allowed for the flow of water from cisterns in the upper city to cisterns in the lower city.

With the arrival of the Roman army at Macherus, Bassus viewed the terrain and pondered how he would be able to move heavy machines of war to the top of the mountain. Battering rams would be needed to assault the fortified and high walls of the citadel. But the deepness of some of the ravines and the steepness of the pathway in various locations would prevent these machines of war from being transported from the desert floor to the top of the mountain. After considering all options he reached the conclusion that the needed machines of war could be moved to the site of the citadel by smoothing out the rugged terrain with earthen embankments at selected sites in a valley that lay on the east side of the mountain. The army then proceeded with haste to build these embankments.[118]

A division then occurred among the Jews living there. Many were newcomers who had gone to Macherus because of the security that it provided. The Jews who lived there viewed these persons as strangers. They separated themselves from them by seizing the upper city (citadel) and forcing the strangers to stay in the lower city where they faced the principle dangers imposed by the Romans. In addition to the safety it provided, the residents had a reason for controlling the citadel. They knew that their situation was perilous because of the strength of the Roman forces, and it was their hope that from a position of strength they might be able to negotiate a pardon from the Romans by agreeing to surrender the citadel.

To strengthen their position, the Jews in the upper citadel began to make sallies against the Romans who were constructing the embankments. The purpose was to prolong the anticipated siege of the citadel and bring cost to the Romans. Each day teams of Jews would rush out of the city through the gates at opportune times and engage the Romans in battle. On some days the Jews were successful, but on others the Romans anticipated their coming and were able to drive them away. A surprising event then occurred

---

118 Some of these embankments built by the Romans are still visible at Macherus.

Chapter 12 The Triumph in Rome

that caused the Jews to give up the citadel. A young man named Eleazar, from an eminent Jewish family, was one of the principal leaders in the attacks against the Romans. He was very bold, and he encouraged the Jews to hinder the raising of the embankments. His management of the attacks caused much mischief to the efforts of the Romans, and he often brought up the rear in the retreat back into the city after a sally. One time he lingered outside the gates and talked with persons who were on the wall, intent upon hearing what they were saying. Then to his surprise, and also to those on the wall, a strong Egyptian by birth, who was part of the Roman army, came upon him suddenly, and carried him off to the Roman camp. Those on the wall were so amazed by the suddenness of the event that they were unable to give Eleazar any assistance. Bassus, the general of the Romans, ordered that Eleazar should be taken to a place where he was visible to those Jews on the walls surrounding the citadel. He was then stripped naked and sorely whipped. The Jews lamented what was happening before their eyes, and there was great mourning in the city. Bassus then ordered that a cross be set up to crucify Eleazar. This caused great grief in the citadel, and the Jews cried out that they could not bear to see Eleazar destroyed in this manner. Whereupon Eleazar shouted to them that they should disregard him, now that he was going to suffer a miserable death. But he exhorted them to save themselves by yielding to Roman power, since all other people had been conquered by them. Moved by what he said, and also because he was from such a prominent and large family, the Jews sent messengers to the Roman general stating that they would surrender the citadel if they would be permitted to leave the city and take Eleazar with them. Knowing that such surrender would stop the need to finish the building of the embankments, and would save the lives of many Roman soldiers, the general agreed to these terms.

When the strangers in the lower city learned of this agreement, which did not include them, they made plans to depart from the city at night time, hoping that they might be able to elude the Romans. Bassus was informed of their intended flight, and Roman soldiers were there to meet them when they came out of the opened gates. Although some of the men were able to escape, about 1,700 were caught and slain. The women and children were made slaves. Bassus then honored the covenant he had made with the Jews who had surrendered the citadel. He restored Eleazar to them and allowed them to depart unharmed.

From Macherus, Bassus marched hastily to the forest of Jarden because he had heard that many Jews who had fled from Jerusalem had taken refuge there. Because they were a formidable force that could be a future problem for the Romans, Bassus surrounded the forest with horsemen to prevent any escape. He then ordered the footmen to cut down the trees of the forest as a means to ferret out the Jews. Realizing the seriousness of their situation, the Jews mounted an attack. But their efforts were futile. Although 1,200 Romans were slain, all 3,000 Jews were killed. Included was Judas, the son of Jairus, who was their general. He had also been captain of a band at the siege of Jerusalem. When the Romans entered Jerusalem, he had gone into an underground vault and eventually had been able to escape from the city. From there he found refuge in the forest of Jarden.

The Siege Against Masada

One stronghold remained, and that was Masada in Idumea on the western shore of the Dead Sea. Although Bassus had full intention of seizing it, he died unexpectedly while in Judea. He was replaced by Flavius Silva, who upon arriving in Judea organized a large army utilizing forces from different places. He then made an expedition against Masada, which was occupied by Sicarii. Their leader was Eleazar, son of Jairus, who was a descendant of Judas the Galilean, founder of the fourth sect of Jewish philosophy. This Judas had urged Jews not to submit to Roman taxation when Cyrenius was sent to Judea by Augustus Caesar to do a census and collect taxes. Eleazar escaped to Masada during the time of the beginning of the civil war in Jerusalem, and before the march on Judea by Cestius,

Chapter 12 The Triumph in Rome

the president of Syria.

Upon arriving at Masada, Silva positioned garrisons at various places and assessed the situation. Because of the barren nature of the area around Masada, food and water for the army had to be brought from great distances, and captive Jews were used for this purpose. The major problem facing Silva was that the fortress was unconquerable by foot soldiers. It was located on top of a large rock with steep sides, so abrupt that even an animal could not climb them. There were only two places where ascent was possible by narrow trails, and these trails were easy to guard by the Sicarii. One passage way was called the *Serpent* because of the narrowness of the trail and the large number of bends (switch backs). This trail was treacherous because a slip of the feet at certain places could cause a person to fall to his or her death. On top of this rock, Jonathan the High Priest, who was the brother of Judas Maccabee, built a fortress and called it Masada. Realizing the potential of Masada as a mighty citadel, king Herod then added to it. He built a wall composed of white stone around the top of the rock about one mile in length. The wall was about 20 feet high and 13 feet thick and contained 38 towers, each about 83 feet high. Herod built a sumptuous palace within the wall. The palace had a wall around it that was high and strong. At each corner were towers that were 80 feet high. The walls and floor were paved with stones of different colors. He also cut deep pits, as reservoirs for water. A large tower built at the narrowest part of the trail leading up the hill (about 1600 feet from the top) made it almost impossible for an enemy to get past that point. Large houses on top were used for the storage of grain and other edible seeds, oil, fruits, and dates. An area on top had soil that was adequate for agriculture, so certain food substances could be grown there, nourished by the water brought from below and stored in the reservoirs, or caught in cisterns during rainstorms. Herod also provided Masada with large quantities of weapons of war, enough for 10,000 men.

Herod built the fortress to his specifications as a refuge for himself. He feared at one time in his life that he might find himself in a war with Cleopatra, who was attempting to have Antony remove him as ruler and place Judea under her control. Herod also feared that the Jewish people might be successful in a revolt against his government, and replace him with a Hasmonean ruler. If either event happened, Herod planned to seek refuge at Masada where he, his family, and his followers could withstand a siege for a long period of time. When the Sicarii seized Masada from the Romans by treachery, they found many of the provisions and weapons of war placed there by Herod. Many of the food substances had been preserved by the dry desert climate and were still edible.

Upon arriving at Masada, Silva built a wall (blockade) around the base of Masada so that the inhabitants on top could not escape. He then pondered how he was going to achieve his goal of destroying the citadel on top of this rock. His army could not ascend the steep and well guarded trails, and even if his army were able to reach the top, in front of them would be the imposing wall and towers. Heavy equipment would be needed to batter the walls and this equipment could not be brought up those trails. Silva noticed, however that in one area there was a broad and prominent outcropping of rock that stood about 500 feet from the highest part of Masada. He reasoned that by using that outcropping as a base, he could build an earthen ramp that would almost reach the top. It was apparent, however, that the construction of such a ramp would be a major and time consuming task. Since there was no other solution, he ordered the construction of the ramp consisting of earth and stones.[119] When finished it almost reached the top of the rock containing the fortress. It was also compact and broad enough so that weapons of war could be brought up the slope and used against the wall. Silva also built on

---

119   Thousands of Jewish slaves, under the watchful eye of Roman soldiers, were used to build this massive ramp made of earth and stones, which is now a landmark at Masada. The almost invincibility of Masada is revealed by the fact that it took over 15,000 Roman soldiers about two years to subdue less than 1,000 defenders, (counting women and children) in the fortress on top of the rock.

top of this ramp a tower 100 feet high plated with iron that was used by the Romans to throw darts and stones at the Sicarii who were on the walls. The Romans were so effective on this tower that the Sicarii were driven away from the wall. A battering ram brought up the ramp was used to bombard the wall, which slowly gave way because of the power of the weapon of war. Knowing from the position of the ramp which wall was vulnerable, the Sicarii had previously built another wall made of beams of wood and earth inside the outer wall, and the Romans were astonished to find this additional wall facing them after the outer wall had been breached. They were also astonished to learn that the battering ram was ineffective against this wall. Cleverly made of beams of wood and earth, it was pliable and became even more firm with battering. Silva then decided that the additional wall could be breached if the wooden components could be burned, so he ordered that torches should be thrown against the wall. It caught on fire and was soon engulfed in a mighty flame. In the beginning, the fire placed the Romans in great danger because a north wind drove the flames towards the Romans, their tower, and their weapons of war. The Romans feared the worst because of this event. But then the wind changed directions dramatically and blew the flames against the wall. Soon the entire wall was destroyed by fire. The Romans celebrated this act of providence with joy, and they returned to their camps resolved to attack their enemy the next day. That night they kept a careful watch to insure that no one would escape from the citadel under the cover of darkness.

When Eleazar saw the walls being breached, he realized that all was lost, and there was no means of escape for his followers and their families. He knew with horror what would happen to their wives and children when captured by the Romans, and he reasoned that the honorable solution was to have no living person in the citadel when it was entered by the Romans. So he called a meeting of the most courageous of his followers, presented his view, and encouraged them to agree with him. He made a long speech reminding them that long ago their group resolved never to be servants to the Romans, nor to anyone other than God himself, who alone is the true and just Lord of mankind. He told them that now is the time to abide by that resolution:

> *"We were the first group to revolt against the Romans and we are the last to fight against them, and although it is plain that we will die within a day's time at the hands of the Romans, it would be more glorious to die at our own hands. Let our wives die before they are abused, and our children before they have tasted slavery. After we have slain them, let us bestow that glorious benefit upon one another mutually. But first we should destroy our money and our fortress by fire, which will cause great grief to the Romans, who are expecting great rewards for their siege against us. Our actions will tell the Romans that we prefer death over slavery."*

Many who heard this speech agreed with his advice, but others were unsure. Even though they knew that death was certain for them, and knew what was in store for their wives and children, they acquiesced at being asked to kill the members of their own families. They did not know if they would be able to carry out this act. They looked wistfully at each other and tears came to their eyes. Eleazar then exhorted them with examples of what was in store for all of them at the hands of the Romans, arguing that death at their own hands was more merciful than the alternative. All then agreed to do what was necessary, without wavering. They worked with a demoniacal fury making preparations for what was to happen, believing that their zeal would be a demonstration of their courage. At the chosen time the men tenderly embraced their wives, took their children in their arms and gave parting kisses to them with tears in their eyes. Then each man killed what was most precious to him. Grief stricken, the men then gathered together all their valuable belongings, threw them into a pile, and set fire to them.

Chapter 12 The Triumph in Rome

By a lottery system, ten men were then chosen to slay all the rest. Each man laid himself down by his wife and children on the ground, threw his arms around them, and offered his neck to one who had been chosen by to be an executioner. After all were dead except the ten, lots were drawn among them to decide who should be chosen to kill the other nine, and then finally to kill himself. The nine offered their necks to the executioner, and each then died next to his family members. The remaining executioner then examined all the bodies to make sure that all were dead. If by chance any person had not succumbed to the wound that was received, he finished the task. When he perceived that all were dead, he set fire to the palace, then ran a sword through himself, and fell dead next to the members of his family.

By this scheme all were killed except an elderly woman and another woman and her five children. This younger woman, who was a kin of Eleazar was superior to most women in prudence and learning. These seven persons had hidden themselves in caverns under ground when the others were being slaughtered. With the exception of these seven persons, a total of 960 were found dead when the Romans entered the citadel the next day.

The next morning the Romans prepared for the assault on the citadel. Expecting a vicious resistance, they were startled when no enemy appeared when they entered the stronghold. With the exception of the fire in the palace, they encountered silence. In an effort to find out what had happened, they made a shout to bring out anyone who might be within any of the buildings. The women who heard this noise then came from the underground caverns and the younger woman informed the Romans what had been said by Eleazar, what was done, and the manner by which it was done.[120]

---

[120] Josephus, who obtained historical records from the Romans of what happened at Masada, gave a gripping and long account, *in his own words*, of what Eleazar might have said in his long speech and what transpired before the Romans penetrated the fortress.

The Romans at first did not believe that such an event could occur, and hurriedly made an effort to put out the fire that was raging in the palace. Upon entering the palace they saw with their own eyes the multitude of slain persons on the ground in family groups. They took no pleasure in what they viewed, even though those who had been slain were their enemy. They were moved by the courage of these persons who lay before them, and their immovable contempt of death, which they demonstrated by their noble actions.

Events Happening in Alexandria and Cyrene Following the Assault on Masada by the Romans

When Masada was taken, the general left a garrison there to keep it, and then he departed for Caesarea because there were no more strongholds of Jewish enemies left in the country. All had been overthrown by the long war, but the unrest due to the Sicarii had not been quieted. Many Sicarii who had been able to flee from the wars in Judea went to Alexandria, where they persisted in encouraging the Jews there to exert themselves, to look upon God as their Lord and Master, and to seek liberty from Roman rule. These vigilant Sicarii were opposed by the Jews of reputation in Alexandria. They feared that their exhortations would be troublesome to the Romans, and all Jews would suffer as a consequence. The members of the senate in Alexandria were also concerned with the events that were occurring. They called for an assembly of the Jews at which the Sicarii were accused of madness and being the authors of all the evils that had come upon the Jewish people. A vendetta was then carried out against the Sicarii. Six hundred of them were captured immediately. Others that had been able to flee into regions of Egypt were eventually caught and returned to Alexandria. Everyone was amazed at the zeal of these Sicarii. Even when they were tortured, they would not name Caesar as their lord, but remained firm to their resolution that only God was their Lord and ruler. What was even more astonishing to the beholders was the courage of their children, for none of them would name Caesar as their lord.

Chapter 12 The Triumph in Rome

When Vespasian was made aware of these events in Alexandria, he became concerned that the actions of the Sicarii might lead to further restlessness of the Jews and eventually to disorder. To affirm that he was their ruler, he gave orders to the governor of Alexandria that he should demolish the Jewish temple in a region called Onion. Up until that time this temple had been a place of divine worship for 343 years.

But this action in Alexandria did not end the influence of the zealots and the extremists among them. A significant event, eventually affecting Josephus, occurred in Cyrene [north Africa]. A weaver by the name of Jonathan, who was a member of the Sicarii, convinced many of the poorer Jews to follow him into the desert, where he would show them signs of what God wanted them to do. Prominent Jews of Cyrene who were suspicious of Jonathan informed Catullus, governor of the Libyan Pentapolis, of the march led by Jonathan into the desert. Concerned that a revolt might be occurring, Catullus sent both horsemen and footmen into the desert to apprehend Jonathan and those who followed him. The Jews were unarmed and they were quickly overcome. Many of the Jews were slain, but others were taken alive and brought to Catullus. Although Jonathan managed to flee away, he was eventually captured following an extensive search. He was then brought before Catullus, but was able to escape punishment by falsely accusing the richest men among the Jews of calumnies. Catullus was pleased to hear these calumnies because it gave him an excuse to bring charges against these Jews. By offering incentives, he encouraged Jonathan and other Sicarii to accuse men falsely. He was hoping to have justification for killing the Jews in Cyrene, and therefore take glory for completing the Jewish war. As a result of the false accusations, Catullus had all the wealthy Jews of Cyrene slain, a total of no fewer than 3,000. The Jews he had quarreled with were among the first that were slain. In an effort to gain praise in Rome for this slaughter, he confiscated their wealth and added it to Vespasian's revenue.

Hoping to obtain additional praise from Rome, Catullus encouraged Jonathan and other Sicarii to accuse Jews of high standing in Alexandria and also in Rome. Josephus was among those that were accused. Jonathan informed Catullus that to further the cause of the Sicarii in Cyrene, Josephus had given him money and weapons. The charge was a serious one, and Catullus brought Jonathan and his companions to Rome to inform Vespasian of the crimes carried out by Josephus and other prominent Jews living in Rome. Catullus assumed that Vespasian would accept what was said, and punish the Jews without any investigation. But Vespasian was suspicious and carried out an inquiry. Titus was also concerned about this matter. Vespasian reached the decision that the charges against Josephus and the other Jews were unjust. Vespasian cleared the Jews of the charges made against them, and punished Jonathan, who was tormented and then burned alive.

Catullus was treated gently by Vespasian and Titus, and received no severe condemnation for his actions. But soon he became mentally disturbed and cried out continuously that he saw the ghosts of those whom he had slain. His distemper increased, and he died a miserable death. What befell him was an instance of Divine Providence and demonstrated that God does punish wicked men.

Josephus in Rome

Upon arriving in Rome, after sailing there with Titus, Josephus was given great consideration by Vespasian, who gave him an apartment in the house where he had lived before he became emperor. Vespasian also bestowed on him the privilege of Roman citizenship, gave him an annual pension, and always honored him. Vespasian also gave him a gift of a large quantity of land in Judea, which provided Josephus a sizable income each year. From time to time, Jewish persons who envied Josephus's privileges attempted to raise calumnies against him, but in each case Vespasian defended Josephus. When the truth was known, Vespasian punished those

Chapter 12 The Triumph in Rome

persons for their mischievous behavior.

The wife Josephus had married in Alexandria gave him three children, but two died, leaving him with a son he named Hyrcanus. Josephus then became displeased with her behavior. He divorced her, and married a Jewess who had lived in Crete. By her, Josephus had two sons, named Justus and Simonides. The second son was also named Agrippa.

When Vespasian died after serving as emperor from 69 AD to 79 AD, he was succeeded as emperor by Titus.[121] Titus, who served as emperor for a relatively short period of time (79 AD to 81 AD), also bestowed many favors on Josephus, and protected

---

121   Following his victory at Jerusalem and his return to Rome, Titus shared jointly with his father in the triumph celebrating victories in Galilee, Judea, and surrounding areas. Titus was made commander of the Praetorian Guard and was given considerable power as sharer and protector of the empire. However, his position as heir to the throne was threatened by his relationship to Bernice, sister of king Agrippa II. During the war in Galilee, Titus met Bernice and became bewitched by her. Following the destruction of Jerusalem, Titus traveled to Caesarea Philippi where he staged games and celebrated his victory. It is conjectured that he went there to be with Bernice. It has also been conjectured that the decision he rendered in favor of the Jews in Antioch after passing through that city on his way to Alexandria and eventually to Rome, was influenced by his infatuation for Bernice, the Jewish Princess. In about 75 AD Bernice and her brother king Agrippa II went to Rome, and Bernice remained there and became Titus's mistress. Titus hoped to marry her, but this marriage was opposed by the populace of Rome who remembered the negative impact of Cleopatra. The Romans would not condone the future emperor being married to an eastern Jewish princess. Titus had to break his relationship with Bernice if he expected to remain heir to the throne, so reluctantly he sent her away. Titus died at age 41 after serving as emperor for only two years. He was succeeded as emperor by his brother Domitian. Titus was married twice. His first wife died, and he divorced his second wife. By his second wife he had a daughter, his only child.

Domitian was eleven years younger than Titus and succeeded him as emperor because Titus had no sons. When Titus became emperor, Domitian assumed that he would have the same powers that Vespasian had granted Titus. But such was not the case, and Domitian became bitter towards his brother. It was also rumored that he was responsible for the death of Titus. Domitian initiated a reign of terror during the latter half of his tenure as emperor. He executed senators and others who opposed him and insisted on being addressed as "master and god." He was assassinated by a conspiracy consisting of various palace officials, ranking members of the Praetorian Guard, and his wife Domitia.

him from his enemies. Titus's brother Domitian, who succeeded Titus as emperor, also honored and protected Josephus. Domitian held the government from 81 AD to 96 AD. As one sign of his friendship, Domitian declared that Josephus's land in Judea, which had been given him by Vespasian, would be tax free. Domitian's wife Domitia also showed much kindness to Josephus.

Epilogue

Josephus spent the rest of his life as a resident of Rome. There is no evidence in his writings that he ever visited Judea even though he owned property there. The Aramaic version of *The Wars of the Jews* was published in 75 AD when Vespasian was emperor, and Josephus was 38 years old. *The Antiquities of the Jews* was published 18 years later in 93 AD when Domitian was emperor. *The Life of Flavius Josephus* appeared in 95 AD as an appendix to *The Antiquities of the Jews.* His fourth major work *Flavius Josephus Against Apion"* has an unknown date, but was published after the appearance of *The Antiquities of the Jews.*

Because the members of the Flavian dynasty were his benefactors, it is understandable, and expected, that Josephus would be complimentary in all his writings concerning them. Thus, the destruction of Jerusalem by Titus was attributed to the evilness of the zealots who were defending the city, and the torching of the temple was done by the fervor of the soldiers, and not by the orders of Titus. Josephus also prudently omitted in his writings any mention of the relationship between Titus and Bernice. He was also careful not to discuss the tyranny of Domitian when he served as emperor. The Greek version of the *Wars of the Jews* was finished when Titus was emperor. According to Josephus, Titus was so desirous that the *Wars of the Jews* would be the primary source of knowledge about this period of history that he signed his imperial name to the books and ordered that they should be published.[122]

---

122   In *The Life of Flavius Josephus,* Josephus makes a point of mentioning that his works were endorsed by both Titus and king Agrippa II. Josephus had rival historians who

Chapter 12 The Triumph in Rome

King Agrippa II was a frequent visitor to Rome and he and Josephus established a close relationship. As distinguished Jews in Rome, both friends of the emperors, they would have had much in common. Josephus mentions in *The Life of Flavius Josephus* that king Agrippa II wrote him 62 letters and attested to the truth of the information presented in the *Wars of the Jews*. Josephus presents statements from two of these letters:

Letter 1
King Agrippa to Josephus, his dear friend, sendeth greeting. I have read over thy book with great pleasure, and it appears to me, that thou has done it much more accurately, and with greater care, than have the other writers. Send me the rest of these books. Farewell, my dear friend.

Letter 2
King Agrippa to Josephus, his dear friend, sendeth greeting. It seems by what thou has written, that thou standest in need of no instruction, (in order to present what transpired from the beginning). However, when thou comest to me I will inform thee of a great many things which thou dost not know.

In the second letter king Agrippa II informs Josephus that he has additional information that he is willing to provide him. The statement, ". . .when thou comest to me" suggests that Josephus planned to visit Agrippa's kingdom. Historical information was undoubtedly contained in some of the 62 letters written by king Agrippa II to Josephus. Because of his loyalty to Rome, king Agrippa's kingdom was enlarged following the destruction of Jerusalem. King Agrippa II served successfully as king until he

---

wrote about various events of the wars between the Jews and Romans. One was Justin of Tiberius who wrote a treatise (now lost) with the title *The Chronology of the Kings of Judah*. It is apparent that his account of some of the events was quite different from what Josephus had written. Josephus viewed him as his enemy.

died in 93 AD.

In the final paragraph of *The Antiquities of the Jews* Josephus declared that he was 56 years old during the thirteenth year (93 AD) of the reign of Caesar Domitian, and if God permitted, he would give an abridgment of the war that befell the Jewish people, and also write three books concerning Jewish opinions about God and his essence, about Jewish laws, and why according to these laws, Jews are permitted to do some things while other things are prohibited. These additional works never appeared. *The Life of Flavius Josephus* was published in 95 AD, only one year before Domitian was assassinated. With the loss of the last of his three Flavian benefactors (Vespasian, Titus, and Domitian), Josephus may not have had the support to complete or publish these works.

Nothing is known about the life of Josephus following 95 AD when he was 58 years old.

References

The Life and Works of Flavius Josephus. The Learned and authentic Jewish Historian and Celebrated Warrior... to which are added Seven Dissertations concerning Jesus Christ, John the Baptist, James the Just, God's Command to Abraham, etc. (Translated by William Whiston, A. M., Professor of Mathematics in the University of Cambridge. Introductory Essay by the Rev. H. Stebbing, D.D.) Published by Holt, Rinehart and Winston, New York.

Baker Encyclopledia of Bible Places (1995). Leicester, Inter-Varsity Press.

Barrett, A. A. (1989). Caligula. The Corruption of Power. London, Batsford.

Garzetti, A. (1974). From Tiberius to the Antoninies. London, Methuen.

Griffin, M. T. (1984). Nero: The End of a Dynasty. New Haven, Yale University Press.

Kreiger, B. (2009). Finding Herod's Tomb. Smithsonian Magazine, August, pp. 37-43. New York, New York.

Painter, J. (1997). Just James. The Brother of Jesus in History and Tradition. Columbia, University of South Carolina.

Scarre, C. (1995). Chronicle of the Roman Emperors. The Reign-By-Reign Record of the Rulers of Imperial Rome. London, Thames and Hudson.

Scramuzza, V. (1940). The Emperor Claudius. Cambridge, Harvard University Press.

Shotter, D. (1991). Augustus Caesar. London & New York, Routledge.

Usebius Pamphili (1953). Ecclesiastical History, Books 1-5. (Translated by Ron J. Deferrari). Washington, D.C., The Catholic University Press.

www.ingramcontent.com/pod-product-compliance
Lightning Source LLC
Chambersburg PA
CBHW052012070526
44584CB00016B/1725